THE CONTEST
FOR
RUGBY SUPREMACY

THE CONTEST FOR RUGBY SUPREMACY

Accounting for the 1905 All Blacks

Greg Ryan

CANTERBURY UNIVERSITY PRESS

UNIVERSITY OF
CANTERBURY
Te Whare Wānanga o Waitaha
CHRISTCHURCH NEW ZEALAND

First published in 2005 by
CANTERBURY UNIVERSITY PRESS
University of Canterbury
Private Bag 4800
Christchurch
NEW ZEALAND

www.cup.canterbury.ac.nz

Copyright © 2005 Greg Ryan

The moral rights of the author have been asserted

ISBN 1-877257-36-2

A catalogue record for this book is available from
the National Library of New Zealand

This book is copyright. Except for the purpose of fair review, no part may be stored or transmitted in any form or by any means, electronic or mechanical, including recording or storage in any information retrieval system, without permission in writing from the publishers.
No reproduction may be made, whether by photocopying or by any other means, unless a licence has been obtained from the publisher or its agent.

Printed through Bookbuilders, China

Author photograph by Neil Macbeth

CONTENTS

Foreword by Gareth Williams	7
Acknowledgements	11
Introduction	13
1. *Creating the Rugby World*	21
2. *Conflicts on the World Stage*	37
3. *Deliberations and Expectations*	52
4. *Making the All Blacks*	69
5. *Healthy Bodies?*	85
6. *Infringing Ideals*	101
7. *Big Matches and Bigger Legends*	118
8. *Serving the Minister for Football*	141
9. *The Fabric Unravels*	160
Conclusion	182
The 1905 Team	185
Statistics	199
Notes	202
Bibliography	221
Index	228

FOREWORD

Gareth Williams is Professor of History at the University of Glamorgan. He has written extensively on Welsh rugby, including a book of essays entitled 1905 and All That. *He also co-authored the acclaimed centenary history of the Welsh Rugby Union,* Fields of Praise.

It was late when the train pulled into Cardiff, and it was fairly quiet. 'The ambush,' writes Lloyd Jones in his novel *The Book of Fame*, 'came in the poorly lit streets around the railway station. We were half asleep, our chins bobbing against our chests, when they flew at us with their goblin language. They reached up, wanting to touch us, shouting and shoving . . . We saw the clenched faces of the police wrestling the crowd back and we held on to our seats with grim smiles. A crowd of 20,000 was later mentioned.' It was December 1905 and the All Blacks had arrived in Wales.

That was a hundred years ago, and it marked a new age. The twentieth century hadn't begun where it was supposed to. It began five years later, with the massacre in front of the Winter Palace and the naval defeat of the Czar's ill-equipped Baltic fleet by the naval power of Japan, whose ships, said the Kaiser, 'were fuelled by Cardiff coal'. This was the year when a small-time clerk in a Swiss patent office revolutionised classical physics; when Wales was swept by a religious revival, and the British Isles were swept by a team in Bible black. 'These Colonials,' enthused a leading Welsh journo, 'are indeed all black. They wear black jerseys, black pants, black stockings, and between the end of their pants and the beginning of their stockings there is a strip of white flesh. The stripe fascinates one. It is the oriflamme of the battle.'

All sports boast their great sides. In rugby football, Dave Gallaher's 1905 All Blacks are so remembered. They landed in Devon in September and during the next four months embarked on a scorched-earth policy of 32 games throughout the British Isles. By virtue of their superior fitness, their positional innovations, their tactical ingenuity and their inventiveness on (and off) the ball, these apparent representatives of the best colonial manhood were undefeated wherever they went – until the end, in Wales. Any goblin with a love of sport, a sense of history and devotion to rugby in particular, will always feel a special *frisson* when the All Blacks run on to Welsh turf. The expectation is always immense. When they first came onto the Cardiff Arms Park, reported the London correspondent of the *Lyttelton Times*, 'clad in their sombre black with the stern faces of men who had a great ordeal ahead of them, the crowd started from their seats and almost tumbled over one another in their eagerness to see the famous All Blacks.'

To a goblin, that game on that December day in 1905 still resonates like some great cavernous, cosmic joke. Did the devoutly religious, temperate and magnificent Bob Deans score that disallowed try against Wales, as he is supposed to have claimed on his death bed less than three years later? Why does Cliff Morgan, scourge of Bob Stuart's 1953 All Blacks, insist that on his mother's knee in the Rhondda Valley he learned three things: the Lord's Prayer, the Welsh national anthem, and that Bob Deans didn't score against Wales in 1905? Why, with Wales 13–0 down at halftime in the first test of Wales' first visit to the Land of the Long White Cloud, in 1969, did one Kiwi announce to the entire press box that he had 'been waiting 64 years for this moment', though he himself had not yet lived that long? And why did the incomparable Carwyn James impress upon his Italian charges, as they prepared to face the All Blacks in 1977, how privileged they were, for 'today we are playing against New Zealand, a *great* rugby nation'? And Carwyn had better reason than most to know it.

Greg Ryan asks none of these questions, though if you read his book carefully you will find he provides all the answers to them. He has questions of his own to ask. He does not deal in myth, sentiment or hagiography. Many in the UK and in New Zealand liked to think the 1905 tourists cemented imperial ties and colonial loyalties. Ryan has a decidedly post-colonial take on that one: the tour generated bitter antagonisms, before and afterwards. Gallaher, immortal captain in 1905 who fell at Passchendaele, was lucky to be selected. Pre-tour, the indispensable Billy Stead (whose absence, owing to the boils he had on his arse, may have cost them victory against Wales) was the current captain and Gallaher himself was under suspicion and recent suspension by the NZRU over financial and other irregularities; he offered his resignation on the boat over. Constantly impeding the opposing inside half by standing alongside the scrum as a wing-forward, throughout the tour he would be subjected to what Ryan calls a 'pitiless fusillade' of barracking. His team were reckoned by some propagandists ('Why do the All Blacks win?' demanded the *Daily Mail*) to be the rugged representatives of a healthy outdoor rural way of life, except that only three of them had any links with the land (one of them was Deans): they were nearly all town- and city-

FOREWORD

dwellers. They didn't leave home with any enthusiastic or optimistic send-off, and they weren't universally admired on tour. The press got after them from the start, whingeing about their perceived illegalities, gamesmanship, and deliberate roughness. And when they got back, their influence on the course of the game in their own country would certainly prove decisive, but for the wrong reasons – they split the rugby community wide open.

Greg Ryan tells us all this and more. As a fellow historian, and a goblin to boot, I don't agree with everything he says. He devotes only one chapter to the Welsh segment of the tour when he could easily have allocated half the book to this worthy end, and even then he wouldn't have unpicked a quarter of its complexities. He has already established himself as a fine historian of sport with his meticulous account of the first New Zealand rugby touring team, the so-called 'Natives' of 1888–89. Now he applies his revisionist scalpel to peeling away the layers of legend, cliché and nostalgia that have become encrusted like coral around the 1905 'Originals' (which they clearly weren't). A lover of the game, of New Zealand and of its rugby, Greg Ryan has researched every match report from Munster to Manawatu. He knows all the stats, but he knows too that any meaningful history of steam locomotion has to be taken out of the enthusiastic hands of train spotters.

However we view them, these New Zealand tourists were superb athletes. As with every touring team, a few of them should have stayed on the boat, but the talk was always, and is still, of the wondrous running of fullback Billy 'Carbine' Wallace, whose boot dispatched the ball like a bullet but who was named after a racehorse; of 'Bronco' Seeling; of the fated Bob Deans; the prolific try scorer Jimmy Hunter; and their phlegmatic, obstructive captain, Davy Gallaher. Greg Ryan wants neither to canonise nor demonise the 1905 All Blacks. He is not in the business of conferring sainthood or exorcising devils. In Wales, the goblins' narrow but deserved victory over these mighty men is part of our collective folk memory, etched into the national consciousness, a cornerstone of our culture. Throughout Britain and New Zealand, rugby was never the same after the All Black tour of 1905. The tour will never be the same either after you have read this fascinating account of it.

Gareth Williams
Pontypridd, Wales

ACKNOWLEDGEMENTS

The writing of this book could never have been a solitary task, and the shaping of its ideas owes much to others. The research benefited considerably from assistance at the British Library Newspaper Library, Colindale; the Macmillan Brown Library, University of Canterbury; the Hocken Library, University of Otago; Christchurch City Libraries; Wellington City Libraries; the Alexander Turnbull Library and National Library, Wellington; the State Library of New South Wales; and the State Library of Victoria. Ron Palenski provided a number of valuable items, including the 1905 tour agreement, correspondence concerning post-tour controversies, and his fasinating compilation of Billy Stead's tour reports for the *Southland Times*. Charles Little, Gareth Williams and Martin Johnes each provided important references and clarifications; and Bob Luxford at the Rugby Museum of New Zealand assisted with illustrations. I am also very grateful to Lincoln University for giving me the time and resources to complete research, and especially to Jim McAloon for his ongoing support of my work. Richard King at Canterbury University Press has constantly encouraged this book and gave it the benefit of his editorial expertise.

At various times over the last decade Luke Trainor sustained this and related projects with fascinating references and ensured that I kept my eye on the wider imperial picture. His deciphering of the 'physical deterioration' debates from almost illegible microcards was invaluable. Geoffrey Vincent, aside from the immense value of his own published work on the 1908 Anglo-Welsh tour, provided transcripts of George Dixon's tour diary and other correspondence, and alerted me to any number of conspiracy facts from the darker side of early New Zealand rugby. Len Richardson, who first introduced me to a broader view of sport, continues, during convivial discussions, to subtly clarify many aspects of my thinking on the rugby world.

Three people are due particular thanks. At a crucial moment Caroline Daley sent me 'The Invention of 1905', a succinct and inspiring dissection of much that has been written about the tour. Her multitude of fresh ideas and reinforcement of many of my own are at the backbone of this book. Tony Collins, as well as providing minutes of the RFU and numerous other references, also read the manuscript and subjected it to his own considerable knowledge of British rugby, the Northern Union and sport generally. Most important is the debt to my partner, Liz Martyn, who sacrificed part of an overseas holiday to be a research assistant, read the entire manuscript, asked for more detail on many things and much less on others, and in so many ways provided a loving and peaceful environment in which this phalanx of ideas could come together as a book in time for the centenary year of the tour.

Greg Ryan
Christchurch, July 2005

INTRODUCTION

The exploits of the 'Original' All Blacks in Britain during the last quarter of 1905 marked the end of innocence for all who viewed rugby as a gentlemanly pastime to be played for its own sake. Rugby cultures that had developed in relative isolation at opposite ends of the British Empire came together in a manner that suddenly and irrevocably transformed the fabric of the international game like nothing else until rugby union finally embraced open professionalism in 1995. To appreciate the magnitude of what happened, it is useful to draw comparisons with another rugby tour a century later. By the time the British and Irish Lions completed an 11-match tour of New Zealand from May to July 2005, the party had contained no fewer than 51 players and at least 30 support staff, including specialist forward, back, defensive and kicking coaches, doctors, physiotherapists, a psychiatrist, a kit technician, media relations experts and a Queen's Counsel. Every aspect of the tour reflected intricate planning and its £10 million budget. Intense media interest highlighted the profile of modern professional rugby as a global game in which every player on both sides was widely known on the world stage. All aspects of the team members' play, their strengths and weaknesses and the pattern to which they belonged, had been carefully analysed by its own strategists and those of the opposition in preparation for a series that was watched by hundreds of millions. As much as this was serious international sport, it was also rugby as a large-scale business and marketing enterprise in which broadcasters, sponsors and fans paid handsomely for the privilege of being involved. And most importantly, despite England's victory at the 2003 Rugby World Cup, and despite obligatory complaints about the standard of refereeing and the supposedly illegal, or at least unethical, methods used by New Zealand players, the All Blacks' comprehensive three-nil defeat of the Lions reinforced the fact that after a decade of professional rugby the consistent strength of the game remained in the southern hemisphere.

By contrast, the 1905 All Black team comprised 27 players, one manager and a redundant coach for a tour that would eventually amount to 35 matches. Before leaving, some of the team members were known to each other and the New Zealand public only by reputation. More importantly, although a British team had met some of the players in New Zealand during 1904, it was 17 years since the New Zealand Native team had toured Britain, and it is safe to say that when the All Blacks first took the field against Devon on 16 September 1905 the number of Britons who had seen any of them play could be counted in the tens. Consequently, everything about them – their appearance, their formation on the field, their tactics – was unfamiliar. While many rugby pundits were quietly confident that the tourists would acquit themselves well in the majority of their matches, many also suspected that they would fall at the four hurdles posed by the international fixtures. Perhaps some others, who viewed rugby as a purely amateur game that ought to be played for its own pleasure, cared little about the results. For all involved this was a journey into the unknown.

By the end of 1905, as conventional wisdom tells, these unheralded New Zealanders had taken Britain by storm, dazzled with their athleticism and innovative style, accumulated a string of huge victories, claimed a moral 'draw' with Wales, and put their young colony firmly on the world map. The tour created the 'All Blacks' name and mystique, and enshrined expectations of international success that show little sign of receding despite the increasingly competitive environment in which the team now plays. So strongly is '1905' and its associated myths and symbols etched in the collective consciousness of New Zealand rugby enthusiasts that the more successful 1924 All Blacks – 'the Invincibles', who avenged the earlier loss to Wales – have attracted nothing like the same attention. In an age of professional rugby, when many perceive that the media-driven game has lost touch with its 'grassroots' and history, the legends of the 'pioneering' and amateur All Blacks, their personal humility, team unity and sensational brand of running rugby satisfy popular nostalgia.

Not surprisingly, the success of 1905 has appealed to a much wider audience than dedicated rugby enthusiasts. During the 1980s, when historians Keith Sinclair and Jock Phillips began to explore New Zealand nationalism and identity, and the ways in which the supposed qualities of colonial life were also used to define New Zealand's place within the wider world, the 'Original' All Blacks naturally loomed large. The achievement of the tour is supposed to have reinforced strong bonds within the British Empire. More importantly, it provided an advertisement for the qualities of New Zealand life. Here was a rural, healthy, egalitarian paradise, a social laboratory that was leading the world into the twentieth century by producing men possessed of admirable physique, natural athleticism, dexterity, adaptability and initiative. Sinclair regarded the tour as being 'famous in the New Zealand secular religion of nationalism'.[1] Phillips declared that 'It was the

INTRODUCTION

1905 tour . . . which created idols of the All Blacks and turned them into formal representatives of the nation's manhood',[2] and that 'the model of manhood represented by the 1905 team was to remain the core of the male stereotype in New Zealand for the next seventy years'. In all of this there was a particular focus on the All Black captain David Gallaher as soldier, athlete and natural leader.[3] During the early 1990s John Nauright extended these themes to a discussion of the way in which the success of the All Blacks was used to counter contemporary concerns about physical deterioration and declining racial virility in the British Empire during the crucial years between the South African War and the Great War. If the core of the Empire was held to be rotting, the colonies were conversely in fine fettle.[4]

Yet much of what has been written about 1905 is an invention that has gained far greater credence over time than it ever held among contemporary observers. There is still much to be said about a tour that is apparently so well chronicled and understood, both within the mythology of rugby and the forging of a New Zealand identity more generally. As much as the All Blacks were eulogised during the last quarter of 1905 and beyond, they were equally subject to criticism and condemnation for their methods and attitudes. This book aims to explain such contradictions between immediate reactions and later interpretations, and to provide them with a context in terms of both the development of rugby and its broader significance within the social history of Britain and New Zealand.

In piecing together the events of 1905, it is easy to get sidetracked in a maze of minutiae and hyperbole, and to lose sight of bigger themes. What follows is much more than the narrative of a rugby tour. For that one need go no further than team manager George Dixon's account published in 1906 (and reproduced in a facsimile edition in 1999). With some crucial exceptions, it is not my intention to grapple with the numerous contradictions between secondary sources or to follow paths of evidence into the dark recesses of rugby folklore. The reader in search of a definitive explanation as to why Simon Mynott replaced Billy Stead for the Wales test, or who tackled Bob Deans and where, will be best served by the wealth of contemporary accounts and by later popular histories. Such things, debated and disputed at the time, are now unknowable. The reasons why these questions have endured are more important than the answers, for sport is an integral part of society – both reflecting and shaping the cultural, political and social values of its admirers and detractors. Every reaction to the 1905 All Blacks was a product of complex historical forces within Britain, New Zealand and the wider British Empire.

The historian of 1905 is not stuck for sources. Newspaper reports of the tour in Britain and New Zealand can be assessed in column miles rather than inches. While much was duplicated, the delving, pontificating and speculation of assiduous correspondents, members of the team and rugby officials produced even more words. Within weeks of the end of the tour, one book appeared and two more followed before the end of 1906.[5] Over the years every rugby historian of note, and many more besides, has had something to say about 1905; statisticians have detailed every aspect of collective and individual endeavour; and even at the dawn of the twenty-first century new light was being cast on the origins of the name 'All Blacks' and the case for Bob Deans' 'try' against Wales.[6]

Consequently, a very deliberate approach to the researching of this book was required to dissect the voluminous sources on the tour and the subsequent interpretations of them. It began with the provincial and national press in Britain. Here can be found the immediate reactions of those watching the matches and interacting with the All Blacks, the views of columnists and critics (many of them former rugby internationals familiar with the nuances of British sport) and the tour's impact presented through the clearly articulated political agendas of publications such as the *Daily Mail*. The search then moved to consider the range of New Zealand comment, locally produced and from New Zealand correspondents in Britain, and the crucial test as to what was, and was not, reproduced from British sources for a New Zealand audience eager to glean every ounce of information in an age before radio or television. Only then was attention turned to the range of secondary literature, both popular and academic, that has fed on these sources.

The value of this approach is that it highlights the filtering of material from one layer to the next, and the points at which selective transmission and shifts of emphasis have occurred. Contemporary descriptions and debate in the British press, a great deal of which was reproduced and discussed in New Zealand, paints a complex and contentious picture of the tour. The books that appeared immediately afterwards were similarly frank in discussing the methods of the All Blacks and the mixed perception of them. So were those that chronicled the inter-war meetings between New Zealand and British teams.[7] Among later accounts, including those by uncritical academic historians,[8] there is some mention of the various controversies of the tour, but without exception these aspects are marginalised in favour of an overwhelmingly positive narrative. Indeed, the more recent the work on 1905, the more selective and one-sided much of it has become. For many, 1905 is something of a creation myth from

INTRODUCTION

which stems a century of largely uninterrupted All Black supremacy and tradition,[9] but this emphasis and interpretation is a long way removed from most of what can be found at the time of the tour.

A further problem with existing accounts is the tendency to seize on '1905' in isolation. Many who have written about the triumphs of the tour fail to balance them against a chain of events, and especially the appearance of rugby league in 1907, that plunged New Zealand rugby into crisis, fundamentally altered relations with Britain and undermined many of the apparent certainties of the 1905 tour. Such contradictions and tensions are embodied in the title of this book – 'the contest for rugby supremacy'. In playing terms, aside from the Scottish international and the Welsh matches, the tour was anything but a contest. Yet it became one in the sense that so many aspects of the tour and its aftermath were very much 'contested' between two continually diverging rugby cultures – one apparently amateur and idealistic, the other increasingly assertive and abrasive.

To understand these 'contests', we begin in Chapter One with the sporting mania that gripped Britain during the nineteenth century and the quite distinct, class-based football cultures that emerged from it. As rugby spread from its cradle among a southern English elite to encompass the rest of the British Isles, it inevitably assumed different, and ultimately conflicting, characteristics as it was shaped to fit the particular local lifestyles and values of its new followers. These differences, manifested most obviously in the rugby split between the north and south of England in 1895 that eventually produced rugby league, were to have a profound bearing on the course of the 1905 tour. Equally, the attitudes and ideals of the All Blacks themselves differed markedly from those of the men who had introduced rugby to New Zealand during the 1870s. Here we need to tread carefully through layers of myth and assumption to examine a colonial game that was rather more fractious and rather less certain of its destiny than some have imagined. As much as New Zealand rugby was characterised by early tactical innovations, or the 'scientific' game, growth was also haphazard and frequently undercut by bitter rivalries derived from class and regional interests. Against this background, Chapters Two and Three trace the emergence of New Zealand rugby onto the international stage, the genesis of the tour, the selection of the team and expectations for it, revealing that the 1905 All Blacks were much less than the unified, confident outgrowth of a secure 'national game'.

As Chapters Four, Five and Six explain, from the moment the tourists took the field against Devon on 16 September 1905, every aspect of their performance and demeanour was subject to intense scrutiny. To some they were a startling breath of fresh air that signalled the way forward after a decade of division and decline in British rugby; to others they apparently represented the salvation of Anglo-Saxon masculinity from 'physical deterioration'. Indeed, these are the most common interpretations of the tour. Yet neither of them pays sufficient heed to a third group – those who criticised the All Blacks' tactics and questioned the morality underpinning them. Just as the political dimensions of the 1932–33 'bodyline' cricket controversy between Australia and England make no sense unless one understands both the laws of cricket and the manner in which they were interpreted, so the interpretation of 1905 lacks substance without an understanding of wing-forwards, positional specialisation and the distinction between 'rough' and 'hard' play. As contemporary observers well understood, all things on the field were instigated by attitudes off it. Rather than seizing on fragments to fit themes, it is critical to follow the course of the tour through Britain, to consider its distinct English, Irish, Scottish and Welsh phases, and to evaluate the ways in which the different interpretations interacted and perhaps collided with each other. As Chapter Seven reveals, these themes were most evident in the four international matches and the final weeks of the tour in Britain.

Undoubtedly, the magnitude of the All Blacks' victories gave many New Zealand observers the confidence to make light of criticism and to quickly forget the tensions that preceded the tour. If there was not quite the crescendo of lasting national euphoria depicted in some accounts, and much of the 'nationalist' rhetoric around 1905 can be revealed as shallow and contradictory, there was nevertheless an acute awareness among public and politicians alike of the immediate potential for rugby to enhance the image of New Zealand within the British Empire. Premier Richard Seddon and the New Zealand government representative in London, William Pember Reeves, constantly mined the tour for propaganda opportunities. But, as Chapter Eight demonstrates, even they were allowed only so much rope. While the triumphal procession of the All Blacks back to New Zealand via North America added a fascinating footnote to the history of American football, it was also a time for sniping at blatant political opportunism and personal aggrandisement.

If the tour was controversial, the aftermath was arguably more so. The sudden appearance of the Professional All Blacks and the beginning of rugby league in Australasia in 1907 was entirely a consequence of 1905. Chapter Nine argues that, rather than uniting New Zealand rugby, the successes of

INTRODUCTION

the tour both on the field and at the gate served to highlight the disparities and evident hypocrisy of amateur rugby. In Britain, the critics of New Zealand rugby were reinforced with new and heavier ammunition. Scotland and Ireland disengaged from contact with Australasia, and an attempt by the Anglo-Welsh to save the soul of New Zealand rugby for amateurism in 1908 did more harm than good. Comparisons with two other colonial touring teams – a much-admired South African one and a generally derided Australian one – further sharpened barbs against the All Blacks to the point where they were not to be welcomed again in Britain until 1924. Few rugby followers in the years immediately after 1905 could have imagined, let alone wanted to imagine, the intensity of the international rivalry played out by finely tuned professional athletes in the stadiums of New Zealand in 2005.

CHAPTER ONE

Creating the Rugby World

THOSE WHO WATCHED RUGBY in the years from the formation of the Rugby Football Union in 1871 to the arrival of the 1905 All Blacks in Britain witnessed fundamental transformations to the players, spectators, laws and ethos of the game. Nothing that happened to the All Blacks in 1905 can be understood properly without considering this turbulent period in both Britain and New Zealand and paying particular attention to the growing tensions between amateur and professional ideals both on the field and off it. To this end, we must briefly examine the origins and organisation of the game, its diffusion throughout Britain and New Zealand and the quite distinct interpretations of the rugby 'ethos' that developed among the different social classes who adopted the game.

The starting point for such a discussion is not William Webb Ellis. As Gareth Williams points out, the Webb Ellis myth tells us more about the late Victorian mind than about the origins of rugby. It was nothing more than a calculated effort to establish elite public school credentials for amateur rugby during the late 1880s when the game was under increasing threat from both its own working-class followers and soccer.[1] The various handling and kicking games from which rugby evolved are centuries older than Webb Ellis's supposed initiative to run with the ball at Rugby School in 1823. But for present purposes, the process of consolidation of 'folk football' into the two most popular football codes of rugby and soccer is not important.[2] It will suffice to say that the handling and running game had emerged as the preferred code of football at Rugby School by the 1830s and that a formal set of laws for the game was drawn up in 1845. Thereafter a number of schools – Eton in particular – issued rules for football games that diverged significantly from the Rugby version. The most popular of these formed the basis for the dramatic growth of soccer during the late nineteenth century.[3]

Why the Rugby game assumed such precedence has been keenly debated. Certainly it was not due to the noted Rugby headmaster Thomas Arnold, who took little direct interest in games – although he did allow boys to play and may have inadvertently created an opportunity for football of some sort by waging war on traditional and competing schoolboy pursuits such as hunting, fishing and general carousing in the neighbourhood of Rugby School. Some have seen the promotion of its game as part of a deliberate attempt by Rugby to boost its status within the English public school hierarchy by adopting a handling game that was distinct from, and apparently superior to, the simpler kicking game preferred by other schools and the wider society. Perhaps closer to the mark is the suggestion that the Rugby game spread through the efforts of innovative young schoolmasters who, having served their apprenticeship in the reformist environment of Arnold's Rugby, went on to make their mark in a growing network of schools that had been established to meet the desire of an expanding middle class to equip their children with a public school education. To them, the discipline and co-operation demanded of team games was an increasingly important element in shaping the character of young gentlemen who would require similar attributes in the serious business of life – whether in the professions or serving the British Empire on its frontiers. In this objective, they, and the profile of Rugby School, were also helped by the publication in 1857 of Thomas Hughes' *Tom Brown's Schooldays* – a bestselling book that was as much a moral message and advocate for the 'games cult' as a novel.[4]

Whatever the exact reason for the emergence of rugby, that game and the various football codes of other public schools were in competition for followers by the 1850s. Inevitably, there was pressure for at least one standardised form of football to allow those from different backgrounds to play together. Although various 'compromise' rules were drawn up, especially at the University of Cambridge, sharp divisions emerged between advocates of the kicking and handling codes – divisions that were as much about school rivalries as the best form of football. In October and November 1863 a series of meetings called to resolve the impasse resulted in the formation of the Football Association and the alienation of those who advocated a handling code. Very much at issue were questions about the acceptable level of violence to be tolerated in football – and particularly the question of 'hacking', or the deliberate kicking of an opponent's shins. Supporters of soccer felt that a less physically demanding, more open and exciting game with simpler rules was better suited to an increasingly civilised society in which men in business and the professions were obliged to take care of themselves. Supporters of the handling game emphasised its manly vigour and were inclined to portray their opponents as somewhat effeminate in their wish to avoid such character-building aspects as 'hacking'.[5]

The advocates of rugby, largely drawn from the southern English middle-class elite, finally came together to form the Rugby Football Union (RFU) in 1871. Their objectives were to counter the popular support for soccer and to standardise the handling rules. In doing so, they quickly abolished hacking, reduced teams from 20 to 15 players in 1875 and made various other law changes to speed up and open up the game.[6] As a reflection of the growth of rugby, the first international fixture, between England and Scotland, took place in Edinburgh in March 1871. Ireland entered the international field in 1875, and Wales in 1881. Yet this growth is not to suggest that the RFU and its administrative counterparts in Scotland (1873), Ireland (1874) and Wales (1881) were committed to fashioning a broadly popular game. To the contrary, they were amateur, elitist and largely opposed to such populist contrivances as numbering jerseys, keeping records, arranging formal fixture lists and providing for spectators.[7]

The concept of amateurism embraced by the rugby establishment was in part a reflection of the developing public school ideal that sport ought to be played for its own sake to foster personal discipline and camaraderie rather than to achieve victory. It was not merely a matter of abiding by the laws of the game, but also the spirit of fair play. Because victory was supposedly of less importance than taking part, the true 'gentleman amateur' saw no need to practise or to manipulate the laws in search of an advantage. Payment for play and the pursuit of trophies or competition points were also alien concepts. But within a nineteenth-century British society that observed pronounced social distinctions, amateurism also worked as a subtle device to exclude those further down the social scale. Prohibitions against payment or any form of compensation for lost earnings automatically removed those among the working class who could not afford to take time for sport. To reinforce this elite position, it was commonly argued that if sport were commercialised or players paid, the game would face a serious struggle for financial survival in which the laws and spirit would be threatened by those needing to win 'at all costs'.[8]

As the efforts of public school old boys spread rugby throughout Britain, and especially to the industrialising north of England and Wales, the game began to attract interest beyond the elite. Decreasing class tensions from the late 1840s, coupled with changing economic and employment conditions, gave workers shorter hours, a higher disposable income and a regular Saturday half-holiday for many from the 1860s. Improved pubic transport, the provision of more public parks, increasing literacy and the growth of the popular press were other factors helping to produce a sporting environment favourable to working-class players and spectators alike. Church, pub, factory and local town teams flourished as rugby initially secured greater popularity than soccer in the north of England and Wales during the late 1870s. At the same time, the pressures of growing civic pride and inter-town rivalries among the burgeoning industrial towns began to force formerly middle-class rugby clubs to become more commercially aware and to entice the best players in order to retain their status and community support. More often than not, the new recruits were working-class men possessing strength, stamina and competitiveness derived from physically demanding employment. Their rugby was more intense and often more violent than the game being encouraged by the idealists of the RFU, but it was also open, innovative and attractive to the paying public.[9] From the mid-1870s various cup competitions and leagues emerged to harness the intensity of northern rugby. Indeed, the importance of rugby as a community focus was such that local Yorkshire Cup derbies during the 1870s attracted 6,000 spectators at a time when international matches in London were drawing only 4,000. In this competitive cauldron, the strength of English rugby shifted decisively north during the 1880s. From 1888–89 Yorkshire won six of the first seven county championships, with Lancashire winning the other, and northern players began to dominate the national team.[10]

These northern developments inevitably prompted severe misgivings from the RFU. Amid increasing industrial unrest and renewed class conflict from the mid-1880s, and growing working-class confidence with the emergence of an independent political labour movement, there was distrust of the rapidly growing strength of the northern clubs, the uncompromising methods of their players and the aggressive intensity of their seemingly vast crowds. Particularly disturbing were the various knockout cup competitions, with their exaggerated emphasis on winning and the distinct possibility that teams would bend the laws and morality of the game and indulge in rough play in order to do so. The RFU feared that the demands of cups and leagues would encourage professionalism, as was beginning to happen in soccer.[11] And in this fear they were right. Aside from good players, Welshmen included, being enticed to the north of England with jobs and other incentives, and successful teams being rewarded in various material ways, many clubs also began to make covert 'broken time' payments to compensate their working-class players who could not afford to lose work time and earnings while playing and training or through injury.[12]

Initially, as the prospect of payment for play was considered so unlikely among the middle-class constituency of the RFU, there was no prohibition against it. Not until 1879 was the first measure against professionalism enacted – by the Yorkshire Rugby Union. This was borrowed from the Marylebone Cricket Club and allowed for legitimate expenses. But as the Football Association moved during the mid-1880s to accommodate professionalism within soccer with very strict controls on wage levels, employment conditions and player transfers, the RFU determinedly set its stall in the other direction. In 1886, in an effort to counter the threat posed by working-class participation, laws were enacted providing expulsion as the likely penalty for anyone found to have taken material benefit from the game. While legitimate expenses were permitted, there was an absolute prohibition on all payments for playing and training, and the employment of players by clubs. Two years later, strict laws were implemented to control the transfer of players between clubs, thus restricting the practice of enticement. That these measures gained strong support among the northern middle class reminds us that the cleavage was much more than a simple north–south divide. Similar tensions between working-class players and middle-class administrators were also evident in the Midlands and southwest of England and in Wales.[13]

As the RFU sought to enforce its laws through increasingly draconian player and club suspensions, it succeeded only in polarising the game with little discernible impact on covert payments. Yet a confident working class was less inclined to tolerate such tactics, and many of the middle-class leaders of northern clubs also saw accommodation with working-class demands as the only way to preserve the game. To them, the option of legitimate and strictly regulated 'broken time' payments and controls on the transfer of players could be used to safeguard amateurism against 'open' professionalism.[14]

All such calls for legitimisation of 'broken time' were firmly rejected at the RFU Annual General Meeting on 20 September 1893 when southern clubs, supported by numerous proxy votes, opted to turn their backs on any prospect for internal reform of rugby. Moreover, the RFU responded with further punitive laws against professionalism – including penalties for knowingly associating with professionals and a 'guilty until proven innocent' approach to the accused. After further acrimonious negotiations, and the rejection of an attempt by northern clubs to apply for membership of the RFU as a separate body with its own concessions to working-class interests, matters came to a head on 29 August 1895 when 21 clubs met at the George Hotel, Huddersfield, to form the Northern Rugby Football Union.[15]

Although the Northern Union moved quickly to legitimise 'broken time', it initially disavowed full-time professionalism. But as it became impossible to stop clubs covertly breaching the six shillings a day 'broken time' limit, professionalism with stringent work and transfer clauses was sanctioned in 1898. In turn, the insistence that all professional players be in bona fide employment outside the game became equally difficult to administer and easy to circumvent. Open professionalism was sanctioned from 1905.[16] For its part, the RFU denigrated the Northern Union as unpatriotic and contrary to the national interests of sport, and declared that any contact with it would professionalise players. As part of a conscious strategy to reconstruct the game on the amateur, public school principles of the 1860s, those in the north remaining loyal to the RFU vigorously pursued and banned anyone with Northern Union connections while encouraging a lenient attitude towards those wishing to repent and return to the amateur fold.[17]

In Chapter Three we shall return to the dramatic changes to the landscape of British rugby caused by the emergence of the Northern Union game, and the remainder of this book will show how the upheavals of the decade after the 1895 split had a crucial bearing on the achievements of the 1905 All Blacks, the way these were perceived, and on the fabric of world rugby in the years immediately after the tour. First, however, it is important to consider the origins and development of New Zealand rugby – a game that soon came to mirror the tensions in Britain and add some of its own.

The 1905 All Black team was obviously a product of the New Zealand rugby environment, but not always in the ways imagined by previous historians of the tour. Indeed, for a game that has been so vital to New Zealand society, little effort has been made to distinguish between myth and actuality. Jock Phillips and a legion of uncritical followers have enshrined rugby as part of a rural pioneering mythology. The stamina, co-operation and tenacity required for such a game was apparently ideal preparation for the many challenges of pioneering life. As with the soldiers who served in the South African War and at Gallipoli, rugby players were typical of a New Zealand male 'type' noted for strength, determination, versatility, initiative and mateship – and in all ways superior to its increasingly sedentary and urban counterpart in Britain. In this context, rugby holds a prominent place in discussions of the elements that shaped a distinct New Zealand identity and projected a positive image of the young country to a wider world.[18] It is claimed that rugby spread rapidly into rural areas, cut across class, race and ethnic boundaries, and was securely entrenched as the 'national game' by the early 1880s – a situation apparently 'confirmed' by Philips's misprinted and frequently quoted claim that there were 50,000, rather than 5,000, affiliated rugby players by the mid-1890s.[19] As Chapter Five explains, this rural imagery is consistent with the tendency of New Zealanders throughout the nineteenth century to glorify the virtues of rural life compared with the perceived ills of the city. It was also used by some contemporary observers, and many more historians, to account for the success of the 1905 All Blacks.

In truth, there is little substance for any explanation of the growth of New Zealand rugby, or the success of 1905, in terms of 'frontier' masculinity, the rural rugby backbone or classlessness. Not only was the game urban in its origins, but its fastest growth and greatest playing strength, in terms of both numbers and results, remained in the four main cities and various larger provincial towns. Of course the game secured a footing in rural areas, but relatively speaking it was beset by obstacles such as poor transport and communication networks, small populations and rural transience. Equally, a range of social and economic factors determined how far players from different social backgrounds could progress in the game.[20] Different explanations have to be found for the successes of 1905.

While rugby was brought to New Zealand in the early 1870s by men of the same public school mould as those who had shaped the game in Britain, it is misleading to see its subsequent growth as a straightforward trickle down from the top of the social scale. Various forms of football, with a tendency towards handling rather than kicking games, owing to the undeveloped state of colonial grounds, were played throughout the country from the early 1850s. Most prominent was the new Melbourne game imported to the Otago and Thames goldfields during the 1860s. Victorian Rules existed side by side with rugby during the 1870s and maintained a noticeable presence up to 1914. The oldest football club in New Zealand, Christchurch, pursued various forms of football from its foundation in 1863 and only grudgingly took up rugby in order to find new opponents during the mid-1870s.[21] In short, there was a football-playing culture during the 1860s upon which rugby could attach itself.

It is commonly accepted that the first game under rugby laws was played in Nelson in May 1870 when Charles John Monro, a product of Christ's College, Finchley, North London, returned home to New Zealand and convinced Nelson College and the Nelson Football Club to adopt the game. During the following year the Nelsonians took rugby to Wellington, where the local club had been playing Victorian Rules. Auckland accepted rugby in 1873 under the influence of several public school old boys familiar with the code. Meanwhile, the Dunedin Football Club, formed in 1872, generally played Victorian rules or soccer. Its eventual conversion to rugby was guided by Professor George Sale, an 1840s Rugbean, and George Thomson, a teacher and scientist who had learnt the game at Edinburgh High School. Such influential patrons surely gave rugby an advantage in the struggle against other football codes – especially as the direct Australian influence on Victorian Rules began to decline with the end of the gold rushes and the departure of many of its most active supporters. The 1870s also witnessed a new wave of British migrants to New Zealand, among whom were men with first-hand experience of the game that the recently formed RFU was working hard to standardise. Yet the formative years in New Zealand were very much rugby in name only. There were considerable variations in rules, team sizes, field sizes, scoring values and length of game throughout the 1870s.[22]

As Geoffrey Vincent explains, the wider embrace of rugby from the mid-1870s was nothing to do with frontier males asserting their strength and vigour. Rather, in the manner of the search for a compromise in England in the 1850s, it was a pragmatic desire within the four main cities to find a common code that would enable teams from distant localities to play each other. The tour through New Zealand by Auckland Clubs in September 1875 was pivotal in turning both Christchurch and Dunedin to rugby rules in order to meet the visitors. This objective overcame the widespread perception that rugby was both too complicated and too dangerous.[23]

In order to understand why the growth of New Zealand rugby was such an urban affair, it is important to consider why rural areas failed to live up to the claims that have been made for them. Many small towns and country areas simply lacked the population and resources to sustain regular rugby of any standard. Consequently, the rural rugby history of the nineteenth century is one in which many clubs enjoyed only a few years of enthusiastic support before succumbing to player shortages and lack of opposition. Hence the first distinction that must be made is one between initial enthusiasm and sustained interest in the game. Phillips suggests that the expansion of rugby into the countryside by the mid-1870s was 'remarkable' – as shown by teams in such places as Temuka, Greymouth, Rangitikei, Oamaru, Pirongia, Greytown, Hawera, Patea, Riverton, Rakaia and Waimate.[24] But a closer examination reveals that the subsequent careers of most of these clubs, and many more besides, were perilous – dogged by player shortages, erratic fixture lists, poor finances and public apathy. The idealism and optimism that characterised most new communities was soon overtaken by the practical and time-consuming imperatives of development or, conversely, the failure of some towns to fulfil the expectations of their founders and promoters. Even areas such as Taranaki, Wanganui and Manawatu that were relatively well served by roads and a rail link to Wellington by the mid-1880s struggled to maintain regular rugby outside their main towns. As Rollo Arnold suggests, aside from the effort required to transform a 'bush burn' into a good playing ground, the constraints of rural work, such as the regular milking timetable in the Taranaki diary industry, also had a significant impact on the availability of players.[25] Many others were simply not willing to lose wages for a day spent travelling to the extremities of a district for an away game. In short, wherever one looks in the various provincial histories of New Zealand rugby – Buller, Poverty Bay, South Canterbury, Waikato and others – the pattern of fluctuation, frustration and rural complaint at urban neglect is the same. Although rural areas generally possessed a stable core of permanent residents, the size of many areas still meant that even small fluctuations of population around this base could signal the end of a rugby club. The departure or ageing of the rural rugby-playing population was not likely to be 'replenished' with the same regularity as in the cities. Nor were these difficulties confined to the early years of rugby in New Zealand. Many clubs, and even some provincial unions, struggled for continuity well into the twentieth century.[26]

The considerable mobility of rural workers, and their work patterns, also posed problems for rugby. The 1891 census reveals that seasonal workers, who were largely rural, constituted perhaps a third of the adult male European labour force, and that more than half were itinerant for some part of the year. This pattern did not alter during the early twentieth century – and was especially true of the young, single males who made up most of the rugby-playing fraternity.[27] Rural working hours also presented a barrier to playing regular rugby. The Saturday half-holiday, or any half-holiday for that matter, was still not standard for rural labourers after the turn of the century, and it seems that many of those who did have a half-holiday viewed it as a time for doing washing and other chores in order to keep Sunday free for rest and recreation.[28] However, prevailing sabbatarianism ensured that organised rugby was not played on Sunday – and would not be until at least the late 1960s.

These obstacles also determined the contribution of Maori to New Zealand rugby. Although historians have been quick to emphasise the presence of Maori players from the early 1870s, and much is made of their willing and welcome adoption of the game, their natural affinity for it, and of the importance of the 1888–89 New Zealand Native team and such talented players as Tom Ellison, David Gage and Jack Taiaroa, it is clear that these players were the exception to the rule. Despite the prevailing rhetoric, the Maori embrace of rugby prior to the 1920s was comparatively limited and largely confined to an elite who had experienced the European school system. The vast majority of the Maori population, until the second half of the twentieth century, was almost entirely rural and frequently located in areas of limited Pakeha population – and therefore areas of limited development for rugby. With the exception of Hawke's Bay (1884) and Wairarapa (1886), those areas with significant Maori population were among the last to establish overarching provincial rugby unions and representative teams – Waikato (1904), Bay of Plenty (1911), North Auckland (1920), East Coast (1921), King Country and Thames Valley (1922).[29] As with Pakeha, it is also probable that economic factors hindered access by rural Maori to regular participation in club and representative rugby. The vast majority of Maori remained economically marginalised on poor land with little available credit for its development and dependant on a mixture of subsistence agriculture and casual or seasonal work.[30] It may also be the case that Maori involvement in the game was determined by the nature of earlier contacts with Pakeha. Tribes such as Arawa and Ngati Porou actively engaged with the Pakeha world and were accordingly perceived as being particularly 'loyal' to the state. Others, such as Taranaki, the Waikato tribes and Tuhoe in the Urewera, harboured significant grievances as a consequence of the wars of the 1860s and sought to remain at a greater distance or actively disengage. While Arawa players from Bay of Plenty made a strong contribution to the formative years of representative Maori teams after 1910, the game made only slow progress in other areas – and especially the central North Island.[31]

To some extent, factors such as mobility and working hours also shaped rugby in the cities. But, at the same time, the volume of population meant that city rugby clubs were much better placed to absorb the impact of these obstacles. The cities also possessed a more diverse occupational base that undoubtedly left more players free on Saturday afternoon. As well as increasing numbers of urban professionals, and a larger community of relatively stable skilled workers, others benefited from the extension of the Saturday half-holiday under the terms of the Shops and Shop Assistants Act (1894) and the Shops and Offices Act Amendment Act (1905).[32]

Finally, the main cities also housed a number of the elite boys' schools such as Auckland Grammar School, Christ's College and Otago Boys' High School that played a vital role in nurturing rugby talent and producing a disproportionate number of provincial players during the nineteenth century. Thus the cities retained a significant continuity among their senior rugby clubs that was not evident in rural areas. Of the eight leading clubs in Auckland prior to 1914, six still held senior status in 1980. Of the nine leading Wellington clubs during this period, eight still held senior status in 1980. In Christchurch, only one of the nine clubs that appeared in regular competition during the late 1880s had ceased to exist as a senior club by 1980. In Dunedin, nine of the senior clubs in 1980 had a continuous lineage to formation dates between 1871 and 1884.[33]

Beginning with Canterbury and Wellington in 1879, Otago in 1881 and Auckland in 1883, 10 provincial rugby unions were established in the North Island and eight in the South by 1893. The emergence of all of these bodies reflected growth in playing numbers and local club competitions and a desire to standardise the laws and procedures of the game within each province and eventually between the provinces. But the struggle of rugby outside the four main cities is further echoed in the uneven pattern of contact between the unions during the nineteenth century. At least half of inter-provincial matches in the period 1880–1900 were between neighbouring rugby unions. A significant proportion of the remaining fixtures were against near neighbours, and contact between North and South Island teams was infrequent and expensive. Not surprisingly, the most fixtures were played by Wellington – the province at the geographical and administrative centre of New Zealand. The next most active provinces were Auckland, Canterbury and Otago, followed by Manawatu, Taranaki, Wairarapa and Wanganui – all provinces that were relatively well served by rail links from the 1880s. By contrast, the least active provinces were the most isolated – Buller and West Coast in the South Island, Bush and Poverty Bay in the North Island.[34]

In sum, rugby rested on a fairly narrow geographical base before 1905 and the opportunities for players depended very much on personal circumstances. Playing at a local or provincial level required access to an active club and province, as well as a Saturday half-holiday or a flexible employer to grant unpaid work leave. No doubt some of the self-employed and those with limited incomes were quickly discouraged. In terms of touring overseas, the field was largely confined to those without dependants – irrespective of the flexibility of their employment. Census data shows that those selected for New Zealand tours to Australia and to oppose Australian teams at home 1884–1900 were seven times more likely than the rest of the male workforce to have 'professional' occupations, and five times more likely during the next period 1901–14. While their representation in the 'industrial' category is fairly consistent with the norm, in the 'primary' sector – mainly farmers and to a much lesser extent miners – the All Black presence is considerably less than that for New Zealand as a whole. The men of the rural myth are a decided minority and, as we shall see in Chapter Three, even more so in the selection of the 1905 All Blacks.

As in Britain, the fledgling New Zealand game soon began to diverge from its elite origins, but with a less cataclysmic result. Public school men, who were influential at the beginning and always retained a conservative stake in the administration of New Zealand rugby, did not have the numbers to remain totally dominant. By necessity, the net had to be cast wider to raise teams from among a smaller colonial population. As Geoffrey Vincent explains, this led to the increasing presence of men with more socially inclusive attitudes. Often drawn from the commercially minded colonial middle class and involved in the management of small-scale enterprises that allowed more common ground between employer and worker, they were less bound by amateur traditions and perhaps possessed a greater tolerance towards elements of working-class culture. But this is not to say that the New Zealand game became the classless paradise imagined by some historians.

We have seen already that geographical and economic factors restricted opportunities for working-class participation at the higher levels. The same factors also meant that, although rugby quickly became a popular attraction, relatively speaking, New Zealand clubs and provinces lacked the numbers of revenue-producing spectators necessary to cover the costs of working-class participation on the scale emerging in the north of England – let alone to contemplate following the lead of the Northern Union after 1895. What emerged, however, was a game marked by some familiar northern characteristics – a strong desire to win, a willingness to pursue tactical innovations, a greater tolerance of 'hard' play and recognition that maximising comparatively limited opportunities for gate money depended on enticing the best players available to exhibit an open game that was attractive to spectators.[35] For a decade after the dramatic schism in Britain, the competing approaches to New Zealand rugby brooded just below the surface, exploding occasionally but never threatening to break, or be pushed, beyond the rugby union fold – at least not until the 1905 tour highlighted stark inequalities and raised other possibilities.

As rugby grew in the cities, tensions among conservative and liberal administrators and between administrators and players took a number of forms. Respectable elements, and especially the increasingly vocal prohibitionist lobby, felt that the spread of the game was delivering it into the morally suspect world of pub culture and associated vices such as gambling. While some of the new clubs found it both convenient and convivial to hold their meetings in pubs, critics were constantly on the lookout for misbehaviour among players. It is significant that the 1891 draft constitution of the New Zealand Rugby Football Union (NZRFU) devoted seven of its 26 clauses to disciplinary procedures, both on and off the field, and that the first annual general meeting in 1893 expressed a determination to 'put down anything which may, in any way, detract from the standing of the game, to secure equal justice to players, while meting out just punishment to offenders, to secure uniformity of rules and practice; to discourage betting and lavish expenditure on the entertainment of teams'.[36] There were also echoes of British debates over the desirability of organised competitions and trophies that seemed to place winning above taking part. During the late 1890s the Otago RFU, in some respects more liberal than its counterparts, accepted and then abandoned a competition trophy. Even the NZRFU only reluctantly accepted the Ranfurly Shield in 1902, and did not organise competition for it until 1904.[37]

Despite the efforts of some administrators to police the laws on professionalism, there is ample evidence in Otago rugby during the 1890s of surreptitious enticements and payments to players in the form of both the arrangement of employment and 'broken time'. Similarly in Christchurch, Sydenham, a predominantly working-class club, was known to present players with useful and expensive gifts on the occasion of their marriage and to make covert 'broken time' payments to its best players.[38] At the same time, gambling also emerged as a threat to establishment ideals. In May 1891 the Kaikorai team became embroiled in a scandal when it was alleged that players had 'thrown' the opening match of the season. Although the accusations could not be conclusively proved, Patrick Keogh, the Kaikorai halfback and one of the early stars of the New Zealand game, admitted to having gambled on games during the previous season and was suspended indefinitely as a professional. These events prompted the Otago RFU to express concern in 1893 that some teams were devoting too much attention to winning rather than participating.[39]

The intensity of the late nineteenth-century game is also apparent in the effort that went into developing tactical innovations and a more 'scientific' approach. But again an understanding of this area requires the debunking of certain popular myths. The most prevalent of these is a depiction of early New Zealand rugby as a very physical game – and one that derived its popularity form this very fact. Jock Phillips places much emphasis on the prolonged 'scrimmaging' that dominated the game of the 1870s and concludes that this was 'rather like an organised hug' that provided ample opportunities for necessary physical contact between men in a pioneering society where most married late and there was a shortage of women.[40] This misses the point on several counts.

First, the strong urban base of New Zealand rugby meant that the game was conducted in an environment where the gender imbalance was hardly a factor. For those of rugby-playing age, even if liberally defined as under 40, the gender imbalance that peaked during the goldrushes of the 1860s was lessening by the 1870s, and scarcely evident in the main centres by the time rugby started its more significant growth in the 1880s. Second, there is something a little incongruous in the notion that those who exerted themselves in physical work would seek further punishment on the sports field.[41] More importantly, while the fledgling and relatively unstructured rugby of the 1870s was certainly very physical, the same can not be said of the developing game of the 1880s, in which the emphasis shifted from brute force in prolonged forward exchanges to a dependence on skill in open play. This was the rugby that began to attract increasing numbers of players and appeal to a wider audience.

It has often been claimed that until the 1888 British touring team introduced the passing game, New Zealand had been restricted by a belief that heeling the ball from the scrum was illegal in that it automatically placed the forwards offside. But this view defies logic. Copies of the laws were widely available in New Zealand, and new players were constantly arriving from Britain with advice on the most recent interpretations of them. Irwin Hunter was in no doubt that heeling was an integral part of the New Zealand game during the early 1880s.[42] It is equally obvious, given that the game in Britain was also undergoing significant tactical developments throughout the 1880s and lacked an absolutely entrenched set of principles and on-field practices, that New Zealanders had the freedom to experiment in similar fashion. Writing in 1906, David Gallaher and Billy Stead even suggested that New Zealanders were more inclined to do so.

It happens in other departments of life that a young colony, beginning things afresh, infuses more energy and thoroughness into its business, and displays a greater fertility of invention and resource than its parent, and whilst in the matter of its football New Zealand fully and gratefully recognises its debt to the Mother Country, and admires the spirit of progress which has animated some sections of players there, it thinks that, as the natural result of its semi-independence, it has possibly displayed a greater keenness in perfecting the science of the game.[43]

Teams were seemingly always on the look out for new arrivals with new ideas, and it was not unusual in this period of experimentation for teams to oppose each other with distinctly different forward and back alignments in which players did not directly mark an opponent in the same position.

There is no doubt that, by the late 1880s, New Zealand tactics had shifted to an emphasis on structure and combination to promote effective back play. Whereas many British teams continued to use nine forwards during the early 1890s, and persisted with a 'first up, first down' approach to packing the scrum until 1905, eight forwards in specialist positions became the norm in New Zealand during the 1880s and was certainly regarded by many observers as being an important element in the success of the New Zealand Native team during its epic tour of Britain, Australia and New Zealand in 1888–89.[44] The objective of the scrum now shifted from pushing and retaining the ball among the forwards to heeling it quickly to the backs. Such a compact and controlled scrum also required only one halfback behind it – whereas two, and sometimes three, had previously been necessary to cover the likelihood of the ball emerging at any point. Experiments by Tom Ellison in Wellington during the early 1890s refined the scrum still further to seven forwards in a 2-3-2 formation with a wing-forward whose main job was to break quickly and pursue the opposition inside backs.[45] Meanwhile in Dunedin, refinements to back play produced, first, a system with four three-quarters, and then a distinctive five-eighths system in which one (and later two) players were positioned as pivots between the single halfback and the three-quarter line. The style of the 1905 All Blacks, aside from being a triumph of specialisation, was regarded as a compromise between the aggressive forward play of the North Island and the attacking back play of the South.[46]

It is obviously a truism to say that the success of the 1905 All Blacks was determined by broader developments within New Zealand rugby. But here it is important to remember that the relatively urban and somewhat middle-class game they represented is not the one that has been conventionally portrayed by its historians. Further, it was a game already showing marked differences in methods and ideals from that cherished by the conservative rugby establishment in Britain. We shall see in later chapters that these differences were critical to the ways in which the 1905 tour was interpreted in Britain.

CHAPTER TWO

Conflicts on the World Stage

Rugby in Britain and New Zealand certainly made dramatic progress during the last third of the nineteenth century. But, as with much progress, there is a sense in which its world became more, rather than less, complicated. The game of the elite had struggled to accommodate new players and playing styles, and an expanding administration had seen progress undercut by rivalries and antagonisms – and ultimately an irreconcilable division in 1895. In New Zealand there was similar class-based antagonism lurking close to the surface. As this chapter explains, such antagonism would become even more apparent as the colonial game expanded its horizons to embrace international competition from the 1880s. For as much as international rugby was a testament to the growing popularity of the game in distant parts of the British Empire, it was also a setting in which different methods and attitudes were starkly opposed to each other. The genesis of the 1905 tour can only be understood against a background of lingering tension from the tour of the New Zealand Native team, the efforts of the emerging NZRFU to unite competing interests within the game and the legacy of the 1904 British team.

From the early 1880s it was evident that New Zealand would command respect on the rugby fields of the British Empire. The first New South Wales touring team to New Zealand in 1882 lost three of its seven matches, and its successor in 1886 lost 10 of 12. The first New Zealand team to tour Australia in 1884, consisting of 19 players from the four main provinces, won all eight matches and startled many observers with its fast and open play.[1] But the pioneering tours of 1888 must be regarded as the true barometer for New Zealand rugby during its formative years – in terms of both strength and attitude. In late April a British team arrived for the first of two tours interspersed with games in Australia. In late June the New Zealand Native team embarked on a 14-month odyssey that amounted to 107 games in New Zealand, Australia and Britain.

The British team secured 13 wins, four draws and losses to Auckland and

Taranaki. While it certainly revealed some tactical innovations, especially in attacking back play, its methods and margins of victory did not overawe its opposition and left ample scope to believe that if a representative New Zealand team went to Britain it would be competitive.[2] In some respects such optimism was considerably enhanced by the performance of the Native team during 1888-89. Although a predominantly Maori combination, and therefore far from representative of the full strength of New Zealand rugby, it secured 49 wins, five draws and 20 losses from 74 outings during a frenetic six months in Britain. Moreover, it met the strongest clubs in England, north and south – a fact that will be considered later in assessing the record of the 1905 and 1924 All Blacks. Upon its return to New Zealand, the Native team also won much praise for its expansive style of play, and the combinations that were refined by Tom Ellison and others during the long tour were to leave an indelible mark on the tactical direction of New Zealand rugby from the 1890s to the 1930s.[3]

But the Native team is significant in several other ways as a prelude to 1905. From the outset the tour was dogged by controversy in New Zealand and Britain. Conceived by its promoters Thomas Eyton and Joseph Warbrick as both a sporting endeavour and a commercial speculation on the appeal of 'exotic' Maori players to a British audience little accustomed to non-white visitors, the Native team was sanctioned by the RFU in England and initially supported by the various New Zealand provincial unions in so far as they agreed to field teams against it. However, unconvincing performances in New Zealand prompted the addition of five Pakeha players to boost its strength.[4] This move was challenged by the provincial unions as a direct threat to their authority over the game – with the obvious implication that the original intention to use only Maori players somehow did not pose such a threat. The Hawke's Bay RFU condemned the inclusions as 'injurious and encroaching upon the functions of the various rugby unions in New Zealand', and asked the promoters to inform those in Britain that the team was not generally representative of the colony and that the Pakeha players had only been added in an emergency owing to a shortage of suitable Maori talent.[5] While any indiscretion by the tourists could be dismissed in New Zealand as the result of an unrepresentative private speculation beyond the control of the provincial rugby unions, the team was at the same time a product of the colony and would surely be identified as such by the British public.

These fears were quickly confirmed. Prior to the first matches in New Zealand, reports surfaced that the promoters and players were at odds over tour conditions and payments. Despite Warbrick's immediate denial that his team was engaged in any form of professionalism and would receive nothing more than 'bare expenses', and a letter from Thomas Eyton to George Rowland Hill, secretary of the RFU, offering to submit the tour accounts for inspection, these accusations cast a long shadow over the tour.[6] When the team returned to New Zealand in August 1889, four players were under suspension while the Otago RFU investigated accusations of match fixing arising from a game against Queensland in which the fullback was reportedly offered £50 if 'he would let the local men go past him occasionally'.[7] Again, exoneration did little to restore confidence in the team.

As the tour unfolded, relations between the Native team and the English rugby establishment became decidedly strained. Reports of early matches against southern county and club teams contain numerous references to 'a certain amount of roughness' on the part of the visitors, and even to 'vicious methods' being used against Kent.[8] Far more serious was the display against England when, after a dispute with referee Rowland Hill, three members of the Native team temporarily left the field in protest. The visitors objected to England's being awarded a try while the majority of their own team were forming a circle around the England captain Andrew Stoddart, 'to protect him from the vulgar gaze' after his shorts had been ripped in a tackle by Tom Ellison.[9] Nevertheless, the RFU extracted an apology under threat to cancel the remainder of the tour and London critics labelled the behaviour of the Native team 'disreputable' and a most 'childish and unsportsmanlike display'.[10] The team was snubbed by almost every leading southern player for its last match in London.[11] Off-the-field conduct was also far from exemplary. Apparently it was difficult to avoid 'constant lushing', one player was arrested for drunkenness in Belfast, and two were found sleeping in a shrubbery owing to the excesses of champagne before an important match against Middlesex.[12]

It is no coincidence that both on and off the field the Native team found solace and support in the north of England and in Wales. As Eyton put it, 'the sporting press of Manchester became almost members of the Maori brotherhood, and on the whole there was no need to complain that we were not fairly criticised'.[13] Elements of the northern press were quick to draw distinctions between 'rough' and 'hard' play in defence of the team and some hinted that the RFU was guilty of 'sharp practice' over events during the England international.[14] These responses indicate considerable similarity between the values of the more socially diverse rugby communities that were emerging in the north and in New Zealand – both of whom found themselves at odds with an establishment that would not, or could not, make concessions to local conditions. These similarities would not be apparent when the All Blacks encountered the conservative rump of British rugby in 1905.

The perceived conduct of the Native team had two important consequences. One, as we shall see shortly, was to undermine various proposals to send fully representative teams to Britain. The other was to give impetus to calls for a centralised administration in New Zealand. The controversies of the tour, and the expansion of rugby generally with increasing interprovincial and international contacts, highlighted the importance of such things as common disciplinary policy and interpretations of the laws among the provincial rugby unions. It has also been argued that the formation of the New Zealand Rugby Football Union, in 1892, was part of a logical process of nationalisation and centralisation that was occurring in many aspects of New Zealand life. Numerous other national bodies, commercial, political, scientific, sporting, emerged during the late nineteenth century as a reflection of both better communications and the gradual replacement of provincial with national identities. But the genesis of the NZRFU was not destined to be so simple.

It is important to remember that the European settlement of New Zealand occurred at different places, at different times and for different reasons. Until 1876 the colony was primarily administered as several separate provinces with their own governments. For much of the nineteenth century travel and communication between them was difficult, irregular and time-consuming. In this setting, the various cultural, economic, political and social differences between the provinces shaped quite distinct identities and strong rivalries that persisted long after much of New Zealand's infrastructure had been centralised.[15] There is ample evidence that interprovincial sporting contests, rugby and cricket especially, emerged as ways in which elements of distinct provincial identity continued to be expressed after the abolition of the provinces. Total interprovincial rugby matches increased from 44 in the decade after the first provincial tour by Auckland in 1875, to 159 in the decade 1885–94, and 334 in the decade up to 1904.[16] But it is equally evident that these were often far from friendly rivalries. While many saw the advantages of centralisation in New Zealand rugby following the Native tour, others saw threats to their autonomy.

Various proposals for a national union had circulated from 1879 but only gained momentum when E. D. Hoben, secretary of the Hawke's Bay RFU, took the lead and arranged a preliminary meeting in Wellington on 7 November 1891. Hoben stressed the need for a body that could establish a consensus on the arrangement of fixtures, interpretation of the laws and resolution of disputes. It was also pointed out that touring teams to New Zealand would find it easier to deal with one authority rather than each provincial union.[17] But South Islanders were considerably less enchanted with the proposals. Some regarded the new body and its intention to affiliate with the RFU as either an effort by Anglophiles to stifle change and innovation in the New Zealand game, or a revenue grab by Wellington bureaucrats. Others saw it as a North Island attempt to launch another speculative British tour on the lines of the Native team. Otago expressed a particular objection to submitting its business to an appeal committee in Wellington. Canterbury, given that it was affiliated directly to the RFU in England, objected to a loss of autonomy if it joined the NZRFU. As a result, Canterbury, Otago and Southland did not affiliate in 1892 and their players were not considered for the first national team sent to Australia by the union in 1893. Although Canterbury and Southland did join in 1894, Southland then withdrew over the refusal of the NZRFU to allow it to play Otago. Otago and Southland both came into the fold in 1895, but Horowhenua soon withdrew for three years when only two of its clubs were favourable to affiliation.[18]

Despite these struggles, New Zealand teams continued to forge a strong reputation in their limited appearances on the field. The first fully representative national team to tour Australia, in 1897, won nine of its 10 matches, and New South Wales was comprehensively defeated during a New Zealand tour in 1901. But the New Zealand team to Australia in 1903 took rugby to a new level. Under the captaincy of Otago's Jimmy Duncan, it scored 276 points to 13 in winning all 10 matches – including a 22–3 victory in the first test match against Australia, played at Sydney on 15 August. George Nicholson, who toured in both 1903 and 1905, was one of many who continued to regard Duncan's combination as individually and collectively the best to leave New Zealand.

> The 1903 All Blacks that toured Australia – that's the best team I ever saw or ever played with, and it also had the best five-eighth combination of the lot. Jimmy Duncan at first five-eighth and Morrie Wood at second were the perfect pair.[19]

It was the short tour by a British team in August 1904 that most sharply focused the attention of rugby followers and also reminded them of the tensions surrounding the New Zealand game. After 1888, a British team toured Australia in 1899 but did not cross to New Zealand, owing to the failure of its promoters to agree terms with the NZRFU. The 1904 combination, under the captaincy of Scotland's D. R. 'Darkie' Bedell-Sivright, was particularly strong in the backs – including the Welsh three-quarters Rhys Gabe, Willie Llewellyn and Teddie Morgan. Also included were two New Zealand medical students, Arthur O'Brien and Patrick McEvedy. But after winning all 13 matches in Australia, and scoring 260 points to 51, the British tourists found that New Zealand rugby posed an altogether tougher challenge. A 5–3 victory over a combined Canterbury-South Canterbury-West Coast XV in atrocious Christchurch conditions on 6 August was followed by a hotly contested 14–8 success over Otago-Southland four days later.[20]

On 13 August 1904 Wellington hosted the first test match on New Zealand soil. Needless to say, interest in the game was intense and preparations were meticulous. As the *Free Lance* put it, 'football is in the air, and everything else is dwarfed in consequence'.[21] Many critics insisted that the importance of the fixture required the New Zealand team to be in training for as much as a fortnight beforehand. Under growing pressure, the NZRFU Management Committee felt obliged to issue a statement pointing out that players in an amateur game could not be expected to devote so much time to training. Moreover, four days' practice before the test was considered sufficient for talented players to develop understanding and combination.[22]

The test attracted a capacity crowd of 20,000 – many of whom had paid considerably more than the face value of their tickets. Also present were the Governor, Lord Plunket; the Premier, Richard Seddon; and several Cabinet ministers. Meanwhile, in various other parts of the country, large crowds began to assemble at telegraph offices to await the result. Late in the afternoon they were told of a tight encounter in which New Zealand eventually prevailed 9–3 through superior forward play, two tries to the speedy wing Duncan McGregor and a penalty to Billy Wallace. With its confidence dented by this outcome, the British team drew 0–0 with Taranaki, lost decisively 13–0 to Auckland and concluded its sojourn in New Zealand with an 8–6 loss in an unofficial fixture against a Maori XV at Rotorua.[23]

Of course much more than rugby supremacy was at stake for a young colony seeking to make its mark on the world stage. For its part, the *Evening Post* viewed the tour in broad imperial terms.

> Second to none among the inter-imperial bonds is the brotherhood of outdoor sport. How much of the Briton's prowess and character are built up in the field of play. How great a part his external exercises, formation

of body, mind and morals, play in maintaining his paramountcy in all parts of the world. And now is seen the peculiar and intensely interesting spectacle of a young Briton of a new land, meeting on his own soil, in the old traditional game, his antipodean rival. Sprung from a common stock, they fight hard, and not always with the gloves on.[24]

But it was the *New Zealand Herald* that perhaps better captured the prevailing mood after the test victory. Although rugby tours were certainly important in encouraging the virility of the British race and in reinforcing bonds of Empire,

> They are also of invaluable benefit in rousing and strengthening that pride of country which has sometimes been said to be wanting among the youth of the colonies, for every young New Zealander to-day will feel an inch taller because of the victory that was won at Wellington by the football champions of the colony.[25]

Not all observers were so enamoured of the New Zealand achievement, and there were ample warnings of the problems to be encountered at the end of 1905. Although Bedell-Sivright conceded that the best team had won the test match, he insisted that the conventional British scrum formation with three men in the front row was still superior to the 2-3-2 and wing-forward used by New Zealand. Later, when safely ensconced in Sydney, he was highly critical of infringements by New Zealand forwards and the failure of local referees to take action. Another team member, Rhys Gabe, objected to the New Zealand spirit of 'win at all costs' and especially the frequent instances of tackling a man after he had parted with the ball. 'Your men are clever enough to win without indulging in these tactics, and it would then be a healthier game and the public would enjoy it better.'[26]

Finally, Arthur O'Brien, a man familiar with the rugby cultures of Britain and New Zealand, condemned the apparent unwillingness to police the wing-forward.

> I can assure you that if you tell a man he is off-side in England, he will mostly get on side at once. It doesn't do much good to tell a New Zealand wing-forward that he is off-side. The referees here seem to have got used to obstruction and that sort of thing. Certainly they don't penalise it often enough.[27]

In retort, the *Otago Daily Times* felt that New Zealanders had learned nothing new from the visitors and 'In some particulars, too, the game played by the British team does not meet approval. Infringements of the rules by its members were frequent and occasionally glaring.' These sentiments were endorsed by *The Press* immediately following the test: 'Breaches of the rules were unfortunately numerous, but in this respect the visitors set our representatives no good example, as they were the more frequent transgressors.'[28]

New Zealanders could undoubtedly derive sufficient confidence from the performances against the British team to counteract some of the negative perceptions of the colonial game, but there was also a strong sense that the task was not complete – that the real test for New Zealand rugby could only come 'at Home'. Just as Australian cricket successes during the 1870s could be dismissed as curiosities of local conditions, and it was the 'Ashes' victory at the Oval in 1882 that truly captured the attention of English observers, so the prevailing view in New Zealand was that success could only be measured with victories in Britain. While Bedell-Sivright's team was certainly a strong combination, it was not reckoned to be the equal of the international teams of the Home Unions. By this measure, most predicted that while New Zealand could win the majority of its matches, success in the internationals was doubtful. Indeed, Teddy Morgan, who predicted that New Zealand would win 75 per cent of its matches, declared that they would be 'no match' for England, Scotland and Wales.[29]

The disagreements that arose from the visit of Bedell-Sivright's team, as had been the case with the Native team, highlight a crucial contradiction in the imperial touring network that would only be exacerbated by the 1905 tour. From the 1870s cricket exchanges between England and Australia, New Zealand, South Africa, India and the West Indies were presented as devices to reinforce imperial solidarity and strengthen cultural bonds of Englishness between the Mother Country and her colonies. Immediately after the turn of the century, and in the context of the burgeoning 'new imperialism', both the Marylebone Cricket Club and the Rugby Football Union saw the touring network as a significant cog in reasserting the unity of the British Empire in the wake of the bitter South African War of 1899–1902. The RFU also viewed it as a means to spread the gospel of amateurism and stifle the Northern Union.[30] Running counter to these ideals, it was often apparent that some of the tours also provided a staging ground for assertive colonialism or emergent nationalism and revealed a growing disparity between the sporting ideals of Empire-minded Britons and those developing in colonial settings. Much in the methods and attitudes of the

Native team drew antagonism from the British sporting elite. In similar fashion, the first quarter-century of Anglo-Australian cricket yielded numerous instances of antagonism and dispute, ranging from the crowd riot at Sydney in February 1879 during the tour of Lord Harris's XI, to English captain Andrew Stoddart's complaint against the 'barracking' of Australian crowds in 1898 that 'We have been insulted, hooted at, and hissed in every match and on every ground without exception'.[31] At the same time, Australian cricket was marked by bitter regional and personal rivalries among players and administrators over team selections and financial control of the game.[32] Such wrinkles in the fabric of imperial sporting relations may also explain the apparent delay in organising the 1905 tour.

Given the prominence of rugby in New Zealand by the late 1880s, and the exploits of the Native team as inspiration, it is perhaps surprising that the provincial rugby unions or the NZRFU did not secure a tour of Britain long before 1905. Their cricketing counterparts in Australia carried out a dozen such ventures between 1878 and 1905. But it seems that the uncomfortable legacy of the Native team and the fractious internal politics of the New Zealand game were difficult hurdles to overcome. Shortly after the Native team departed in August 1888, plans were afoot for a second Maori team to tour Britain and North America. When these collapsed, a group of Wellington enthusiasts announced plans in April 1889 to assemble a fully representative New Zealand team. But several provincial unions, no doubt with the embarrassment of the England international walk-off and other stinging criticisms of the Native team fresh in their minds, immediately condemned the idea and insisted that any subsequent tour must be under their authority. The Otago RFU also felt that frequent touring would encourage professionalism because the participants would spend long periods devoted to playing rather than working. It was to be four years before another team left New Zealand, on a tour to Australia under the auspices of the newly formed NZRFU.[33]

The formation of the NZRFU in 1892 re-ignited proposals for a tour of Britain. With the NZRFU and some provincial unions having direct affiliation to the RFU in England, negotiations were conducted directly with that body rather than the wider International Board, which also included Ireland, Scotland and Wales. In 1893 Cecil Wray Palliser, a permanent staff member of the New Zealand Agent General's office in London and recently appointed NZRFU delegate to the RFU, presented the case for a tour and stressed that it would be under entirely different auspices from the private and troublesome Native team. However, his best efforts were sabotaged by

Samuel Sleigh, the Otago representative to the RFU, who pointed out, with the aid of a map, that because the main South Island provincial unions were not affiliated to the NZRFU its team could in no way be representative of New Zealand rugby.[34] Strangely, although the recalcitrant unions had joined the NZRFU fold by 1895, there is no evidence of another approach to the RFU during the next seven years. It was perhaps the case that the spectre of professionalism hanging over the Native team had not entirely evaporated.

In 1898, when prominent politician and sporting administrator Alfred Newman raised the possibility of a tour, Tom Ellison presented an obvious stumbling block and a simple solution.

> I see one difficulty only, and that is getting the best men away without giving them some allowance over and above their actual hotel and travelling expenses – a difficulty due to the stringency of the laws as to professionalism. Personally, I think that these laws were never intended to apply to extended tours abroad. Such tours were never contemplated at the time the rules were framed. However, if I am wrong in this view, I think that the law, under certain circumstances, should be relaxed.[35]

It is hard to imagine that anyone in Britain would have sanctioned Ellison's proposal so soon after the emergence of the Northern Union. To the contrary, the RFU position had been made very clear in 1888 when Jack Clowes, a member of the British touring team, was suspended for allegedly accepting payment of £15 for clothing and other tour items from one of the promoters. The RFU also expressed concern that other members of the team had infringed the laws, and all were called upon to provide an affidavit stating that they had received no pecuniary benefit from the tour.[36]

When a new tour proposal did emerge in 1902, it merely demonstrated the fragile unity of the NZRFU and the clashes between idealism and pragmatism that were becoming more evident in New Zealand rugby. At the AGM on 25 April 1902, W. Coffey of Canterbury moved a motion to take definite steps towards a tour of Britain no later than the end of 1903. Without a vote being taken, the matter was referred to the provincial unions for comment – a move that incensed Coffey, who sought a legal opinion on the validity of the decision to postpone the motion. As the *Lyttelton Times* described the acrimonious proceedings, 'Strong statements and tardy withdrawals were the principal characteristics of the debate.'[37]

The particular point of contention was revealed at a special general meeting on 5 June, when Coffey echoed Ellison's position in stating that a special dispensation would be required from the RFU on the laws of professionalism as each player in a representative team would require a £3 a week living wage in order to tour. While he was no advocate of professionalism, Coffey hoped the RFU would 'meet' the New Zealand request, as it was unfair to ask players to tour without wages when many had dependant relations. He added that the New Zealand government could also be asked for a financial contribution to the tour, as it had done so for riflemen who attended the Bisley Royal National Rifle Association tournament. Another delegate moved an amendment that the RFU should be asked to waive the laws on professionalism only to the extent necessary to allow a tour. Neil Galbraith of Wellington further proposed that the NZRFU should be given absolute discretion over the level of travel and other expenses allowed to players during the tour. Finally, R.M. Isaacs of Otago suggested that the tour could be fully financed by public subscription. But the majority declared that such proposals were 'professionalism of the worst kind', and it was pointed out that any presentations to players beyond basic expenses would make them professionals. All of the motions were lost.[38] Nevertheless, it is testimony to the relative accommodation of working-class interests in New Zealand rugby that elements within the NZRFU were willing to propose such flexibility at a time when the spectre of the Northern Union was inflicting severe damage on English rugby.

In late June 1902 a subcommittee comprising George Dixon, A. C. Norris and Coffey was appointed to draft a letter to the RFU and to consult William Pember Reeves, the New Zealand Agent General in London, and Joseph Ward, the acting Premier, regarding prospects for a tour. When the letters were approved on 24 June, A. W. Thomson of Wanganui voted against that to the RFU because it referred to the need for 'reasonable expenses beyond those actually required for transit and board'.[39] Precisely what transpired in the subsequent correspondence has not survived. But on 30 September 1902, with positive replies from Reeves and the RFU to hand, the NZRFU Management Committee expressed the opinion that a tour would be possible under the existing laws of professionalism. Providing that satisfactory finance could be secured, provincial unions were now requested to forward names of players willing to tour at the end of 1903.[40]

In April 1903 the RFU suggested postponing the tour until the end of 1904. The following January it called a further postponement until the end of 1905, as the Home Unions' international calendar for the 1904–05 season was already in place.[41] In a letter to the NZRFU in March 1904, Rowland Hill, secretary of the RFU, outlined various financial requirements for the tour – including the willingness of England and Wales to guarantee at least £500 each for an international match. Scotland offered the whole gate but no guarantee – a point worthy of note given the manner in which its position was subsequently manufactured as a controversy.[42] On 14 March 1904 the tour subcommittee presented a report estimating that a 25-member, three-month tour would cost £5,000 – a figure that increased to £6,000 by early 1905. It was hoped to secure £2,000 from guarantees and the issue of debentures in New Zealand, leaving £4,000 to be obtained from gate revenue in Britain and from preliminary matches in Australia and New Zealand. In Britain the terms were 70 per cent of gate receipts or a £50 guarantee from each match.[43] The NZRFU would provide £300, the larger provincial unions would contribute £100 and each be responsible for the sale of £150 worth of debentures. The smaller unions were asked for £100 in total and the disposal of £400 worth of debentures between them. Unnamed 'public spirited' men in Hawke's Bay were apparently willing to contribute funds towards the tour, and there was also reason to believe that 'special aid' would come from the government. Any profit from the venture would be used to redeem debentures and then refund the provincial union subscriptions pro rata.[44]

On 6 May 1904 a lively NZRFU AGM formally approved a tour of Britain at the end of 1905.[45] But again the endorsement was hardly unanimous. Otago opposed the venture on several grounds:

(1) That the visit would not benefit New Zealand football (vide Native team); (2) that the work of the New Zealand Union is the conservation of football and not the advertisement of the colony; (3) that football is at such an ebb in New Zealand as to render the movement inopportune; (4) that it would be impossible to form such a team without constituting the members thereof professionals; (5) that the surplus funds of football in New Zealand will be better directed to the more frequent visits of football teams from England; (6) that such a trip may spoil the lives of many of the participants (vide Native team); (7) that there has been no invitation received from Home for a team to visit England, all the representations having been made from New Zealand.[46]

While various other delegates ignored Otago's objections and enthusiastically endorsed the tour, the question of amateur status again provoked debate. Here the most revealing statement came from the NZRFU President, G. F. C. Campbell, who insisted that if friends contributed money to enable a player to tour, this was more in the manner of a private loan between one man and another and was no business of the union. A breach of amateur status would only occur if players were paid directly by the NZRFU. Others dissented from such a liberal interpretation and the debate ended inconclusively.[47] Finding itself in the minority, Otago subsequently agreed to provide a share of the financial guarantee, but only if the government was not involved in financially assisting the tour in any way. Similarly, Canterbury declared that it would be 'most degrading to sport to go to the Government for money' and that its £250 would only be forthcoming if such an appeal was not made. Taranaki, South Canterbury and Wanganui, while supporting the tour, declared their inability to assist with any part of the financial guarantee.[48] As for the government, although the manager of the touring team, George Dixon, travelled to Britain with a letter of introduction from Premier Richard Seddon,[49] the details of any financial contribution are uncertain. In June 1906 a report emerged that £1,963 had been contributed.[50] However, there is no evidence of this in the accounts for the British section of the tour – suggesting that, if the claim was true, this amount represented the controversial subsidy arranged by Premier Seddon to parade the team through North America in February 1906.[51] Certainly those charged with balancing the NZRFU books in 1904–05 saw no sign of a subsidy. Nor did they meet their expectations in terms of debentures, with only £1,722 of the projected £2,000 being sold by the time the team left New Zealand.[52]

In what would later emerge as one of the most keenly debated aspects of the 1905 tour, the NZRFU announced in early December 1904 that all team members would receive an expense allowance of three shillings per day while absent from New Zealand. Given that it was commonly known that Bedell-Sivright's British team had toured under the same terms, the announcement produced not a murmur. Indeed, so assured were the players of the legitimacy of the payments that one, Billy Stead, wrote to the NZRFU asking whether further provision could be made for married men and whether the existing allowance was to be paid for Sundays. The union replied: 'No and Yes'.[53] Potentially more controversial in light of the debates in 1904 were reports in July and August 1905 that 'purses of sovereigns' were presented to several players to assist them during the tour. H. J. 'Simon' Mynott of Taranaki reportedly received 70 sovereigns from well-wishers – a gesture that antagonised at least one critic, who remembered the inability of the Taranaki union to contribute to the tour fund during the previous year.[54] Apparently these payments had been reported from New Zealand to the RFU with a view to having the players declared professional on arrival in Britain. Rather than denying the veracity of the reports, the *Otago Witness* went on the offensive: 'The strict view of the laws in regard to professionalism in England and Wales would undoubtedly point to the recipients being classed as professionals, but it appears to be the view of every commonsense person in our democratic colony that the rule is positively ridiculous and wants wiping out altogether.'[55] While the purses of sovereigns, if they existed, drew no comment or censure from the RFU's consistently vigorous investigators of professional transgressions, the attitudes of a number of New Zealand administrators and commentators towards the financial arrangements for the 1905 tour ensured that a collision between amateurism and professionalism was not far away.

A snapshot of New Zealand rugby in 1905 presents a very mixed picture. In playing terms, New Zealanders had every reason to believe that while their team was not invincible, it would certainly be competitive in Britain. Since 1884, representative New Zealand teams had won 38 of their 41 matches against Australian opposition and their only encounter against a British team. Provincial teams had also enjoyed consistent success over their New South Wales and Queensland counterparts, Auckland had comprehensively defeated the 1904 British tourists and Taranaki drawn with them. At domestic level there were 40 inter-union matches in 1905, including Auckland reclaiming the Ranfurly Shield from Wellington, and Otago University became the first New Zealand club side to tour overseas when it visited Sydney. Shortly after the departure of the All Blacks for Britain in July 1905, the first fully representative Australian team arrived for a seven-match tour, which included defeat by a New Zealand team containing several of those unavailable or unlucky to miss the major selection. These achievements stemmed from a player base that had reached approximately 7,000 registered adult players in 1904.[56]

In other respects, however, followers of New Zealand rugby were less sure of themselves. In May 1904 the annual general meeting of the Canterbury RFU contained lengthy discussion about increasing incidents of rough play and foul language, and concern that the British team may refuse to play Canterbury if such behaviour continued.[57] In June there were frequent reports of violence at club matches in Wanganui and Wellington, and a Wellington player died after receiving a kick in the head. In July, Auckland rugby was gripped by a gambling scandal involving the leading clubs City and Newton, and claims that players were receiving money from bookmakers to perform badly. The Auckland RFU eventually suspended two players, including 1903 New Zealand representative A. J. 'Paddy' Long, for 10 years, and one bookmaker was 'warned off' all grounds under the control of the NZRFU.[58] The annual report of the NZRFU in April 1905 was suitably pessimistic.

> Regret is expressed that the game is not free from the ills that from time to time bring odium upon it, but there are satisfactory indications that the unions are alive to their responsibilities. There is, however, a tendency to leniency, and an appeal is made to create a higher ideal of play. Consideration might be given to the question of modifying the laws so as to enable wider observation to be brought to bear on the field of play to cope with the evils everyone knows to exist.[59]

At the annual meeting, Dr Thomas Hunter of Otago complained that money was looming too large in New Zealand rugby, that too many testimonials were being given to players and that it was questionable whether these constituted breaches of the laws on professionalism. He also criticised rough play and lax refereeing. Press reports for 1904–05 abound with references to bad behaviour and the suspension or disqualification of players for various indiscretions.[60] Nor, it seems, had the internal politics of the NZRFU improved significantly since the mid-1890s. The appointment of Edgar Wiley as secretary in 1905 led to parochial friction at the annual meeting. Later in the year Canterbury proposed to move the NZRFU headquarters from Wellington, and Southland proposed a five-year rotation around the main centres.[61] For its part, the NZRFU felt that its authority was being undermined by those unions such as Otago that were still directly affiliated to the RFU. Finally, after an Otago request directly to London for a clarification of the laws on rough play, the 1904 NZRFU annual report reminded all affiliates that any communication with the RFU had to go through Wellington and not directly from individual unions.[62] Against this background, any portrayal of the 1905 All Blacks as the logical outcome of a coherent and united 'national game' is to miss many important points.

CHAPTER THREE

Deliberations and Expectations

HAVING COMMITTED TO a tour of Britain at the end of 1905, the NZRFU then embarked on the search for players of suitable ability and, as importantly, suitable character. But, despite the importance of the undertaking, the process was beset with controversies and acrimony, and appears distinctly haphazard in several respects. The final selection of the team, the decision to appoint Jimmy Duncan as coach, decidedly patchy performances during preliminary matches in Australia and New Zealand, and the strained relations that emerged between members of the touring party during the six-week journey to Britain, all point to the 1905 All Blacks as the product of a divided game. Moreover, although the fortunes of British rugby had declined significantly since the visit of the Native team in 1888, public expectations for the New Zealand team were muted at best.

In November 1904, after nominations from the provincial unions, a selection committee composed of George Fache (Wellington), Walter Garrard (Canterbury) and Henry Harris (Otago) compiled a list of 50 players from which the team would be selected. Three more were soon added. While the players were asked to confirm their availability by 31 December 1904, their unions were also asked to submit a confidential report on the character and general conduct of each.[1] Five members of the eventual touring party – Abbott, Gillett, Smith, Cunningham and McDonald – were not included on the original list.

By early January 1905, 41 of the 53 players had confirmed their availability, although David Gallaher, the eventual captain of the team, was not among them. Aside from doubts about his ability to secure work leave, he was currently under suspension by the NZRFU until it received a satisfactory explanation for the £4 14s expenses he had claimed from the 1904 British match.[2] Among those definitely unable to tour were Ernest Fookes, Colin Gilray and the 1903 New Zealand representative Reuben Cooke. Born in Wairoa and initially educated at New Plymouth Boys' High School, Fookes went to England in 1890 to complete his education and eventually graduated in medicine from Manchester University. He played for Halifax but was the only active player to leave the club when it joined the Northern Union in August 1895. Transferring to Sowerby Bridge, he made his debut for Yorkshire against Lancashire in the first match after the split, captained the county in the 1896-97, 1897-98 and 1898-99 seasons and won 10 England caps 1896-99 as a wing or fullback. Returning to New Zealand in 1900, he played four seasons for Taranaki, including an appearance at fullback against the British team.[3] Gilray, who represented Otago 1904-06 and New Zealand against Australia in August 1905, went to Oxford University on a Rhodes Scholarship in 1907 and subsequently won four caps for Scotland in 1908, 1909 and 1912 – at a time when players moved rather more easily between countries of the British Empire than later International Rugby Board regulations would allow.[4] In February the 1904 New Zealand halfback Peter Harvey also declared himself unavailable. The importance of his job as a lip-reading teacher at the Sumner School for the Deaf, near Christchurch, meant that he could not be spared despite representations to the government on his behalf.[5]

On 27 January 1905 the selectors submitted the names of 24 players to the NZRFU Management Committee – including five who did not subsequently tour and one, Donald Stuart, who was not on the original list of 53. At the same time, George Dixon, an Auckland accountant and newspaper manager and loyal servant of the NZRFU Management Committee, was unanimously appointed manager of the team. All of those initially selected, but whose names had not yet been made public, were also warned that their place on the tour would depend on form during the early part of the 1905 season. Within the week, and without any public explanation, it was decided to expand the touring party to 26.[6] In mid-February, with his suspension lifted, Gallaher finally confirmed his availability if chosen, and it was also reported that George Smith, a prominent jockey, leading athlete and star back of New Zealand teams in 1897 and 1901, had resumed his sporadic rugby career with the hope of gaining selection.[7]

At the end of February the selection of 17 players, subject to passing a medical examination and retaining form, was confirmed to the public. These certainties were Booth, Corbett, Deans, Glenn, Harper, Hunter, Johnston, McGregor, Mynott, Nicholson, O'Sullivan, Roberts, Seeling, Stead, Stuart, Tyler and Wallace.[8] A month later, Gillett, Smith, Thompson, Scobie Hay-McKenzie of Auckland and David Whisker of Wellington (the last two of whom did not tour) were provisionally added.[9] The supposed remainder of the touring team – Casey, Gallaher, Glasgow, Mackrell, McDonald and

Newton – were finally confirmed after the inter-island match at Wellington on 3 June.[10] In the meantime, in late May, Donald Stuart of Otago was informed that he had failed the medical examination because of a weak heart resulting from typhoid and was unable to tour. Initially he was not replaced.[11]

Why the NZRFU approached such an important selection task in so haphazard a fashion is hard to understand, and inevitably the union left itself open to a good deal of public condemnation. In December 1904 the *NZ Referee* criticised the decision to select the team six months before departure, as it was possible that some could lose form during 1905, while others could come to prominence.[12] In January, before any names had been announced, the *Otago Witness* attacked the apparent non-inclusion of Bob Bennet, who confirmed that he was not one of the original 53 to be contacted: 'The Alhambra player, if the selectors had known their business, should have been one of the first chosen.'[13] In early February a Wellington correspondent for the *Witness* launched a stinging attack on NZRFU selection methods and the recently announced decision to take a manager and two extra players: 'The management in recent years has been just about as feeble as it is possible, and it is apparently little better now.' At the same time the Wellington RFU submitted a formal protest against the non-selection of Joseph Calnan,[14] a loose forward who represented Wellington on 49 occasions 1895–1906 and played nine games for New Zealand in Australia in 1897. His absence probably stemmed from a two-year suspension incurred for drunkenness and bad language during an incident in Auckland when the team returned from Australia.[15] That such considerations were uppermost in the minds of the NZRFU also seems apparent from a rebuke delivered by the normally conservative James Hutchinson of Otago, who informed the 1905 annual general meeting that he objected strongly to players having to pass 'a social or moral test, as it were, and their reputations hawked all over the colony'.[16] Finally, when the selectors revealed their complete team after the interisland match, and Auckland's Hay-McKenzie was the only back from the winning North Island team to miss selection, after being provisionally included, several accusations of southern bias appeared in the northern press.[17]

The final phase of the selection process suggests that the lack of public confidence in NZRFU methods was entirely justified. When the team arrived in Sydney for a preliminary tour in July, they had no idea who had been selected as lock – a vital position to bind the 2-3-2 scrum. Experiments with John Corbett and Fred Newton could not transform a weak forward effort, with the result that Bill Cunningham of Auckland was belatedly added to the touring party the moment it returned to New Zealand.[18] During the week before departure the Taranaki wing Harold 'Bunny' Abbott also joined the team, while the Otago halfback James King was given until 26 July, four days before departure, to indicate his availability. When King declared himself unavailable, no further steps were taken to find a second halfback and the team, which had now expanded to 27, was confirmed almost by default.[19]

The NZRFU took even longer to confirm the leadership of such an important venture. No more than three days before the team departed Wellington on 30 July, David Gallaher was appointed captain and Billy Stead vice-captain. A veteran of the South African war and of Auckland rugby teams since 1896, Gallaher appears to posterity as a natural leader and a man of considerable integrity. Yet his appointment as captain was by no means clear-cut, as witnessed by his strained relationship with the NZRFU towards the end of 1904 and questions over his availability. Moreover, Stead had captained New Zealand against the British team in 1904, and Jimmy Hunter, who led the preliminary tour to Australia in the absence of both Gallaher and Stead, was also considered a prospect.[20]

If the NZRFU was less than efficient in assembling its touring party, it appeared to leave nothing to chance in the tour agreement that all players were obliged to sign before departure.

> WE the undersigned members of the Football Team about to tour Great Britain and Ireland under the auspices of The New Zealand Rugby Football Union do hereby in consideration of the New Zealand Rugby Football Union paying our passage money and travelling expenses and paying the daily allowance for out-of-pocket expenses hereinafter mentioned agree with the said New Zealand Rugby Football Union and with G. H. Dixon the representative of the said New Zealand Rugby Football Union travelling as Manager of the said Team in manner following that is to say: –
>
> 1. THAT we will each of us well and cheerfully obey all reasonable requests, orders and instructions of the said G. H. Dixon in the capacity of Manager of the said Team relating to training, travelling arrangements and general conduct.
>
> 2. THAT we will remain on tour with the said team and will not without the consideration of the said G. H. Dixon leave the main body thereof at any time until the conclusion of the series of matches which the New Zealand Rugby Football Union has undertaken to play in England, Wales, Ireland and Scotland has been completed.

3. THAT we will throughout the tour conduct ourselves in a quiet, orderly, sober and respectable manner and will do all in our power to uphold the good name of the said Team and the credit of the Colony.

4. THAT we will abstain from betting on the results of any match to be played by the said Team and will not receive any moneys or payment or equivalent of any kind whatever from any person or persons dependant on the result of any match to be played by the said Team and will strictly adhere to all the rules as to Professionalism as laid down by the Rugby Union of England.

5. THE New Zealand Rugby Football Union shall manage and pay for all travelling expenses, board and reasonable washing for the members of the said Team and will allow to each member of the said Team Three shillings (3/-) per diem as and for out-of-pocket expenses incurred on the said tour, such allowance to commence from the date of departure from New Zealand and to be paid weekly until arrival back at any port in New Zealand provided that such daily allowance shall not be payable after the expiration of nine weeks from the date of the last match in the United Kingdom.

6. ANY member failing to adhere to the conditions or any condition herein set out or in any way misconducting himself may at the discretion of the said G. H. Dixon be sent back forthwith to New Zealand and also may have his daily allowance mentioned in paragraph 5 hereof wholly stopped or suspended for any length of time.

7. THE New Zealand Rugby Football Union shall in no way be deemed to be responsible or liable for any accident that may befall any member of the Team either whilst travelling or whilst taking part in any match.[21]

Mostly this agreement was a reflection of the NZRFU's determination to maintain firm control over its players and ensure that the tour was free of indiscretion. But as we shall see in Chapter Nine, the apparent generosity over expenses in clause 5 was to produce no small amount of controversy. But from the players' perspective, the parsimonious approach embodied in the final clause would return to haunt Australasian rugby in ways that none could have imagined in 1905.

Perhaps the most charitable view of the final selection came from 'Full-Back' in the *Otago Witness*: 'Taking the team as at present chosen, it must be regarded by the unbiased as a strong combination – one likely to do the colony credit both on and off the field . . . They are all men of splendid physique who can play a hard game from end to end.' But with strength in the forwards rather than the backs, and a notable weakness at halfback, the team ought to be regarded as solid rather than brilliant.[22] Dixon later claimed that several other players were entitled to selection and New Zealand was therefore much more than a one-team colony.[23]

Despite its controversial non-selections and the unavailability of other undoubtedly talented players, the touring party contained a core of experience. Smith had toured Australia in 1897, and Cunningham had played at home against New South Wales in 1901. Of the outstanding team to Australia in 1903, Gallaher, McGregor, Nicholson, Stead, Tyler and Wallace were included, while Deans, Glenn, Harper and Seeling had been capped against Bedell-Sivright's team. Abbott, Booth, Casey, Corbett, Gillett, Glasgow, Hunter, Johnston, Mackrell, McDonald, Mynott, Newton, O'Sullivan, Roberts and Thomson were all new to international rugby.

In light of subsequent explanations for their success in terms of rural pioneering virtues, it is important to consider the origins of the 1905 All Blacks as much for who they were as who they were not. As the previous chapter demonstrated, nineteenth-century New Zealand rugby was a largely urban game. While the proportion of the total population resident in the four main cities increased from nearly a quarter to slightly less than a third in the years 1881–1911, two-thirds of All Blacks selected prior to 1914 came from the four main cities. Using a broader definition of urban areas that includes New Zealand's 20 largest towns and cities, which accounted for slightly more than 40 per cent of the population, nearly 90 per cent of the All Blacks were drawn from urban clubs. The 1905 team, with 66.66 per cent from the four main cities, and 85.18 per cent (23 of 27) if the larger towns are included, are entirely consistent with this pattern. That six of the team came from Taranaki, a relatively well-developed province in terms of its rugby infrastructure in and around New Plymouth, and the province that contributed more pre-1914 All Blacks (26) than any other outside the main four, is similarly unsurprising.[24] Nor is the 1905 combination typical of either the supposed formula for All Black success or the occupational profile of the New Zealand population as a whole. Aside from Deans, Hunter and O'Sullivan, all farmers defined as being part of the primary sector, 15 came from blue-collar industrial backgrounds, six from broadly professional occupations and three from transport, whereas the 1906 census reveals that for males aged 20–25, 32.44 per cent worked in the primary sector, 36.63 per cent in industry, 9.18 per cent in transport and communications and only 4.65 per cent were professional. In terms

THE 1905 ALL BLACKS

Backs	Province	Club	Occupation
H. L. Abbott	Taranaki	Star	blacksmith
E. E. Booth	Otago	Kaikorai	journalist
R. G. Deans	Canterbury	Old Boys	farmer
G. A. Gillett	Canterbury	Merivale	tramways employee
E. T. Harper	Canterbury	Christchurch	solicitor
J. Hunter	Taranaki	Hawera	armer
D. McGregor	Wellington	Petone	railway worker
H.J. Mynott	Taranaki	Tukapa	tinsmith
F. Roberts	Wellington	Oriental	clerk
G. W. Smith	Auckland	City	meatworker
J. W. Stead	Southland	Star	bootmaker
H. D. Thomson	Wanganui	Wanganui	civil servant
W. J. Wallace	Wellington	Poneke	ironmaster

Forwards			
S. T. Casey	Otago	Southern	storeman
J. Corbett	West Coast	Reefton	baker
W. Cunningham	Auckland	Ponsonby	blacksmith
D. Gallaher	Auckland	Ponsonby	foreman
F. T. Glasgow	Taranaki	Eltham	bank staff
W. S. Glenn	Taranaki	Waimate	auctioneer
W. S. Johnston	Otago	Alhambra	iron worker
W. H. C. Mackrell	Auckland	Newton	printer
A McDonald	Otago	Kaikorai	brewery worker
F. Newton	Canterbury	Linwood	railway fitter
G. W. Nicholson	Auckland	City	bootmaker
J. M. O'Sullivan	Taranaki	Okaiwa	farmer
C. E. Seeling	Auckland	City	slaughterman?
G. A. Tyler	Auckland	City	boatbuilder

of occupational types the 1905 All Blacks certainly do not epitomise the rural rugby backbone imagined by some contemporaries and perpetuated by Phillips and others. If anything, the backgrounds of the players and the scientific playing methods being developed in New Zealand ought to have drawn more comment akin to that of English commentators who sought to explain the tourists' subsequent success through industrial imagery and the efficiency of the All Black 'machine'. But even Phillips concedes that 'little is made of the All Blacks' use of specialised positions, which might have been seen as a perfect model for the modern division of labour; and the insistence on sheer physical strength and pioneer adaptability looks backward to a frontier past rather than forward to an organised, urban future'.[25]

It is also misleading to characterise any of the 1905 farmers as paragons of the backblocks. Bob Deans, of a long-established and wealthy pioneering Canterbury family, played for the High School Old Boys club in Christchurch and worked on the family property at Riccarton – very close to the centre of the city. Only after the 1905 tour did he become manager of his family's rural property at Homebush.[26] Jimmy Hunter, educated at Wanganui Collegiate School, came from a Taranaki farming family prosperous enough to allow him to join Deans and Eric Harper in each contributing a weekly £2 to assist the finances of 'less fortunate' team members during the tour. Jimmy O'Sullivan was also reported to be a contributor.[27]

If the selection of the 1905 team was fraught and somewhat chaotic, the decision to add a coach triggered internecine rugby warfare. In October 1904 the NZRFU received several unsolicited applications for the position of trainer with the team. After referring the matter to its finance committee, it was eventually decided that no trainer would be sent.[28] However, at the 1905 annual general meeting it was also announced that Jimmy Duncan of Otago would accompany the team as coach. A veteran of 50 games for Otago 1889–1903, including the last six seasons as captain, and New Zealand captain in 1901 and 1903, Duncan was widely regarded as the leading rugby tactician in the country – not least for his role in developing the five-eighths system of back alignment. He had also won much praise for his effort in preparing the New Zealand team in 1904, and the desire of the NZRFU to include him in the tour is surely a reflection of the increasingly 'scientific' and competitive pursuit of rugby that had emerged in New Zealand.[29]

For once Otago supporters were pleased with an NZRFU decision, though their counterparts in Auckland were furious. In a letter to the

NZRFU in early June 1905, the Auckland RFU claimed that the players unanimously objected to the inclusion of Duncan instead of another player and that his presence would cause 'ill feeling' within the team. With support for its position from Southland and later Hawke's Bay, Auckland insisted on a special general meeting of the national body to resolve the matter.[30] 'Full-Back' of the *Witness* immediately lambasted the Auckland RFU for 'causing strife', and pointed to the evident hypocrisy of many who had praised Duncan's efforts in 1904 and yet condemned him less than a year later. He also doubted whether objections to Duncan, especially among the southern members of the team, were unanimous.[31] Nevertheless, on 18 July the full NZRFU Council met to review the management committee decision to appoint Duncan. C. E. MacCormick, secretary of the Auckland RFU, claimed that Duncan was not liked and had caused a major rift in the 1903 team. Others defended Duncan and suggested that the rift was more a broader north/south issue than a personal matter. A motion from Auckland 'that in the opinion of this meeting the appointment of a coach by the Management Committee is a grave error and ought to be cancelled' was eventually lost 34–15.[32] A columnist for the *Canterbury Times* later claimed that it was entirely wrong to saddle Duncan with blame for friction on the 1903 tour: 'What friction existed was brought about by an official of the New Zealand Rugby Union whose excessive pampering of certain Auckland members of the team raised the ire of the southerners, and justly so. In other ways the northerners made themselves responsible for bickerings on the field.'[33] Whatever the truth of the matter, the open acknowledgement that a rift had existed in 1903 among a touring team that contributed six members to the present side was hardly an encouraging sign before the tour had begun.

When the team departed for Britain on 30 July, George Dixon wrote in his diary: 'Duncan appears quite happy with rest of team and gives impression of being shrewd and a leader – decent fellow – don't anticipate any trouble in this direction.'[34] But the problems surrounding the coach refused to go away, despite the ultimate succcess of the tour. During the preliminary visit to Australia, Jimmy Hunter apparently informed the acting manager, Neil Galbraith, that Duncan's presence would create friction. When the team arrived in England there were some questions in the press, although not from rugby authorities, as to whether his appointment as coach and payment of expenses to him on the same terms as the players breached the laws of professionalism.[35] More damaging were reports that reached New Zealand in December supposedly based on private letters from Otago players to their Dunedin friends. These claimed significant friction in the team between Auckland and Otago players regarding Duncan. David Gallaher had assumed responsibility for coaching the forwards, and Billy Stead was coaching the backs, with the result that Duncan was generally ignored at training and unable to assert any authority. The dispute was also reported to be having an impact on selections, with accusations of bias against Otago players and a claim that one of them had given an Aucklander 'a good thrashing'.[36]

While Stead strenuously denied all rumours in his column for the *Southland Times* during the tour, and an examination of the match totals for each player reveals no evidence of a selection bias, it is nevertheless revealing, as the *Witness* pointed out, that the columns of adulation for the team throughout the tour contained no mention of Duncan.[37] Nor do Gallaher and Stead mention him anywhere in the book largely devoted to coaching and rugby strategy that they wrote at the end of the tour.

But these uncomfortable relationships lay in the future. For the moment the newly assembled team faced the task of convincing its critics that justice would be done to New Zealand's rugby reputation on the field.

Although the NZRFU was keen for preliminary matches in Australia, as much to 'blood' its new team as to boost its finances for the British tour, the venture was initially stalled by haggling with the New South Wales RFU over terms.[38] On Monday 3 July, after a 9–3 victory by New Zealand over Auckland at Alexandra Park on the previous Saturday, 19 of the 25 selected players embarked for Australia under the captaincy of Jimmy Hunter and management of Neil Galbraith, the NZRFU treasurer. For various work and personal reasons, Dixon, Deans, Gallaher, Harper, Mackrell, Stead and Tyler remained in New Zealand, and it soon became apparent how important Gallaher, Tyler and the yet-to-be-selected Cunningham would become to the team. For in the two matches against New South Wales and one against Metropolitan Union there was little other than criticism of the efforts of the forward combination. As one 'Ex-New Zealander' observed from Sydney:

> It seems a joke to call them representative. Whatever may be the cause – prejudice or incapacity on the part of the selectors – it is ridiculous to set them up as a combination worthy to uphold the fine standards of New Zealand forward play. The backs, when they are in the mood, are bright

and dashy, but they need the protection that they will never get from this sluggish, amateurish team of forwards.[39]

Most other critics felt that the forwards were markedly inferior to those of the 1903 combination.[40]

When the team returned to New Zealand for another three matches, reactions were similarly discouraging. On 22 July it was lucky to escape with a 10-10 draw against Otago-Southland. Of the 21-3 victory over Canterbury five days later, *The Press* observed that 'The match was rather disappointing both as an exhibition of play and as an indication of the New Zealand team's strength'. Clearly not all of the best players were available for the tour, and some of those selected on their 1904 form had not retained it in 1905. On the other hand,

> It may not be quite so good individually as the team which beat the Englishmen last year, but it will have the advantage of greater combination than was possible with that brilliant fifteen. The team leaves with the good wishes of the countless supporters of football who look to it with confidence to uphold the credit of New Zealand both on and off the field.[41]

Two days later the tourists travelled to Wellington for their final fixture before departure. Here they were greeted by bitter cold, torrential rain, an extremely wet Athletic Park ground and a match that was delayed for some time by the absence of a ball. Although the 3-0 defeat at the hands of Wellington reflected something of a lottery in these conditions, one reporter felt that 'the chosen players of New Zealand made so poor a showing as to give cause for grave reflection upon what may happen to them if they meet some of the strong home teams on wet turf'.[42]

With hindsight, and after some early victories in England, the *Lyttelton Times* offered the intriguing suggestion that the poor form shown in Australia and New Zealand reflected the desire of the players to avoid injury before the main tour.[43] Yet the more immediate reaction towards the tourists and their prospects seems to have been both sceptical and muted, with the farewell smoke concert at the Wellington Town Hall on Saturday 29 July drawing a smaller than expected attendance. In the first of his many pronouncements on the team, Premier Richard Seddon tamely observed that they would certainly represent the honour of the colony and that the tour would bring New Zealand closer to Britain by drawing attention to its various qualities. He also announced that arrangements had been made for the New Zealand High Commission to cable news and results to New Zealand through the Premier's office.[44] Yet George Dixon recalled that

'The team left Wellington for London . . . under circumstances that were in the highest degree depressing, the weather being so keenly cold and showery that there was only a small assembly of enthusiasts to see them off'.[45] Nothing in the preliminary stages of the tour carried the hallmark of a team that some have imagined as epitomising a highly developed national game.

In his book *The Triumphant Tour of the New Zealand Footballers*, Dixon describes an uneventful journey by a happy team who entered fully into the social round of the SS *Rimutaka*'s six-week voyage via Monte Video and Tenerife to Plymouth. Once the weather settled, the days were filled with sports gatherings with other passengers, formal rugby training, generally under the direction of Bill Cunningham and George Smith, and meetings to discuss laws and tactics. Players ran around the decks and practised ball skills and passing, scrum formations and lineout drills. Boxing was also a part of the training regime, and some players maintained their fitness by stoking the ship. Passengers usually watched the training and some, including two women, even joined in. Evening amusements revealed that several in the team possessed musical talent. Aside from minor injuries and illness, and Gallaher briefly suffering the recurring effects of enteric fever contracted in South Africa, the team reached England fit and well.[46]

A reading of Dixon's tour diary adds some vital dimensions to this picture, however, not least of a manager who appears anxious to control his charges. On 5 August he informed the team that success depended on loyalty and that they should not discuss the tour with outsiders. There was to be no contact with the press except through Dixon. On 15 August he observed, 'somehow don't fancy Corbett very much, seems to have very vague idea of scrum work & doesn't appear to take same keen interest in game as other members'. The next day he recorded his anxiety at the behaviour of team members as one passenger had complained about noise – although this was not supported by others. On 20 August, Dixon warned the team about practical jokes that made work for others, especially the stewards, and reminded them that morning and afternoon training was essential. By 27 August – 'looking forward to end of voyage & for that matter, to end of trip' – he seemed to have reached the end of his tether.[47]

The greatest challenge to Dixon's authority, and potentially to the future of the tour, came on 5 August. At a team meeting Gallaher resigned the captaincy because he believed that the players wished to have a choice in the appointment. Stead also resigned as vice-captain. But Dixon declined to accept the resignations, as the appointments had been made by the NZRFU and the team was bound by its decision. Nevertheless, Frank Glasgow moved 'That this meeting heartily endorse appointments made by the managing committee'. Although Dixon also refused to accept this gesture, 17 members of the team voted in favour – certainly a majority, but hardly a complete endorsement of the authority of the NZRFU on the verge of its most important hour.[48] Dixon's final shipboard entry on 7 September was somewhat ambiguous:

> Had meeting of team today & congratulated them on record up to date & expressed hope that records would be as good at end of tour – impressed upon them that every individual was responsible for keeping himself in form & that if anyone by his own act rendered himself unfit, then the consequences whatever they might be would be on his own head.[49]

At 4 a.m. on Friday, 8 September 1905 the *Rimutaka,* containing the New Zealand football team as they were still commonly known, arrived at Plymouth. The party was met by Cecil Wray Palliser of the New Zealand High Commission, officials of the English, Devon and Somerset Rugby Unions, and a number of journalists eager to cover the New Zealanders' arrival and speculate on prospects for the tour.[50] Dixon informed them that the team would render a good account of itself because the players had been selected on form rather than reputation, rugby was strong in New Zealand and was enhanced by intense interprovincial rivalries.[51] After disembarking, the team travelled to its first base in the quiet town of Newton Abbott. The following afternoon it returned to Plymouth to watch Devonport Albion playing Torquay. Although not entirely impressed with the standard of play, the visitors acknowledged that it was still very early in the season and they had no grounds for complacency. Indeed, the first week in England established a pattern of practice and tactical discussion in the morning and visits to local tourist attractions in the afternoon.[52]

It was almost 17 years since the arrival of the New Zealand Native team – the only other overseas rugby team to visit Britain – although sports tours of other kinds were nothing new. One Aboriginal and 12 white Australian cricket teams had visited since 1868 – including one that was currently five days short of completing a rather unsuccessful tour in which it lost the test series two-nil and failed to regain the Ashes. A West Indian and three South African cricket teams had also toured, as well as various baseball, cricket and lacrosse teams from North America.[53] But, as we shall see shortly, no visit since the Australian cricket team of 1878 caused quite such a reaction as that of the New Zealand rugby players during the last quarter of 1905.

Naturally, while much of the speculation and prediction about the tour was centred on comparisons with the Native team, it is vital to remember that the British rugby landscape in September 1905 was radically different from that of 1888–89. The emergence of the Northern Union had drained the English game in particular of the vast majority of its best and strongest clubs and players, while both codes were being dwarfed by the dramatic and seemingly unrelenting rise of soccer. In 1893 the Rugby Football Union had 481 affiliated clubs, including more than 150 in Yorkshire and a large number in Lancashire. By 1905 this had been reduced to 250 – including various Oxbridge colleges, a handful of schools and some overseas clubs such as Calcutta. Not until 1925 would the RFU regain something like its former numerical strength.[54] At its 1898 annual general meeting the Lancashire County Union could muster only eight affiliated clubs, and Yorkshire only 14 in 1901. Having won six of the first seven county championships up to 1895, Yorkshire did not regain the title until 1926, and Lancashire until 1935.[55] England, which dominated international competition during the 1870s and 1880s with teams increasingly composed of northern players, failed to win a triple crown – victory over Ireland, Scotland and Wales – between 1892 and 1910.[56]

The year 1905 also marked a significant turning point for the Northern Union, which had experienced decidedly mixed fortunes since 1895. Having initially refused to embrace professionalism, the inability to enforce the broken-time limit of six shillings per day eventually led to its acceptance, although with stringent work and transfer clauses, in 1898. In 1905 these too were abolished and open professionalism was legalised.[57] By this time there were at least 169 clubs in full membership, and in February 1906 a leading official, J. H. Smith, claimed a total of 420 clubs including schoolboy and works teams.[58]

Beyond England, there was arguably even stronger support from Ireland and Scotland for the avowedly amateur position of the RFU. Indeed, the Scots had already established a reputation as the staunchest defenders of amateurism. The game took root within socially exclusive Edinburgh academies that remained decidedly conservative in outlook, restrictive in membership and careful in their choice of fixtures against like-minded social equals. Certainly, Borders rugby displayed greater communal involvement and an intensity similar to that in northern England, and a Border League was established in 1903. But as much as Borders players were crucial to the competitiveness of Scottish teams from the late 1890s, the region maintained an antagonistic relationship with the Scottish Football Union (SFU).[59] Likewise, the Irish game remained very much the preserve of higher education institutions and public school old boys' clubs. But here unity and conservatism was reinforced by the overtly political agenda of the Gaelic Athletic Association, which accompanied its promotion of Irish nationalism and the broader Irish cultural revival by sustained hostility to English games and their cultural mores. As far as it was able, Irish rugby insulated itself against political and sectarian conflict, and as Richard Holt explains, 'The Irish, more than any other of the Home Unions, have retained something of the old morality of the game – the dash, the daring, and the idea of enjoying the game "for its own sake".'[60]

Wales, however, was a rather different proposition. While the game had arrived in South Wales during the 1870s through the same networks of public school old boys as elsewhere, its arrival also coincided with industrial growth and high wage levels that attracted rapid migration – especially to the coalfields. Just as in the north of England, rugby percolated downwards from the middle class and became a focus for identity in, and rivalry between, developing working-class communities. Cup competitions soon followed – replete with intensity, hard and often violent play, and large parochial crowds. Regular fixtures between Welsh clubs and those in the north of England were common from the 1880s. Inevitably there was the same public pressure for clubs to secure and retain good players, and to circumvent the laws on professionalism in order to do so.[61]

Confronted with the same challenge as the RFU in terms of how to accommodate working-class interests, the Welsh Rugby Union (WRU) responded with greater pragmatism and tolerance. With a much smaller population from which to sustain a successful national team, and one that became increasingly important in asserting Welsh national identity, the WRU engaged in what Gareth Williams describes as a certain amount of 'blindside remuneration' in order to retain its best players. This stance inevitably antagonised the other unions – and especially in 1896 when the WRU sanctioned a testimonial for its star player Arthur Gould, who was then presented with the deeds to his house. Such an apparently flagrant breach of the laws of professionalism prompted the International Board, a body representing the four Home Unions but effectively a puppet of the RFU, to threaten the expulsion of Wales from the international fold. The impeccably amateur Scots then refused to play Wales for two seasons.

Although the dispute was resolved in 1898, the WRU remained 'flexible' on matters of professionalism. Meanwhile, the Northern Union provided an outlet for those wishing to engage in more overt professionalism, and numerous Welsh players took the opportunity. Indeed, the Northern Union organised international fixtures between teams designated 'England' and 'Wales' from 1908.[62]

But regardless of the considerable differences and tensions within and between the two rugby codes, they faced a common obstacle – the rise of soccer. As the football codes expanded beyond their public school base during the last quarter of the nineteenth century, the relative simplicity of soccer rules and the appeal of its open style of play to spectators gave it a considerable advantage in attracting support from those, especially among the working class, who did not possess a particular football playing tradition from their schooldays. From its establishment in November 1863, the Football Association expanded to 10 affiliated clubs in 1867, 50 in 1871, 1,000 in 1888 and more than 7,500 by 1905 – including 578 in the British Army alone. Estimates for 1910 suggest that England had as many as half a million amateur footballers and 6,800 professionals among its seven million males aged 15–39. Scotland had as many as 150,000 amateurs and 1,650 professionals, and the game was continuing to grow rapidly throughout Ireland and Wales.[63] Although the figures are not precise, it is safe to say that there were 10 to 15 times more men playing the round-ball game than the two handling codes combined. Moreover, while rugby had showed a clear regional split, soccer was a national sport – a crucial advantage at a time when improved communications and the mass-circulation press were reducing regionalism and shaping a more national perspective.[64]

The rapid growth of soccer in the north of England during the 1890s was keenly felt by the young Northern Union. As soccer took hold in schools and increased its spectator base, the previously buoyant economy of northern rugby began to decline. In conjunction with sustained hostility from the RFU, the Northern Union became increasingly 'proletarianised' as its middle-class backers and sometimes whole clubs began to defect to soccer. In this environment, the costs of maintaining grounds and attractive competitions became increasingly difficult to sustain.[65] Thus, following an unsuccessful two-division league competition from 1902–03, the Northern Union sought to counter the football challenge with various experiments to increase the speed and attractiveness of its game. Gradually, what had been a professional version of rugby union was reshaped as a distinct code in its own right. While the most revolutionary transformation to a 13-a-side game with play-the-ball rules would not come until June 1906, after the departure of the New Zealanders,[66] there was apparently already enough difference in the game, to say nothing of its move to open professionalism, to draw the attention of some among the tourists – with dramatic consequences for the immediate future of New Zealand rugby.

All of these developments had a profound impact on the itinerary prepared for the 1905 tour compared with that of the Native team. At least 40 of the 74 fixtures played by the Native team in Britain were against clubs that subsequently joined the Northern Union or against representative teams drawn from these clubs. Among them were 19 of the 21 pioneering clubs of 1895. The England team for the controversial international at Blackheath contained eight Yorkshiremen and two Lancastrians.[67] By contrast, the 32 matches arranged for the All Blacks in Britain included only five against northern club or county sides – Durham County, Hartlepool Clubs, Northumberland City Clubs, Cheshire and Yorkshire. The once-strong Lancashire union declined to accept a fixture because of the £50 guarantee required.[68] Moreover, even allowing for the comparatively limited resources at its disposal by 1905, there was some dissatisfaction with the itinerary arranged by the RFU and a sense that it was serving English interests rather than those of British rugby as a whole. Many thought it regrettable that the potentially most attractive and challenging Welsh fixtures were scheduled late in the tour, that Ireland and Scotland had been allocated only two matches each, and that in all cases the internationals were before the minor fixtures – leaving no opportunity for locals to assess the New Zealanders' tactics. The leading Scottish clubs felt particularly slighted at not playing against the tourists.[69]

In all respects, then, the genesis of the 1905 tour had not been an easy one. At every step it highlighted the competing cultures and differing expectations of the rugby world. Although they were about to compile a record that, in purely statistical terms, was beyond argument, it is naive to imagine that the differences swirling around them would simply disappear.

CHAPTER FOUR

Making the All Blacks

O<small>N</small> M<small>ONDAY</small>, 4 September 1905 the *Athletic News*, the leading sports paper in the north of England, presented somewhat muted expectations for the forthcoming tour.

> Unhappily, or happily, according to the point of view, there are two codes of football, so that even if the New Zealanders should prove quite as skilled exponents of rugby football as the Australians are of cricket, their visit cannot excite the same general interest. To the rugby enthusiast, however, the approaching appearance of the New Zealanders is of supreme moment, and although the sound of bat meeting ball still awakes the English echoes, the probable effect of the tour on our methods of play is already being eagerly and anxiously discussed. Will the New Zealanders revolutionise the game? Will their system of back play supplant the Welsh system just as the latter ousted the 'three three' game?

Basing his coments on New Zealand's success in 1904, this critic felt it likely that the greatest impact of the tourists would be on techniques of forward play, but it was important not to interpret the superior skills of individuals to mean that the system of play they used was necessarily superior.[1]

Yet within a very short time the *Athletic News* and all of its contemporaries were in no doubt that the visit *was* exciting quite extraordinary general interest and genuine surprise. In New Zealand the much-maligned touring team also restored the faith of its critics. During the first four weeks of their itinerary from 16 September to 14 October, the New Zealanders won each of their nine games and scored a phenomenal 341 points while conceding only seven. At the same time, the relatively unheralded New Zealand football team went a long way to becoming the All Blacks of enduring legend. We shall also see in the next chapter that such success apparently also had a role to play in debates about the quality of British manhood. But although there is much to confirm such accounts of admiration and enthusiasm during the first half of the tour, this period also provides a platform for a fuller consideration of both the achievements of the team and the debates and controversies, to be outlined in subsequent chapters, that were soon to settle on the tour. To be swept along, as some historians have been, by the initial excitement is to entirely underestimate what was, without being in the least clichéd, an increasingly bitter end. It is important, then, to examine the beginning of the tour in some detail.

On the morning of the opening match of the tour, against Devon at Exeter on 16 September, the *Western Times* predicted an even contest. While the Devon side soundly defeated by the Native team in 1888 was little known in rugby circles, the improvement of the county over the last decade needed to be balanced against a feeling that the present New Zealand combination was considered inferior to its predecessor.[2] George Dixon recalled a similar mood among his players.

> In view of the expressions of opinion in some of the leading newspapers which were disposed to doubt our prospects of success, the prevailing feeling in the team was simply one of modest self-confidence. We knew our own strength, and we were prepared for equal strength on the other side, but we shared the opinion of the public and the football critics that the chances were fairly even. We were destined, however, to change our opinion before the first ten minutes of play had expired.[3]

In front of about 8,000 spectators, including various RFU committee members and a number of New Zealanders who had travelled from London, the tourists fielded most of what became their strongest international combination. As Dixon observed, they started with 'dash and brilliancy' and the forwards 'fairly smothered the Devonians'. Within three minutes halfback Fred Roberts passed from a scrum to Billy Stead, who passed to his five-eighths partner Jimmy Hunter, who 'in one of his characteristic dashes' beat a tackle easily to score the first of his 42 tries in Britain. Billy Wallace converted the try and then, as if to confirm that the visitors were not yet ready to take liberties with their opponents, landed a penalty from a difficult angle. There were to be no more penalty goals until 4 November, and only four during the entire tour. For now the New Zealanders began to score tries at a rapid rate – another to Hunter, three to Wallace, four to Smith and 12 in total. The only Devon response, late in the game, was a dropped goal – making the final score 55–4.[4] After the game the teams dined together amid numerous speeches including one from David Gallaher, who, despite the result, modestly claimed that his team were merely sons of Empire and did not pretend to be able to show the British anything about rugby.[5] The New Zealanders then attended a performance of *Maritana*. When they returned to Newton Abbott at 11.45 p.m. they found, to their considerable surprise, a large cheering crowd waiting to welcome them. They were accompanied to their hotel by a brass band, and Dixon felt it necessary to make a further speech of thanks to the assembled throng before noting in his diary: 'This has been a memorable day & should establish the success of our tour.'[6]

On Monday morning the press analysis and post-mortem began in earnest. While most scribes conceded that there was something to admire in the pace and combination of the tourists, especially among the forwards, few were overawed. Assessments of their true abilities were also tempered by the particularly poor display from Devon. The most praise came from the *Western Times* of Exeter:

> Devon's unpreparedness was painfully apparent throughout. Equally obvious was it that the New Zealanders were in the pink of condition . . . Alert, fleet of foot, skilful in accepting and giving passes, with a thorough conception of the science of the game, and above all with a complete understanding between them, they compel admiration and it will take the best we can produce to inflict defeat upon them.[7]

Hamish Stuart, a prolific columnist who was soon to emerge as a thorn in the side of Australasian rugby, wrote in the *Athletic News* that the margin of victory was largely due to very poor play by Devon. Certainly there was plenty of pace and 'individual cleverness' in the New Zealand team, 'but their combination does not approach the best Welsh standard'. Indeed, Stuart was disappointed that there appeared to be no novelty, originality or particular style in the play of the visitors.[8] The *Daily Telegraph* critic was similarly unimpressed: 'Much of their passing was slow and faulty, the ball often being parted with in a somewhat reckless manner, and though at times their general combination was admirable, it unquestionably fell short of the Welsh standard.'[9] *The Field* added that although they were a 'fine body of men' the tourists did not possess the 'phenomenal physique' of the Native team. In the backs their formation and tactics were little different to established Welsh systems, but they displayed much greater 'science' in the forwards.[10] From this point onwards, the spectre of strong Welsh opposition later in the tour, rather than retrospective comparisons with the Native team, was to provide the most frequent reference point in assessing New Zealand performances.

Two other comments on forward play against Devon are worthy of note at this stage, although we shall return to the controversies surrounding one of them in much greater detail in Chapter Six. From the outset there was much discussion of both the use of specialist positions for players in the scrum, as opposed to the 'first up, first down' method common in Britain, and the position of Gallaher, or his understudy George Gillett, as wing-forward. 'The wing forward', wrote Hamish Stuart, 'had something to do with the success of his side. He is an obstructionist, neither more nor less, and if he is penalised off his game and out of existence the one blemish in the New Zealand game will be removed.'[11] And from *The Field*:

> Amid all this excellence which stamped the football in the first match, every exception must be taken to the startling innovation of a wing forward; he makes no pretence to scrummage, but simply hangs on the fringe of the pack to obstruct the opposing half back. An equitable administration of the off-side rule ought to very quickly make this players position untenable.[12]

Meanwhile, in New Zealand the first result of the tour was awaited with nervous anticipation. According to the *Otago Witness*, many in Dunedin expected defeat because the team's form in Australia and prior to departure suggested that it was a 'very ordinary' combination. The crowd who gathered outside the *Witness* office on Sunday evening to await the cable containing the score could hardly believe what came through. Nor could some of those who repeatedly telephoned the *New Zealand Herald* office in Auckland.[13] But there was also a reluctance to get too excited. As the *Southland Times* pointed out:

> Devon is not a football stronghold, and the New Zealanders probably had one of their easiest matches on Saturday. In the second place, the British season has just opened, if it can properly be said to have opened yet, and while the New Zealanders are probably in very good condition, the English Ruggers can hardly have struck form. This advantage should show in the results of the early matches and to it a portion of Saturday's score must be attributable. After all allowances have been made, however, the victory is eminently satisfactory and should encourage those who were somewhat dubious of the prospects of the tour.[14]

This would not be the last time a New Zealand performance would be downplayed with claims that they had arrived at the start of an English season.[15] Yet, and notwithstanding the comprehensive training regime on the journey to Britain, it ignores the point that the touring team had just spent six weeks within the confines of a ship. Moreover, those teams who suffered substantial defeats against the tourists in October and November had ample time to prepare.

The visitors having disposed of Devon so easily, there was naturally even greater press and public interest in the second match, against Cornwall on 22 September. With five changes, mostly among the backs, the New Zealand team was, if anything, more convincing against stronger opposition. Eleven tries were scored, and only the limited success of Wallace's goal kicking kept the score to 41–0. As *The Cornishman* enthused:

> Their success was due to tactics as intelligent as they are original – superior in every way to anything witnessed in English football. Backed up as they are by running, passing and kicking of the highest class, it is indeed difficult to say what British team will check their victorious career.

Although Gallaher at wing-forward was 'closely watched', there were few penalties against him and he appeared to be a valuable attacking element.[16] Hamish Stuart, however, informed his readers that there would be an early 'collision' between the methods of the wing-forward and the interpretation of them by referees.[17] R. G. T. Coventry, the Oxford University halfback, in the first of his significant contributions to the *Daily Mail*, immediately warned English teams against trying to alter their tactics to emulate those of the New Zealanders:

> It would be laughable, were it not so pitiable, to see this country of such glorious rugby traditions adopting first one system and then another in a vain endeavour to regain her lost supremacy, shutting her eyes to the fact that it is players and not position that she lacks.[18]

But Dixon felt that 'after the second decisive win, the newspaper critics were more inclined to give the New Zealanders credit for superior play, and less inclined to attribute the home defeat to want of preparation or loss of head'.[19] To his diary he confided: 'Great fault of English forwards so far as we have seen them, indifferent following up, weak tackling & general want of initiative.'[20]

When the team arrived in Bristol on 22 September it was already apparent that the tour was gaining a momentum out of the ordinary. Many local junior fixtures scheduled for the Saturday of the game had been cancelled in recognition of the educational value that could be gained from watching the New Zealanders.[21] Dixon also noted the presence of various

Welsh officials and selectors, adding 'they are beginning to "think" about us'.[22] But it is also evident, to judge from the *Bristol Echo*, that his charges were not getting carried away with the gathering euphoria:

> Quietly clad in dark jerseys and knickers with black stockings and black boots or shoes, there was nothing remarkable about the appearance of the colonials when in the most modest and unassuming manner they entered – almost ambled – into the arena.[23]

To its credit, Bristol conceded only nine tries and won a good deal of respect for its determination. As the *Western Daily Press* put it: 'There was a vast difference between the skill of the two teams, but in stamina, pluck and perseverance the players of the old country fully held their own with the representatives of the far away colony.'[24] Indeed, from this point there was a relative improvement in the opposition. Northampton conceded eight tries, Leicester only six, and the first appearance of the tourists in London, in front of 16,000 spectators against Middlesex at Stamford Bridge on 4 October, yielded another eight. But if the New Zealanders' scoring decreased slightly after the first three games, the victories continued and the superlatives showed no sign of abating.

The *Northampton Daily Chronicle* found it

> very difficult to pen an impression of the New Zealanders who are overwhelming in their brilliance both individually and collectively. Every man is an expert who can run, kick, dodge, handle and defend up to the highest standard. Each man has his definite game to play, and yet each is part of the whole and the combination is wonderfully developed, the passing being splendid.[25]

A Leicester critic described the tourists as

> men endowed with nature's best gifts, and it is their strength of body and mind combined that enabled them to triumph so easily over their opponents. They are a team of giants without the clumsiness of giants.[26]

Three days later the same observer insisted that

> However divergent our views may be as to the system of New Zealand football, I think we shall agree that the team demonstrating its effectiveness is one of the best we have ever seen on a football field.

The New Zealanders would give a great boost to rugby in the Midlands and as many local players as possible should witness their next appearance at Leicester against Midland Counties on 28 October.[27] In the *Daily Mail*, A. O. Jones, the leading English referee, claimed that 'In appearance it would be impossible to imagine men of more suitable physique for the rugby game, though the dark clothing worn scarcely conveys to the ordinary eyes the imposing appearance they would otherwise have'. While their combination as a team was inferior to the best Welsh clubs, Jones felt that they were individually superior.[28] According to *The Sportsman* after the defeat of Middlesex:

> The remark that rugby football has suffered in quality during the last decade has been drummed into our ears times out of number. One might go back, however, to its very best days, allowing the critics to be correct, and then fail to find anything more dashing and brilliant, skilful and clever, than the display given by the winning team yesterday.[29]

There were others, however, who remained less convinced or overawed. From the opening fixture against Devon, various critics argued that there was no particular uniqueness in the New Zealand methods, and some, such as E. H. D. Sewell, felt that the team had merely revived the best features of the British game as played in the 1880s or that perfected by the Scots and Irish around the turn of the century.[30] While the New Zealand back formation and five-eighth game was unusual, some critics felt that their tactics were fairly conventional – and generally inferior to the best Welsh combinations.[31] And, as we shall see in Chapter Six, the spectre of the wing-forward was never far away from the minds of those who were not seduced by New Zealand supremacy.

Finally, on Saturday, 7 October, the New Zealanders encountered genuinely strong opposition in the form of Durham, the current county champions. Aside from being restricted to four tries, the tourists also conceded their first – one of only two scored against them in England and just seven during the whole tour. Not that the fixture had an auspicious start. Two Durham players missed their trains and, after a quarter-hour delay, the game was started without them. Although the full Durham complement was eventually assembled 10 minutes later, Hamish Stuart mused that 'Really, some modern footballers ought to be taken to the grounds in apron strings.'[32] Much as Durham provided a stern defence, it was again the attacking flair of the tourists that drew admiration from local observers:

> Two features that stood out conspicuously where nearly everything reached perfection were the dash they infused into their play, and their brilliant passing. They were up to an opponent almost as soon as the ball reached him – not one, but several of them – their following up being decisive. The forwards are nearly as fast as the backs, and fall into a

scrum as though they had been 'made to order', their formation being almost rigidly compact. Indeed, this machine-like precision seems to animate the whole team.

The wing-forward was described as 'unique, but not alarming', and Durham also adopted the position for this game, as did Northumberland a week later.[33]

Four days later, as if stung by the comparative setback against Durham, the tourists exacted revenge with no fewer than 15 tries against a hapless Hartlepool Clubs XV. *The Field* described the local combination 'as completely outclassed and absolutely bewildered by the swift passing and the dashing tactics of the New Zealanders who were well suited by the fast and even ground'.[34] Another nine tries followed on 14 October against Northumberland Clubs – taking the total in nine matches to 82.

There is no question that, by rugby standards, the tour was becoming phenomenally popular and quickly drew the attention of many who knew little or nothing about the game. Crowd estimates are always rather haphazard, and the different reports for each match often varied markedly. Yet, based on attendance and revenue figures provided by Dixon to the NZRFU at the end of the tour, it seems that the average crowd for each match was at least 9,000 during the first month of the tour, 12,500 for all games in England and 15–16,000 for the tour as a whole when an average 32,000 for each of the five games in Wales is included. At a conservative estimate, 500,000 saw the 32 matches in Britain. While these figures do not stand comparison with the rapid rise in soccer attendances that had begun during the 1890s, or the 15–20,000 who regularly attended the most important Northern Union fixtures,[35] they were consistently the largest seen at rugby union grounds up to that time, and in many cases the largest since the visit of the Native team. During the first month of the tour, attendances for midweek fixtures were noticeably smaller than those for Saturday. But these soon caught up. Much temporary seating was built for the Somerset match, and an entire new stand was erected at Bedford, where leading employers closed businesses and factories at midday to enable attendance. For the Midland Counties fixture, stand tickets were sold out two days beforehand and many spectators travelled long distances for the occasion. Amid concerns about the 'crush' of spectators, reports of ticket forgeries and the presence of scalpers, both Oxford and Cambridge Universities banned the sale of tickets in the streets before their games.[36]

Among those who were determined to see the tourists were a significant number of expatriate New Zealanders, including members of an Association of Young New Zealanders, who, for the match against Blackheath Club on 4 November, reserved an entire section of the stand.[37]

In a letter to the NZRFU, Dixon noted that good weather and good results had contributed to the increasing attendances. But he was frustrated that only six shillings admission was charged at many grounds, and that a significant number of rugby club members were admitted free, as were some country cricket club members if grounds were shared. The Somerset RFU declined to use the county cricket ground in Taunton precisely because of this issue.[38] Nevertheless, with New Zealand taking 70 per cent of the net profit from each game, or a minimum £50 guarantee, it was clear within the first few weeks that the tour would be lucrative. We will see later that the eventual profit of £8,908 10s 4d was to provide something of a rallying point against the NZRFU among players who felt entitled to a share of the return from their efforts.

Given the unprecedented interest in the tour, it is no surprise that advertisers also saw an opportunity to capitalise. Cadbury's promoted its cocoa as 'Scoring All Points' with an image of a New Zealand player. BDV Cigarettes also claimed to have the endorsement of Dixon and the team, and offered a substantial £50 prize for the best limerick about them published in the *Daily Mail*. In New Zealand, R.B. & Co. of Wellington began advertising an 'All Black' suit range early in 1906.[39] For its part, the New Zealand government also began to use the success of the tour to promote the colony as a destination for settlers. Advertisements for reduced fares to 'the settler's ideal home' or the 'home of the New Zealand footballers' began to appear beside match reports in the British press and on posters around the towns where matches were played.[40]

The growing popularity of the tour produced another consequence – one that has had considerably more significance since 1905 than it did at the time. It gave the New Zealand footballers a name. The first published use of 'All Blacks' appeared in the *Express & Echo* after the opening match against Devon, when the local paper referred to 'the All Blacks, as they are styled by reason of their sable and unrelieved costume'. This initial use was not reported in New Zealand, and the term was not apparently used again in Britain until after the Hartlepool match on 11 October. Thereafter it was picked up by the *Daily Mail*, in which J. A. Buttery referred to 'the All Blacks, so dubbed because of their sombre football garb', and came into increasingly common usage by early November.

Although the English press linked the name to the New Zealanders' uniform, there has been continued debate over the origins of what has become the most iconic feature of New Zealand rugby. As Ron Palenski reminds us, it was always common in the press to refer to teams on the basis of the colour of their uniform. The 1894 Wellington RFU *Annual* referred to the 1893 New Zealand team to Australia as 'the Blacks', and George Dixon's tour diary describes the 1905 team in the same fashion. But others point out that no other international rugby team has acquired a name based on its playing colours. Billy Wallace, the longest-lived of the touring team and something of a custodian of its legends, always maintained that the name derived from 'All Backs', on account of the spectacular running game played by the tourists, and only became 'All Blacks' owing to either a printer's error or a misreading of a cable to the *Daily Mail*. Yet this version of events is undermined by Billy Stead, a very thorough chronicler of the tour for the *Southland Times*, who noted the suggestion of a journalist, probably Major Philip Trevor of *The Sportsman*, that the name should in fact be changed *from* 'All Blacks' *to* 'All Backs' on account of their playing style.[41]

Whatever the origin, the name stuck throughout the tour, though it did not win universal approval after it reached New Zealand in late November. The home press remained just as likely throughout the tour to refer to the 'New Zealand footballers' and occasionally the 'Maoriland footballers'. After it was reported in New Zealand that the success of the tour had prompted a Welsh club side to adopt the name 'All Blacks', the *Otago Witness* observed, 'It is a laborious title at best even applied to such a team as the New Zealanders proved themselves to be.'[42] Of course, as Caroline Daley points out, the real significance of the name should rest not in its origin but in the fact that the common usage of such an important national symbol derives from the British press rather than the NZRFU or the New Zealand public.[43] The 1906 Springboks and the 1908 Wallabies both chose their own names – although in the later case it was partly to counter the intention of some in Britain to call them 'Rabbits'.[44]

In New Zealand, reactions to the performances of the team also began to gather a momentum mirroring the intense coverage in the British press. Initially, however, there was growing frustration as very brief cables from the Press Association and the New Zealand High Commission indicated remarkable results but gave little supporting detail. In late September the *NZ Referee* complained bitterly about brevity and the numerous discrepancies between accounts.

The reports which have been furnished by the Press Association of the New Zealand team's matches to date have been meagre in the extreme, and very disappointing to the thousands of rugby enthusiasts in the colony. If the London representative would only expand on the doings of the New Zealand footballers about one quarter of the time and attention which he gave to the Australian cricketers, the result would be a vast improvement on the present unsatisfactory state of affairs'.[45]

Almost immediately the Canterbury RFU sent a letter of complaint to the NZRFU, with the result that the Australian Cable Association agreed to supply prompter and fuller information.[46]

The first summaries from the British press and direct correspondence from the team did not appear until 18 October. Thereafter, the pages of analysis and debate swelled to unprecedented proportions – as much concerned with chronicling the tour as trying to gauge the merit of each victory. The increasingly detailed cables, reports from a wide variety of British, Australian and other New Zealand newspapers, various columns from 'special correspondents' with the team and letters from players and other New Zealanders in Britain were compared and cross-referenced. Every game was anticipated by lengthy examination of the record of the opponent during previous seasons and its performance against others on the New Zealand fixture list. Every aspect of the games themselves – size of the crowd, weather and ground conditions, composition of the teams and chronology of the play – was reported in lavish detail. Longest of all were the post-match evaluations of individual players and the collective efforts of the forwards or backs, and both together. In the four to six weeks that elapsed between cable reports and the fuller accounts of matches, the void was filled by a vast array of opinion, speculation, supposition and trivia. Readers were also encouraged to take part in 'guess the score' competitions and columnists such as 'Full-Back' of the *Otago Witness* endeavoured to answer specific queries from readers.[47] To provide a more direct view of the tour, West's Pictures were also trying to secure a 'cinematograph' of the international matches for screening in New Zealand.[48] In every respect this was more voluminous and detailed coverage than that for the tour of the Native team or any of the New Zealand teams to Australia.

In the next chapter we shall also begin to examine the somewhat contentious contribution made by the New Zealand Premier, Richard Seddon, and the High Commissioner in London, William Pember Reeves, as they tried to exploit the tour for political purposes. But we should be cautious in assigning too much importance to the tour either as a vehicle for expressions of emergent New Zealand nationalism or as a symbol of imperial unity. Such an interpretation is simply not a dominant element in the press coverage.

Certainly some imperial sentiment can be found. At the first formal reception of the tour, hosted by the Devon Constitutional Club on 14 September, Dr R. H. Crimbly declared that 'For the time those present had no party politics, but were brothers. The New Zealanders were the same flesh and blood and were as such as much units of the British Empire as the Britishers.'[49] In early October the *Yorkshire Post* described

> a wonderfully agile, speedy and resourceful body of men. They represent, in short, that fine self-reliant, athletic type of Britishers that made itself so prominent when the old country had far more serious matters afoot in recent times . . . full of indomitable pluck, coolness and resolution, they seem to one as a team that would play any game as only a Britisher is expected to play it.'[50]

Finally, the arrival of the team in Swansea towards the end of the tour inspired the *Cambria Daily Leader* to observe that

> These capable men from the Antipodes are the true missionaries of Empire. By their intercourse with the youth of the mother land, they strengthen the fabric of the sacred bonds of brotherhood and common feeling which bind our many lands.[51]

But such reactions were very much in the minority. Moreover, it is evident that some critics viewed such imperial themes with a good deal of scepticism. As the *Lyttelton Times* reported an interview between a *Daily News* journalist and the secretary of the New Zealand High Commission concerning the importance of the tour: 'next morning Mr Kennaway was considerably astonished and amused to find himself reported as saying, "It is an excellent idea. The team is, so to speak, yet another instrument for the welding together of the Empire" – a piece of flowery rhetoric which had its origin in the interviewer's own imaginative brain.'[52]

Such cynicism reminds us that, even where it does exist, the rhetoric linking New Zealand sporting success to broader imperial and national themes is shallow and contradictory. Anyone tempted to read the pride and excitement that greeted the success of the All Blacks in 1905 as being indicative of a confident young colony beginning to assert itself on the world stage needs to balance this against such events as those on 18 March of the same year, when a New Zealand cricket team lost to Australia by an innings and 358 runs. As I have argued elsewhere, the continued failure of New Zealand cricket to achieve any international success until late in the twentieth century produced a rhetoric that constantly emphasised ties to Britain and New Zealand's junior role within Empire. Typical is T. C. Lowry's claim at the start of the 1927 tour to England that the New Zealand team he captained were 'Britishers anxious to appear on the cricket map, and accordingly came Home not to beat the best sportsmen but to learn the rules as England taught them'.[53] Not only was this position entirely at odds with the claims that some contemporary observers made for rugby, the rhetoric was frequently being written by the same editors and columnists – changing their sentiments as the seasons changed.[54] The obvious contradiction between these two positions has not been reconciled by historians of New Zealand's national identity, who seem determined only to use those aspects of sport that serve a positive narrative. We shall return to their selective interpretation in more detail in the next chapter.

Another feature largely absent from reactions to the tour, especially in light of the numerous comparisons with the Native team that accompanied the arrival of the All Blacks in Britain, is any discussion of the ongoing role of Maori players in the development of New Zealand rugby. Admittedly, George Dixon observed shortly after arriving that the standard of Maori rugby had markedly deteriorated since the tour of the Native team.[55] Yet both Billy Stead and Bill Cunningham were identifiably Maori players who would later make a significant contribution to the first New Zealand Maori teams, assembled by Ned Parata from 1910.[56]

The All Blacks also performed Te Rauparaha's haka, 'Kamate', although it is not clear whether this was done before every game. Certainly it was performed against Wales, although neither Cunningham nor Stead was in the team to lead it. Moreover, a surviving photograph suggests that it was a decidedly loose arrangement, far removed from the highly choreographed spectacle of recent times. First used by the 1897 New Zealand team to Australia, this haka became a prominent feature of All Black rugby only later in the twentieth century. It was not performed by the All Blacks in Australia in 1907, the 1924–25 'Invincibles' used another haka, and the 1935–36 All Blacks to Britain did not perform one at all.[57] Perhaps the most significanct legacy of the 1905 haka was that both the Springboks and Wallabies were encouraged to perform a 'native dance' before games for the entertainment of the crowd. Of the performance by the Wallabies, their captain Paddy Moran bitterly remarked:

Now we were being asked to remind British people of the miserable remnants of a race which they had dispossessed and we had maltreated or neglected. We were officially expected to leap up in the air and make foolish gestures which somebody thought Australian natives might have used in similar circumstances, and we were also given meaningless words which we were to utter savagely during this pantomime. I refused to lead the wretched caricature of a native corroboree and regularly hid myself among the team, a conscientious objector.[58]

But as had been the case with the Native team, although the performance of the haka and its imitators seems to have been popular, it attracted little comment from the British press.[59]

The most difficult aspect to assess is how the players reacted to events on the field and how they experienced the tour off it. We have seen already that Gallaher's appointment as captain, and that of Jimmy Duncan as coach, created some friction within the touring party. It would be naive to suggest that this simply evaporated after the team meeting of 5 August at which Dixon reiterated that all were bound by the decisions of the NZRFU. Perhaps after these events, and with the somewhat tarnished off-field reputation of the Native team firmly in mind, he was determined to exert firm control over the team. There is little in Dixon's private diary to suggest problems. Billy Stead's fascinating but uncontroversial account of the tour for the Southland Times reveals numerous outings to factories and places of historical interest and evening spent at theatres. For example, in Cornwall the tourists visited the Dolcoath mine and, before the Bristol match, toured the Wills Tobacco Company, where each player was presented with tobacco and cigarettes.[60] There were various other outings to factories and evenings spent at theatres. In November some were reported to have attended divine service at St Paul's or Westminster Abbey.[61] The only evidence for anything more adventurous emerged in an interview with an unnamed Otago player after the team returned to New Zealand, in which he observed that particular women could have enticed some members to remain in Britain.[62] Given that Deans, Harper, Hunter and possibly O'Sullivan apparently paid £2 each Monday to help their 'less fortunate' companions, it is perhaps the case that many of the team could not afford a sustained social round or excursions in their free time. But generally their off-field activities seem to have been kept firmly out of the public eye. Aside from Stead, whose account is notable for how little it says concerning rugby, the other players who supplied copy to the New Zealand press throughout the tour confined their observations almost entirely to rugby matters. Meanwhile, some in the British press became rather exasperated at an inability to secure interviews with players or to get beyond Dixon's reticence and insistence that the team was in Britain to play football rather than talk it.[63]

There are signs throughout the tour that its continued success brought the All Blacks together, kept them firmly focused on the task at hand and ensured that they were abstemious by choice. In late September, Dixon wrote that various players were 'dodging' after-match functions or leaving early – 'boys keeping very steady indeed' – and that he had requested post-match dinners and smoke concerts to end early.[64] Two weeks later, after the hard game against Durham, he added: 'Find it very tedious work filling these functions out, most of boys don't.'[65] Later in the tour, although happy to attend post-match dinners, they were still continuing to decline other social invitations and 'prolonged sittings', prompting the *Athletic News* to report that 'it is evident in conducting themselves the team lighten Mr Dixon's duties to a minimum'.[66] On 13 November the *Yorkshire Post*, even allowing for its general tendency to praise virtuous behaviour by amateur rugby union players, informed its readers that:

> One hears very little of what may be called the inner life of the New Zealand football team. They are a modest family, with a dislike of parade and entertainment. It is not their desire to figure at large in interviews and contents bills, the luncheon room and dining hall are their pet aversions. For this, as much as for their wonderful football prowess, they will carry away with them the respect of all well-balanced British minds.[67]

J. A. Buttery in the *Daily Mail* drew a clear parallel between success and an apparent absence of social distinctions within the team: 'Ability to play football, and the intense desire to win, is their standard of comradeship, and to this is largely due their perfect understanding on the field.'[68]

If any distinction did emerge within the team, it was one based on playing ability and availability. Fifteen players appeared in at least 20 of the 32 matches in Britain, while seven appeared in 13 or fewer. The most notable absentee was hooker Bill Mackrell, who arrived in England with flu, did not take the field until 28 November and made only six appearances in total. Various leg injuries took a heavy toll on the wings Bunny Abbott, Eric Harper, Duncan McGregor and Mona Thompson. Loose forward Massa Johnston missed the last 14 matches owing to various injuries and a throat infection that eventually forced him to remain behind when the team left Britain. Dave Gallaher and George Smith also missed international matches because of injury.[69] On the other hand, the apparently fit John Corbett and Billy Glenn were simply not selected on a regular basis.[70] As with the Native team before them, it seems that the tour selectors were determined to put their strongest team in the field as often as possible. Aside from Fred Roberts, who, as the sole halfback selected, was rested for only three matches in Britain, Billy Stead missed six matches and Frank Glasgow, Bronco Seeling and Billy Wallace eight each. Dixon's reservations about Corbett's ability, noted on board the *Rimutaka*, perhaps indicate a lack of confidence in the depth of the team.

Although the 1905 All Blacks won praise for their combination and understanding as a team in which forwards and backs combined with ease, several players quickly emerged as 'stars' of the tour. Among the backs, Roberts, Stead and Smith attracted much praise, but it was Hunter and Wallace who really stood out. Of Hunter, E. H. D. Sewell later wrote, 'He seemed to glide rather than to run, and to go through the opposition as might a snake.' Another critic spoke of his 'zigzag, eel-like bursts for the goal line'.[71] Of Wallace, Sewell claimed, 'The ease with which [he] turned up at the right moment to cap the movement was that of a master player who had nothing to learn at this game.'[72] Among the forwards, as we have seen already, it was the formation rather than the individuals within it that attracted most comment. But Seeling was repeatedly singled out for his speed, ball skills and ferocious tackling. As Sewell later put it, 'this splendid specimen of manhood had everything necessary to the composition of a forward. Search where one may, a better forward than Seeling does not exist.'[73]

It is, of course, pointless to speculate on how different the selections and results may have been had all of the players been fit. Touring rugby teams are seldom, if ever, afforded such a luxury. But even without their full strength, the achievements of the All Blacks during the first month of the tour were already remarkable. Now, as the next chapter explains, they were about to trigger a frenetic debate in some sections of the British press on themes much bigger than the winning and losing of rugby matches. This debate is critical to our understanding of the tour, but not in the ways that most historians have suggested.

CHAPTER FIVE

Healthy Bodies?

O N 12 OCTOBER 1905, the day after the 63–0 rout of Hartlepool Clubs in the eighth match of the tour, the London *Daily Mail* dispatched a cable to Richard Seddon, Premier of New Zealand: 'British public are amazed at the brilliance of the New Zealand footballers. Could you kindly let us know what New Zealand thinks of their remarkable success.' At the *Daily Mail*'s expense, Seddon, an ardent imperialist who never missed an opportunity to boost New Zealand's profile within the British Empire, replied immediately:

> Am not surprised at the British public being amazed at the brilliancy of the New Zealand footballers. The British team visiting the colonies in 1904 was beaten by New Zealand and in two other matches. This gave an index of the standard of rugby football in England and augured success for our pioneering teams visit to the Mother Country. It is confidently anticipated that the present team will prove equal to the strongest teams in England, demonstrating the advancement of scientific rugby football in the colony. As indicating the public interest taken here, information respecting the contests taking place in Great Britain is awaited almost as earnestly as news of the late war in South Africa and the results are received with great enthusiasm. The natural and healthy conditions of colonial life produce stalwart and athletic sons of whom New Zealand and the Empire are justly proud.[1]

Implicit in this exchange are a number of themes of colonial or emergent national identity crucial to the way some contemporary observers understood the tour but, more importantly, crucial to the way historians have interpreted it. It is necessary, then, to step aside from the triumphant progress of the All Blacks through England to consider the wide-ranging contemporary debate that emerged among many who were considerably surprised by their success. For some the explanation for their results rested with events and strategies on the field. For others such as Richard Seddon, who have attracted the most attention from historians, it was very much in terms of the broader qualities of colonial manhood and the apparently uncertain position of the British Empire within the world. We shall see that for contemporary observers the less complex explanations generally prevailed. Some historians, however, have taken a different view.

Previous chapters have explored the misleading links between the rural, pioneering environment of New Zealand and the success of its rugby teams, and the particular focus by Keith Sinclair and Jock Phillips on the 1905 All Blacks as exemplars of an ideal, physically superior colonial male 'type' that served the cause of New Zealand's emergent nationalism by projecting the country onto a world stage. During the early 1990s John Nauright added another dimension to this interpretation of the tour when he argued that the All Blacks had a central role to play in the 'physical deterioration debates' in Britain immediately after the South African War 1899–1902.[2] That it had taken more than two years for 450,000 British and imperial troops to subdue 40,000 largely untrained Afrikaners apparently raised significant questions about the standard of military recruits and, by implication, the standard of British manhood as a whole. In particular, observers pointed to the depopulation of the countryside, the rise of crowded, unhealthy cities and the urban degeneration of working-class men who constituted the bulk of the fighting force. Sir Frederick Maurice, in an influential article in the *Contemporary Review*, claimed that 60 per cent of those seeking to enlist in Britain were rejected as unfit. In addition, the emergence of Germany as a major power, especially in naval terms, provided evidence that the British economy was weakening and losing market share. Widespread fears of Anglo-Saxon population decline and the rise of Asia, epitomised by the victory of Japan over Russia in May 1905, further reinforced perceptions of decadence and the vulnerability of the British Empire after more than two decades of 'New Imperial' progress.[3] Between 1900 and 1904, various commissions of enquiry were convened to look at the military shortcomings revealed in South Africa and to consider the health of Britain more generally.[4] In this context, the success of the All Blacks and their evident physical superiority was apparently seen as something of a reassuring safety net. As the *Daily Telegraph* explained in early October 1905: 'the colonial physique and health are so superbly good that they testify with comforting eloquence to the betterment of the transplanted and blended Britisher, and the steadiest progress of this wonderful Empire'.[5] That is to say, the physical virility of the British Empire was in safe hands in its colonies, if not at its core. While Britons bemoaned the consequences of urban degeneration, the New Zealanders were the embodiment of a land with ample space, an absence of urban congestion and a generally higher standard of living.[6]

This contrast between urban and rural remained the staple explanation for New Zealand rugby success long after 1905. As with the 'Anzac legend' that developed around the achievements of New Zealand soldiers in two world wars, the stereotype of the successful New Zealand rugby player, epitomised by Colin 'Pinetree' Meads, was of the tough, 'backblocks' farmer conditioned for the game by his working environment. Moreover, the accuracy of this portrayal remains unquestioned among a wide section of the New Zealand public, media commentators and documentary makers. The failure of the All Blacks to progress beyond the semi-finals of the Rugby World Cup in 1999 and 2003 prompted both a lament for the absence of 'hard men' in the team and a call for the 'back to basics' physical training epitomised by farm work, as a counter to the 'softness' of pampered, urban, professional players.[7]

The first attempt to debate such themes in 1905 failed to gain any momentum. On 16 September, the day of the opening match against Devon, a letter from P. A. Vaile, formerly of Auckland and now resident in London, appeared in *The Spectator*. In it Vaile referred to the 'general tonelessness' and lack of originality and initiative in Britain compared with the athletic qualities produced by an 'unconstrained' colonial life. But, in a blunt reply, F. W. Payn, a former Scottish tennis champion, stated that the British were used to such accusations by those failing to recognise the natural reticence, conservative disposition and sense of tradition in Britain. Moreover, 'Many people might consider, with good reason, that Mr Vaile's tirade against English youths . . . is sufficiently contrary to the facts to obviate any necessity for a reply.'[8] Vaile defensively replied that he had only presented his impressions. The editor then declared the correspondence closed.[9]

We have seen already that there was praise for the physical prowess of the New Zealanders from the outset of the tour. After the first three matches, in which the scores had decreased as the methods of the All Blacks became better known, the *Yorkshire Post* concluded that physical superiority undoubtedly contributed to their success.[10] When the team first appeared in London in late September, *The Sportsman* commented: 'Finely built and apparently in splendid condition, the visitors looked one and all a body of thoroughly trained men. Not an ounce of superfluous flesh was carried by the heaviest of the crowd and even the manager himself appeared in perfect trim.'[11] But, as Caroline Daley observes, such praise for the physique of the All Blacks did not necessarily detract from their opposition. The early match reports tended to emphasise how evenly matched the teams were and freely conceded that opponents such as Devon, Cornwall and Leicester looked heavier, were 'a fine stamp of men' or looked 'big and fit'.[12]

To understand properly the direction of the debate beyond this point, it is worth remembering the wider agenda of the *Daily Mail* – the newspaper in which most of it was conducted. Founded in 1896 by Alfred Harmsworth (later Lord Northcliffe), the *Daily Mail* was arguably the first national newspaper – using new technology and rapid distribution by rail to appeal to a mass audience throughout Britain. While it aimed for respectability, the *Mail* also had an eye for the sensational, provided 'talking points' on every page and gave saturation coverage to sport in a style that was as much 'gossip' as analysis. And its political agenda was unashamedly imperial. According to Northcliffe's biographer, 'His political philosophy combined Tory populism, Disraelian imperialism and a firm belief in "the Anglo-Saxon future".' He was sympathetic to any group supporting the British Empire and personally became involved with numerous imperial organisations.[13] The mounting popularity of the 1905 tour fitted perfectly with Northcliffe's views on the superiority of colonial 'stock' to that in an overpopulated, sedentary Britain.[14]

It is no surprise, then, that the *Daily Mail* took a keen interest in the tour from the outset. It was the *Mail* rather than any of its numerous competitors that approached Seddon for comment on 12 October. Among newspapers that provided estimates of crowds at tour matches, those of the *Daily Mail* were consistently the largest. It was also the *Mail*, rather than one of the specialist sporting publications, that produced *Why the All Blacks Triumphed* in January 1906 – a collection of match reports and columns on the tour, replete with cover illustration of a lion in the beak of a moa. The book sold out within hours and a second printing was done – 10,000 copies of which were apparently sent to New Zealand. Finally, the Harmsworth Magazine Publishing Company paid David Gallaher and Billy Stead £100 to write *The Complete Rugby Footballer on the New Zealand System* – a 270-page book completed in little more than a week before the All Blacks departed for North America.[15]

In early October, and especially after the massive Hartlepool victory, some contributors to the *Daily Mail* began to broaden the discussion of the All Blacks into one that emphasised not only their physical qualities but also suggested that these were lacking among their British counterparts. On 9 October, in a review of the early stages of the tour, the Oxford University halfback R. G. T. Coventry wondered whether 'national physique' was deteriorating:

> Our national character and physique are nowhere more plainly evidenced than in our games and personally I am inclined to think that we have lost a good deal of our ancient robustness and sturdy independence, qualities that are nowhere displayed to a greater advantage than on the Rugby football field. New Zealand's success is, in fact, a confession of physical inferiority.[16]

At the same time 'Ex. County Captain' criticised the average Englishman for 'becoming more and more a flabby specimen of humanity (in work as in play) [who] avoids as often as possible hard knocks, danger and much self-sacrifice' and lacking the dedication of the New Zealanders in training and preparation:

> We Englishmen seem to be fast losing our historical grit, allowing 'fat and flabby' to take its place. Until the Boer War, with its too numerous instances of white flag surrender by unwounded officers and men, knocked the conceit out of us, we used to claim that one Englishman was worth two of any other country . . . Let us in football, as in the serious walks of life, try to regain our fast disappearing reputation for zeal and efficiency. New Zealand is indeed the object lesson of efficiency. Happy is the man that learns it.[17]

The following day, having been rebuffed by *The Spectator*, P. A. Vaile again entered the fray with simultaneous letters to *The Times* and *Daily Mail*. While he did not wish to deprecate the quality of British manhood, and doubted that the New Zealand team had given the matter much thought, it was nevertheless the case that successful football required all of the qualities that were necessary to make an 'ideal Britain'. There were also, as Vaile explained to the *Daily Mail*, clear environmental reasons for the physical superiority of the visitors on the field:

> 1. The New Zealander lives a more natural life than the Englishman, spends much more of it in the open air, and is therefore stronger. 2. The men of the Antipodes team almost certainly have much more outdoor physical exercise than those they are called on to meet in this country. 3. They are full of originality and resource and do what occurs to them on the spur of the moment so that it is hard to anticipate their movements.

> They are therefore far more 'tricky' than their opponents. This is shown in their scrum work, their dodging and other important points. 4. They are full of an overflowing vitality and virility – an abounding mental and physical force – which gives the team a moral which is delightful to see in these days when enthusiasm and virility are negligible quantities.[18]

To *The Times* Vaile declared that 'these lusty athletes from the land of the Moa are full of an abounding vitality and vigour that is conspicuously lacking in their opponents'. More importantly, they were not simply engaged in a struggle on the rugby field.

> [I]t is the question of the manhood of the nation, the physical and mental vigour of the parent stock and the sapling that has sprung from it, and realizing this it behoves the men of England to show that the bond and brain of the motherland are as good as ever they were.[19]

Following Seddon's cable of 13 October, William Pember Reeves, Canterbury fullback of the late 1880s and now New Zealand's High Commissioner in London, offered his own explanation to the *Daily Mail* in which he emphasised the qualities of environment and lifestyle that lay behind the success of the All Blacks:

> The climate is a great factor . . . brisk, breezy and bracing with a combination of sea and mountain air. Our country is peopled with a race inheriting the sporting instinct of British stock, with vaster opportunities . . . Even in the four most populous cities . . . the inhabitants do not live packed together, house touching house.

They also enjoyed plentiful food, shorter working hours and more leisure, universal education, small and healthy families.[20] To this, noted critic and rugby chronicler Leonard Tosswill added an emphasis on the mental superiority of the All Blacks:

> The writer has seen the New Zealanders play several of their matches, and the conclusion is irresistibly borne in upon him after every match that they are not only better men physically, but quicker in conception, possess much more initiative, and, moreover, a greater amount of resolution . . . What is the reason? Has the decadence of the English athlete really set in?[21]

Such 'physical' and 'rural' explanations for the achievements of the 1905 All Blacks and their successors are clearly at odds with a New Zealand rugby environment that was largely urban and somewhat middle class. But more than this, they are at odds with the full course of the debate during late 1905, a debate in which notions of physical 'deterioration' or 'superiority' were actively rebutted and in which, even in the *Daily Mail*, they were ultimately relegated to fairly minor positions among the range of explanations for the All Blacks' dominance. Furthermore, there was a far from unanimous understanding of what was meant by 'physical deterioration', and official investigations of the matter before 1905 did nothing to clarify this. Nor was it apparent to many at an official level that colonial males, rugby players or otherwise, should be regarded as the salvation of the British Empire.

Contrary to Nauright's linking of the All Blacks with the 'physical deterioration debates', it is important to remember that the tone of the various official enquiries reveals rather more about a narrow range of middle-class opinion, articulate propaganda and perhaps a little hysteria – the sort of thing the imperial-minded *Daily Mail* was good at – than any set of realities about the state of Britain or the empire. In the first place, the Deterioration Committee that reported in 1904 was very sceptical about the figures for unfit recruits presented by Frederick Maurice and others. Rather than a general physical deterioration among the British working class, the committee members were inclined to see the problem as a lack of fitness, which is certainly not the same thing.[22] Further, the committee only briefly alluded to possible links between sport and a better physique as a solution to this problem. Its focus, and ultimate recommendation, was largely directed towards the provision of gymnastics and military drill – as distinct from organised sport – in schools.[23] But even this emphasis on a militaristic path to health needed to be approached cautiously. It sat very uncomfortably, and was *known* to sit very uncomfortably, with growing numbers in Britain who had either opposed the South African War from the outset or come to disapprove of the brutal 'scorched earth policy' methods employed to finish it in 1902.[24]

It is also doubtful whether there was unqualified admiration for white colonial manhood in the years before 1905. While there was much public enthusiasm for men from the dominions who rushed to volunteer for military service during the early stages of the South African War, the response from the British Army and conservative politicians in Britain was certainly more cautious. For a start, the very use of colonial troops implied doubt about the quality of the British military effort.[25] It was also widely perceived that colonial troops, who were almost all volunteers and not professionally trained soldiers, were lower class and prone to riotous behaviour. Various Australian accounts of the South African War reveal ample evidence of indiscipline and disrespect for the British command structure.[26] One of the strongest examples here is the court martial and subsequent execution of the Australian 'Breaker' Morant in 1902 – a case in which his supposed conduct in shooting Boer prisoners highlighted a serious disjuncture between British and colonial social and military mores.[27] We shall see in later chapters that in 1905, and again in 1908, the behaviour of New Zealand and Australian rugby players confirmed many of the suspicions that some of the British establishment already held about the performance of their counterparts on the battlefield. Indeed, it was the methods of the All Blacks' apparently obstructive wing-forward and captain David Gallaher, a veteran of the South African War, that drew the strongest condemnation from British observers. In short, it is doubtful whether those who exerted most influence in terms of forming official policy, as distinct from those who outlined fears of physical deterioration in the columns of *The Times* or *Daily Mail*, ever regarded sport in general, or Australasian rugby players in particular, as a working model to improve the quality of British manhood – if it needed improving.

Such doubts about a general deterioration are also apparent among those who tackled this issue during 1905. As discussed earlier, many were content to acknowledge the physical prowess of the All Blacks without feeling the need to denigrate their opponents. Even Vaile, as he had done in *The Spectator*, later felt the need to clarify and qualify his position – insisting that his criticism was not so much of a general physical deterioration among the English but a comparative lack of initiative and mental adaptability among their rugby players, especially compared with the New Zealanders.[28] Similar sentiments came from prominent journalist E. H. D. Sewell in a lengthy article early in 1906. While claiming that climate and the sedentary occupations of British players meant they were unable to compete with the fitness of New Zealanders – 'Both come of the same magnificent blood that nothing can alter. Only one cannot flourish in fog and stuffy offices as well as the other that always breaths fresh air' – Sewell also stressed that he was not one to 'croak' about physical deterioration. He was in no doubt that British rugby possessed good players, but for the most part they had failed to adapt to recent innovations by the leading Welsh clubs. Such was the apparent tactical weakness of the game in England that he was inclined to wonder why the New Zealanders were not even more successful.[29]

Nauright's reading of the debates in late 1905 is also highly selective in its emphasis on physical-deterioration themes and reveals a determination to place the tour within late twentieth-century interpretations of masculinity. In the same week that Coventry, Vaile and others outlined the apparent contrast between superiority and decadence, the *Daily Mail* stated that it had received numerous letters, in fact more than could be published, offering a wide variety of explanations for the success of the All Blacks.[30] All, explicitly or implicitly, rejected physical deterioration as a factor. Some, as we shall see in the next chapter, turned to the questionable methods of the tourists. Others, such as A. O. Jones and former England international E. W. Dillon, emphasised 'scientific rugby', combination, tactical astuteness and the quality of the New Zealand backs. Another critic, E. W. Taylor, stressed the need for strong forwards to restrict the New Zealand attack.[31] Ernest Ward in the London *Referee* focused on New Zealand's adherence to 'the gospel of fitness' and insisted:

> There is no novelty in the New Zealanders' football. They have merely worked out afresh a few of the forgotten principles of the real rugby game; they have put them to the test, and pace and fitness have given to their game its crowning mark of efficiency.[32]

Very quickly attention turned to the limited resources available to British rugby – and particularly in relation to the growth of soccer and the split with the Northern Union. As one correspondent wrote on 12 October, the success of the All Blacks was not due to deterioration but to the decline in popularity of rugby: 'The flower of Great Britain and New Zealand athletes are playing under different codes and therefore not meeting each other – hence the New Zealanders' uninterrupted success.' Moreover, as evidence that all was well with British manhood, no teams outside Britain were anywhere near equal to the best it had to offer in soccer.[33] Later in the tour *The Scotsman* observed that

> In England it is well known that amateur rugby is not a successful game. Professionalism withdraws many of the best athletes, but Association football absorbs more. Thus no inference as to the decadence of athleticism and diminution in the bone and muscle of the nation can be drawn from the Colonials' success in England.[34]

The other factor restricting rugby union, as discussed in the previous chapter, was the Northern Union game. On 18 October 'A.B.' wrote to the *Daily Mail* advocating a reconciliation between the two rugby codes to challenge the All Blacks: 'The Northern clubs have the cream of our British talent and the match would be an eye-opener to the flabby Rugby Union exponents of the game. A team from three Lancashire clubs only could lower the New Zealanders' number.' 'Northern Unionist' added that if an 'entente cordiale' could be established between the two rugby codes, 'the visit of the colonial team will have done a service to British sport that can not adequately be estimated'.[35] An anonymous member of the Northern Union committee claimed that 'There is no getting away from the fact that rugby football of to-day is but the flickering of the dying embers of what was once a great blaze of football of the best quality'.[36] J. J. Bentley was equally sure that the Northern Union would give a much better account against the All Blacks, but was in no doubt that such a fixture was utterly impossible until the RFU stepped down from its 'lofty pedestal' and offered a compromise.[37] That no compromise would come during the All Black tour, or at any other time, was made abundantly clear by Percy Coles, secretary of the RFU:

> You can take it from me, and I speak with emphatic certainty, that the idea of amalgamation of the Northern Union with the Rugby Union is impossible. The idea is not to be entertained. It is absurd. It could not happen, at least not as the Rugby Union is at present constituted.[38]

From early in the tour the New Zealand audience was also made aware of these debates. A report in the *Otago Witness* on 25 October stated that the All Blacks' victories lacked magnitude owing to there being two football codes in Britain – to say nothing of soccer. But as the *Witness* piously reminded its readers:

> The Counties which broke away from the English Union, and formed a Northern Union, playing professional football, have themselves to blame that they are not included in the New Zealand team's tour. Had they been playing amateur football, no doubt they would have met the New Zealand team.[39]

But as we shall see in Chapter Nine, the prospect of a true test against the real strength of British rugby was to play some part in defections from the New Zealand amateur rugby ranks in 1907.

Of course, it can be argued that even if the numbers playing rugby union in Britain were small, they were still larger than the New Zealand player base and the difference in standard between the two was therefore still remarkable. In response, the emphasis of some critics shifted to consider both the nature of amateur rugby and the particular advantages of a touring team. 'Old Rugbyite' insisted that it was not valid to compare club players with a trained international team and that the real test would come only when the All Blacks met such opposition.[40] Harry Alexander, former England international and regular *Daily Mail* columnist, strongly resented accusations of slackness and unfitness levelled at amateur rugby players – describing them as a destructive, rather than constructive, response arising from the tendency of professional football and spectators to demand each match as a 'gladiatorial combat'.

> But the amateur rugby player has given no sort of guarantee of the class of entertainment he will provide, nor any undertaking as to what his own condition will be. He is perfectly free to play utterly untrained and unprepared and to be as superfluous as may be, just as long as his club selects him. No critic, therefore, has a right to do more than express an opinion on the general unfitness of such and such a player and is certainly going outside his province, and serving no good end, in allowing his remarks to degenerate into the scurrilous abuse to which we have lately been subjected.[41]

In reply, 'Anglo-Scot' suggested that Alexander's comments would only hold true if 'pat-ball' were being played behind closed doors, but the gates had been opened to the public and admission charged:

> In so far as our games reflect the character of the nation, the spectators cannot but feel that the matches hitherto played against the New Zealanders only confirm those pessimists who see decadence in every department of English life. No man cares to be wounded in his feelings of national self-respect.[42]

Hamish Stuart was another who did not endorse the 'superlative mania' for the All Blacks. It was impossible to compare teams of the past and present, and other teams may have had similar success if given the same opportunities to practise and perfect their methods.

> What I maintain is that many sides of the past (and one might add of the present) if given the same opportunities and imbued with the same determination to scorn delights and live laborious days would have accomplished the same striking series of successes as now stand to the credit of the New Zealanders in the annals of the game. What national fifteen have ever enjoyed the chance of playing together like a club side or of devoting their whole attention, and of sacrificing every other interest, business and social, of life to enable that perfect mental and physical condition which makes for football of a sustained excellence, far above the ordinary whether regarded from the individual or collective point of view?[43]

In similar vein, 'E. G.' wrote to the *Daily Mail*:

> Much of the criticism on the alleged decadence of modern British rugby football is, to put it mildly, 'utter rot'. Will these loud-voiced pessimists tell me what the result would be if a picked team from any of our countries

were to play against ordinary club and county teams under the same conditions as the New Zealanders are now doing – i.e. practically living for football and nothing else.

It was 'nothing short of imbecility' to expect amateur players, who had to work throughout the week, to compete against carefully selected and trained international opposition. 'To conclude that all the home men are demoralised and emasculated on such evidence is at least illogical and I, for one, consider that these critics may as well ask town and country cricket clubs to beat the Australians.'[44] 'Anti-Craze', who described Vaile's articles as 'perfect lunacy', offered another parallel with cricket:

> All these physical deterioration cranks are rampant with delight quite forgetful of the fact that when the Australians beat county after county, no comment was made. Of course an international team will beat local or county teams ... What have the deterioration cranks to say in reply to the fact that all of the armour in the Tower of London is too small for most people of the present day ... It is high time a check was placed on all this prevailing hysteria with regard to deterioration. If an English team were to go round beating New Zealand piecemeal at cricket, I don't think they would conclude that their nation was a set of effeminate wrecks.[45]

The crucial point here is that as recently as the 1902–03 season an English cricket team had comprehensively defeated all opposition in New Zealand and, although there was a great deal of lamentation about the state of local cricket, there was no 'deterioration' rhetoric to accompany it.[46] Moreover, according to 'Anti-Craze', the success of this and other English cricket teams, especially against Australia in 1903–04 and 1905, and the success of Englishmen in other sports, provided ample evidence of strength and stamina. The success of the 1905 All Blacks merely indicated the necessity to learn and adapt – as lessons had previously been learned in war and other sports.[47]

Amid the many and varied theories, the most novel explanation for the All Blacks' success came from those who could offer nothing more than a frank admission that they were superior opposition. As Major Philip Trevor wrote in *The Sportsman*, 'Their lessons are simplicity itself and it is the too curious amongst us who have discovered deep and obscure meanings.'[48] A week later he added that numerous theories and constant predictions that the tourists would be beaten 'in the future' or 'in Wales' revealed a basic inability to admit that they were better players.[49] Similarly, 'Judex' wrote in the *Sporting Life*:

I think the rugby player is now as fine a man as ever he was. I do, however, think that many of us have been ungenerous in our comments on the New Zealanders' victories in seeking out excuses for our defeats . . . We are, and will continue to be, beaten by the finest team that has ever played rugby football, and in this lies our only excuse. And what better one could any sportsman have?[50]

Following the All Blacks' victory over England, the *Westminster Gazette* re-iterated that theories of 'fitness' and 'superiority' had been rejected 'and the methods rather more than the men are receiving the credit which is due to the side'. The fact seemed to be that the New Zealanders were individually 'players of remarkable physical aptitude and skill' who played 'a more intelligent game than do our own men, hampered by a stereotyped scheme of combination (and that not a very good one), and seldom daring to make innovations'.[51]

Perhaps the most comprehensive indictment of the 'deteriorationists', and of British rugby more generally, came from *The Field* in a leading article of 11 November. While the manner in which New Zealand had exposed the weakness of the British in one of their national games was certainly comparable with the 'stuperfacaction' caused by the Australian cricketers in 1878,

> Then, as now, a kind of sleepy complacency prevailed which was thoroughly ripe for a rude awakening; an art which was supposed to have culminated was revolutionised by the display of original methods coupled with a novel application of both physical and intellectual energy.

Nevertheless, this realisation had been obscured by the volume of theories, opinion and advice coming from those uninformed about sport. As *The Field* sarcastically explained:

> There is never any lack of patriots willing and able to save their country by writing to The Times; and it is to be hoped that the Rugby Union will not fail to profit by the discrepant exhortations that have been showered upon them. They have only to determine whether national decadence in football is due to old-fashioned adherence to scrummages lasting a quarter of an hour, to a slow-witted preference for defence over attack, to the pedantic insistence of referees on the off-side rule, to obstinate disregard of the spectators right to see a bright and open game, to the players luxurious aversion to train like a prize fighter for six months at a time, to his slowness to recognise the merits of the simple life, vegetarian diet, ju-jitsu, somebody's system of muscle culture, and wing forwards. In

circles that may comparatively be termed esoteric, the New Zealanders triumphs are variously ascribed to their brilliant and accurate passing, to their pace and weight, to the superior intelligence or physique of colonials in general, and to their innovations in formation and tactics.

It was also inevitable that a well-trained, well-selected team from a country where rugby was a major sporting passion would succeed against those in a comparatively minor sport limited by its amateur restrictions. Moreover, compared with the Association game, rugby

> is handicapped by the obscurity of its laws and its inatractiveness to men of a logical and intelligent character. Legislators who cannot draft a comprehensive or grammatical clause, are perhaps matched with thick-witted players who fail to develop the possibilities of their art.[52]

As *The Field* and many other observers were increasingly aware, those who looked for British failings or inherent colonial exceptionalism were also ignoring the fact that the dominance of the All Blacks reflected the fact that they trained more often and more scientifically than any other amateur rugby team up to that time. As Chapter One explained, 'scientific rugby', specialist positions, careful tactical analysis and practice had been a part of New Zealand rugby from the 1880s. The insistence in 1904 that the New Zealand team should have ample time to train before meeting Britain is an obvious reflection of these developments. So too, as we have seen already, was the emphasis that was placed on both physical conditioning and tactical appreciation during the six-week voyage to Britain, and the dedication with which the team practised and avoided excess throughout the tour. There was no hint in the All Blacks' demeanour that success came naturally or merely because they had grown up in New Zealand. Here Caroline Daley also places particular emphasis on the role of Eugen Sandow, the founder of modern body-building. Through his London Institute of Physical Culture, *Sandow's Magazine*, various books, stage shows throughout the world, and through the sale of exercise equipment, Sandow had established a reputation as the leading 'physical culturist' and advocate of systematic exercise as a means to both personal health and development, and to produce trained and conditioned athletes. He had conducted an extremely successful tour of New Zealand in 1902–03, attracting large crowds and leaving a legacy of devoted followers.[53] Now in 1905, Sandow claimed that the success of the All Blacks was entirely due to their adoption of his methods. Moreover, if given another 15 players to train for six months, he was sure that he could produce a team that would 'run off their feet any Rugby football team within the Empire'.⁵⁴ However, aside from Billy Glenn's apparently taking a Sandow Developer, a form of chest expander, with him, there is no conclusive evidence that the team followed Sandow to the letter – as distinct from the more general virtues of exercise and training.⁵⁵

The final element undermining links between the All Blacks and debates concerning British and colonial manhood is the abrasive response to Richard Seddon and William Pember Reeves. In early October both had informed the *Daily Mail* that the success of the tour was in part due to the 'natural' and 'healthy' colonial environment – as a sharp contrast to the urban congestion of the Mother Country. A number of those who rejected the notion of deterioration in Britain implicitly rejected such claims. Others did so more directly and sarcastically. In late October the London *Daily News* declared:

> Our old friend Mr 'Dick' Seddon will be more cock-a-hoop than ever. His mutton has long filled our butchers' shops and his wit and wisdom have increased the gaiety of nations. He has pointed out a hundred ways in which we fall short of the country he governs with a naïvete that always reminds us of Sancho Panza. Hitherto, however, we have never realised our inferiority. Perhaps we have never even felt it. But to-day we are humbled and abased. Mr Seddon has scourged us with football scorpions.⁵⁶

Towards the end of the tour, and after the All Blacks' loss to Wales, *Punch* launched a further scathing response to Seddon's environmental determinism, mocking New Zealand's apparent extremes of heat and cold 'that are so injurious to the system; geysers at one end of the thermometer and frozen lamb at the other' and suggesting that the Premier was hardly an ideal advertisement for the qualities of colonial life:

> Finally, in the person of the Rt Hon. Richard Seddon, New Zealand's ideal figure, we have a standard of physical culture that makes for national obesity. His bodily dimensions (quite apart from his tendency to mental tumidity) can not but have exerted a baleful influence upon his loyal subjects, discouraging that abstinence and self-restraint which are essential to a perfect training and more than counter-balancing the admirable example offered by the svelte and almost ascetic figure of the Hon. W. P. Reeves, High Commissioner for the colony. These drawbacks notwithstanding, and above all, though the football players of New Zealand may have had a hand in the establishment of female suffrage, frozen lamb, and Mr Seddon, yet they can not be held responsible for

their premier's proportions, nor for the geysers - I must believe that this promising young country, by strict attention to its physique, will eventually distinguish itself and send out a combination worthy to cross shins with the all conquering cymry.[57]

We shall see in Chapter Eight that this was not to be the last criticism of Seddon – the self-appointed 'Minister for Football' – and his efforts to capitalise on the success of the tour by using it for nationalist propaganda purposes in Britain and North America.

It is clear that the range of explanations offered for the success of the 1905 All Blacks was much wider than those few seized upon by historians determined to link the tour with preconceived notions of colonial masculinity and national identity. It is equally important to remember that the debate in all of its perspectives, eccentricities and parodies was extensively covered by a New Zealand press that, as we have seen in the previous chapter, eagerly devoured everything to do with the 1905 tour. As Caroline Daley conclusively demonstrates, there is absolutely no substance for James Belich's claim that aspects of the tour coverage in Britain were 'culled out' to enable New Zealand audiences to retain an untarnished perception of their rugby team and relationship with the Mother Country.[58] Indeed, as the next chapter will argue, the mounting volume of criticism of the All Blacks' methods and attitudes was to leave no doubt among all observers of rugby, in Britain and New Zealand, that this was a highly contested and controversial tour.

CHAPTER SIX

Infringing Ideals

WHILE CONTRIBUTORS to the British press keenly debated the reasons for the success of the tour, the All Blacks continued a relentless march through England. If the margins of victory were not always as large as they had been in the first weeks of the tour, the tourists nevertheless scored 67 tries among 271 points in total from the 10 matches from 19 October to 15 November. A penalty goal by Devonport Albion and a converted try by Midland Counties were the only eight points in reply. Many commentators continued to search their dictionaries for superlatives; others developed the various explanations outlined in the previous chapter; but another group, who had been brooding quietly since the opening match against Devon, now began a vociferous attack on the All Blacks' methods. To them, the ideal amateur athlete was supposed to possess a healthy body and a healthy mind. He not only required the physical attributes to succeed at games, but also the correct attitude in terms of personal conduct, observation of the rules and respect for opponents. Yet many argued that the All Blacks clearly subverted this ideal in that their success depended on suspect methods and competitive instincts that represented a blot on the gentlemanly ethos of a game that ought to be played for pure enjoyment. The most frequent target was the wing-forward, and the regular occupant of that position, David Gallaher.

The debate around the wing-forward – the use of an unbound player 'roving' on the side of the scrum to harass the opposing inside backs and to shield his own when on attack– is much more than one between rugby buffs over the merits, or otherwise, of a particular playing strategy. Just as the particular 'bodyline' fast-bowling tactic employed by Douglas Jardine's touring cricket team triggered considerable controversy and a broader 'imperial crisis' between England and Australia during 1932–33,[1] so the methods of the wing-forward reveal much about the divergent British and New Zealand rugby cultures and the different social settings that shaped them. Some historians in search of broader meanings for the 1905 tour have been swayed by the magnitude of the scores without stopping to consider carefully the means by which these were achieved. It is essential, then, to explain the origins and purpose of the wing-forward position, its divisive impact on New Zealand rugby and the full range of reactions to Gallaher's play in 1905. As important, the contrasting ideals and concepts of sportsmanship epitomised by the wing-forward debate were to trigger strained rugby relations between Britain and New Zealand for more than a quarter of a century – not least in terms of a sometimes bitter struggle between the traditionalists of the International Board in Britain and the desire of the increasingly powerful dominions to have a stake in the running of the game. All of this produced a rather more critical and contested legacy for the 1905 tour than the reams of praise and admiration that emerge from the nostalgia of later years.

Despite the early success of the tour, George Dixon was not inclined to get carried away. On 16 October he informed the *Daily Mail* that while the team was glad it had 'fulfilled its mission' thus far, there was a long way to go yet, and a different story may have to be told after the internationals. 'You must not forget that at the commencement of the tour we caught some of our opponents scarcely fit, and that as the season advances we may go off, while the others may come on.'[2] Later, following the victory over Midland Counties, he diplomatically rejected a suggestion that his team had come to Britain to 'teach' football:

> No we have not come over to teach you football, but to remind you of some of the things you have forgotten. English footballers first taught us how to play the game. We closely studied their methods and tried to improve upon them, and if to-day we can in any way help them to further the interests of the grand old game we shall be more than repaid.[3]

As it was, few of their club or county opponents showed signs of 'coming on' or learning. Gloucester City Clubs and a Bedford XV conceded 10 tries each, Blackheath conceded seven, Somerset, Devonport Albion, Midland Counties and Richmond five each, and Oxford University, traditionally a strong rugby combination, conceded 13 in a defeat that would have been much larger than 47–0 if any more than just four kicks at goal had been successful. Only Devonport Albion, which won praise for its willingness to attack rather than contain the All Blacks; Surrey, defeated 11–0 at Richmond; and Cambridge University, which succumbed 14–0, provided truly competitive opposition – although the Cambridge effort was as much due to an understrength All Black team, with several players appearing out of position.[4]

Naturally these results produced yet more admiration for the New Zealanders and criticisms of the state of the English game. Dixon's account of the tour, although undoubtedly selective, nevertheless contains numerous extracts from critics who were seemingly mesmerised by the speed, combination, adaptability and unorthodoxy of the All Blacks. Some, such as Captain Southwall Fitzgerald in the *Sporting Life*, were unrelenting in their admiration.[5] After the Somerset match, former test cricketer and county rugby player S. M. J. Woods claimed that the tour would give a considerable boost to rugby, but it was essential that all players in local teams had to be fit:

> There is too little 'devil' and go among our players, and the New Zealanders play is an object lesson for us. Our forwards of to-day can also take a lesson in kicking and passing from them. Their backs do not hesitate to make an individual effort to get through – and often do so.[6]

With considerable optimism, the Oxford captain declared that 'if our rugby clubs would only adopt the style of the New Zealanders, the game would in the course of time – Rome was not built in a day – oust Association from public favour'.[7] The *Daily Mail* also reported a supposed exchange between undergraduates in which the younger asked, 'Why don't our men tackle them?' The response from his older colleague – 'My son, if you read the rules, you would know that you are not allowed to tackle a man until you have caught him'[8] – embodies the widespread acknowledgment that the New Zealand backs, Jimmy Hunter, George Smith and Billy Wallace especially, were simply too fast and too evasive. But although the backs scored 181 of the 215 tries in Britain and France, and Hunter accumulated a remarkable 42 in only 22 appearances, it was the forwards who soon began to monopolise press coverage – and not merely because a solid forward platform is essential to effective back play.

As we have seen in Chapter Four, both the New Zealand scrum formation and the methods of Gallaher as wing-forward attracted unfavourable comment from the outset. Ideally, the task would be to read everything written in the British press during and immediately after 1905 to determine whether, on balance, the All Blacks won more praise or condemnation for their methods and demeanour. Such an assignment is probably beyond any researcher, even with years at their disposal. It is also difficult to assess the merit of much that was written. Some critics, such as the numerous former international players who watched the All Blacks regularly and wrote for the specialist sporting press, were undoubtedly well versed in the laws of the game and qualified to venture an opinion. Others, many of them local editors and journalists who saw the tourists on only one or two occasions, were no doubt swept along by immediate euphoria and the smallness or vastness of a particular score without necessarily understanding the intricacies of rugby tactics. But if the balance is hard to establish, what can be said with absolute certainty is that the emphasis in existing historical accounts of the tour has been far too preoccupied with adulation, to the detriment of a proper examination of those who found considerable fault with the All Blacks.

Every New Zealand account of the tour makes some mention of the wing-forward and related controversies. But equally apparent is a belief that such problems evaporated as the tour progressed and that the All Blacks ultimately won over their critics with their brilliant performances. As Ron Palenski puts it:

> In context, the fuss over the wing-forward did not then loom large, not half as large as the disputed result against Wales and was insignificant in the huge influence of the tour itself – on the New Zealand public back home, on the players who undertook the tour and on the players they opposed. The tour set yardsticks by which all others would be measured.[9]

Writing immediately after the tour, George Dixon presented a rather mixed recollection. Early in his book he claims that British press views gradually changed in favour of New Zealand and that controversies died down as the tour progressed – until they reached Wales. Later, he refers to many in the British press who

> seemed jealously indisposed or incapable of giving us the credit for our victories that was justly due to us. On the other hand, of course, there were other writers, and they were in the majority, who were most generous and magnanimous in their praise of the New Zealand team and its exploits. To the hostile critics, I have made no reply because the continuous succession of victories was an effective answer in itself to carping criticism'.[10]

At the end of the book he notes that many negative critics were still persisting at the end of the tour, although they were not reinforced by any British players or critics of 'standing'.[11] However, this is rather disingenuous. For one thing, it was precisely the 'method' of achieving victories that drew criticism – and from a number of observers who did possess strong rugby credentials. Further, as we shall see in the next chapter, Dixon was sufficiently stung by their 'carping' to respond directly in the Welsh press and, despite Palenski's claim, the apparently 'disputed result' against Wales was the least of his concerns.

To unravel the wing-forward controversy, we must begin with the origins and purpose of the position and remember that, contrary to popular belief, it was not a New Zealand invention. As Tony Collins points out in the context of the greater specialisation, training and scientific play that shaped northern English rugby from the early 1880s, there was a long history of wing-forward play in Yorkshire. Thornes, winners of the Yorkshire Cup in 1882, used specialist forward positions and a wing-forward. Brighouse Rangers used two wing-forwards as late as the 1893–94 season. But the position was widely condemned as a spoiling tactic in that the player frequently got himself offside around the scrum when pursuing opposition backs and appeared to do little more than obstruct when protecting his own.[12] For this reason, wing-forwards gradually disappeared from northern rugby. As the rather conservative *Yorkshire Post* observed of the All Blacks in early October 1905, there was nothing new in tactics 'that were responsible for so much ill-feeling that by common consent the wing-forward was abolished'.[13] In fact, the first rule change of the Northern Union in 1896 had been specifically designed both to force the halfback feeding the scrum to retire behind the scrum as soon as the ball was put in and to forbid his opponent from advancing beyond the feet of his props until the ball was out. This reduced obstruction around the scrum and enabled the ball to be cleared quickly, thereby removing one of the supposed requirements of having a wing-forward to shield the inside backs.[14]

But at the beginning of the 1904–05 season, perhaps in light of British experiences in New Zealand during 1904, a number of critics advocated the use of a wing-forward by England against Wales. One argued that English prestige could only be restored if they reverted to a formation using three three-quarters in the backs and one 'winger' rather than four three-quarters, adding that 'A wing-forward is of infinitely more value in spoiling the opposition half-backs than a fourth three-quarter can be'.[15] Such ideas seem to have been forgotten by the time the All Blacks arrived for the following season.

The genesis of the wing-forward in New Zealand owes something to English traditions. As Chapter One noted, new players arriving in the colony during the 1870s and 1880s brought with them the latest strategies and interpretations of the laws. No doubt these were reinforced by the tour of the Native team in 1888–89. Tom Ellison, once of its most prominent players, was soon developing patterns of aggressive forward play revolving around a 2-3-2 scrum and distinct wing-forward in Wellington teams from the early 1890s. He saw the role of the wing-forward as putting the ball into the scrum, protecting his halfback as the ball rapidly emerged and staying onside while his team advanced. There was no room for complaint, and ample scope for open play, if the system was used correctly.[16] At the end of the 1905 tour, Gallaher and Stead argued that the wing-forward was 'simply a detail of the natural development of the New Zealand game in the direction and with the object of the greatest possible economy of speed and power in the team, and for the purpose of exercising the full measure of its resources in every contingency'.[17] The magnitude of Ellison's strategy is neatly captured by Arthur Swan, the doyen of New Zealand rugby historians:

> This radical change, which did so much to assist future New Zealand sides, and incidentally to heap abuse upon players chosen in the position, entirely altered the playing aspect in New Zealand rugby.[18]

But the wing-forward did not win easy acceptance in New Zealand from those who perceived that aggressive and obstructive forward play was contrary to the spirit of the game. In 1897, after an acrimonious clash between Otago and a Wellington team dubbed 'the butchers', the Otago RFU asked the NZRFU to seek clarification from the RFU regarding the legality of the wing-forward. The NZRFU refused to forward Otago's letter on the grounds that there was nothing in the laws against the position and ample penalties for obstruction already existed to contain it. When the Otago RFU forwarded the letter directly, the RFU replied that it was unable to rule.[19] In 1901 the New Zealand referees conference passed a motion requesting that the NZRFU abolish the wing-forward. Again the union replied that objectionable features of the position would be removed if referees strictly enforced the laws.[20] In 1902 Ellison insisted that the criticisms stemmed from the ignorance of those playing as wing-forwards rather than from the position itself:

> The so-called wing-forwards of to-day are nothing more than aimless off-side jostlers, who do more harm to their side than anything else. They seem to think that their duty is to do nothing but harass their opponents and to play off-side and jostle.[21]

At the end of the 1905 tour, Jimmy Duncan, who had been on the receiving end of Wellington's tactics in 1897 and had just spent three months watching Gallaher, was highly critical of the obstructive tactics of the wing-forward and wanted the position abolished in the interests of open play.[22] Thus the wing-forward was a contested position long before the All Blacks took the field against Devon and it is consequently somewhat misleading to follow Dixon's portrayal of jealous and carping British critics.

Another context for understanding objections to the wing-forward rests in the importance of muscular Christianity to the dominant middle-class sporting view of Edwardian Britain. Although prone to a shifting definition, the notion of muscular Christianity outlined in the mid-nineteenth century by Thomas Hughes, Charles Kingsley and others, and which emerged as a central tenet of the sporting ethos of the English public schools, emphasised the bond between sport, manliness and godliness – linking honesty, maturity and a strong sense of moral duty with robust energy and physical vitality. What is most important to note here is the connection between qualities of body *and* mind – between physical prowess and the possession of a strong moral character.[23] For a game to be played well, results had to be accompanied by the right amateur spirit and style. As we have seen already, middle-class objections to excessive physicality and competitiveness, and a tendency to follow the letter rather than spirit of the law, were as much a part of the split between north and south in British rugby as were issues of player payment. We must keep these two components of muscular Christianity firmly in mind when considering the increasingly antagonistic reactions to the All Blacks. For although, as the last chapter argued, there is some contemporary evidence and more historical writing to suggest that they were healthy physical specimens, this must be balanced against the not insignificant perception that in many other respects they failed to accompany these attributes with a healthy frame of mind – with *esprit de corps* and an appropriate devotion to the principles of amateurism, fair play and gentlemanly sporting conduct. Their playing methods, as with the Native team, were more akin to those in the north of England, which had apparently departed from the accepted form of rugby. And yet many of the opponents and critics the All Blacks encountered in 1905 were from a rugby world that had been purged of its 'problematic' northern element. In short, whatever the All Blacks achieved on the scoreboard, there were many who regarded them as less than true sportsmen.

From the opening match against Devon, the All Blacks were left in no doubt that the wing-forward position was unpopular with many observers.

The *Morning Post* critic wrote: 'There is one blot on the game as played by the New Zealanders and one which is against every canon of rugby union football. This is in the work allotted to the "wing" forward.' Moreover, the term 'winger' was usually a slur in English rugby for those not doing their share of scrum work.[24] The *Manchester Guardian* described Gallaher as 'a professed obstructionist' who was lucky to escape greater sanction from the referee.[25] Many critics predicted trouble ahead for the wing-forward. Following the next fixture, against Cornwall, Dixon wrote in his diary:

> Afraid newspaper reporters here one-eyed – they started off with preconceived notion that winger was offside abomination & are allowing their judgement to be run away with – As a matter of fact Cornish 1/2 and winger (they brought a man out of the scrum) were more frequently at fault than Davey.[26]

Preconceived or not, the criticism gathered momentum – epitomised by the *Illustrated Sporting and Dramatic News* describing the wing-forward as an abomination: 'His principal work seems to be to plant himself in front of the opposing half, and we find it difficult to regard an obstructionist as a footballer.'[27] Against Somerset on 21 October Gallaher was again frequently penalised for offside play – a reaction that drew much praise from a local reporter:

> [T]he strict manner in which Mr Davies held the impetuous 'All Blacks' back was not altogether to their liking, and they were inclined to question some of his decisions. But the refereeing, however unpalatable to colonials, was decidedly good and based on correct interpretations of Rugby Union rules.[28]

Four days later, the first full reports of the developing controversy were published in the New Zealand press. Included was the *Daily Chronicle* description of the wing-forward as

> such an irritating person ... [who] plays such a decidedly unlawful game, from our point of view, that his prudence in wearing shin-guards may be commended. The winger showed a fine scorn of certain sections of Rule 11, and if he had met with his deserts he would have been penalised into ineffectiveness.[29]

New Zealand readers saw no shortage of such assessments over the ensuing months.

The debate intensified after the All Blacks defeated Surrey on 1 November. Under a headline 'Whistling Fantasia by the Referee', and a claim that it was 'probably the greatest rugby football farce in the history of the game', the *Daily Mail* mocked the match as more an open-air concert to the tune of the whistle than an athletic display, as referee W. Williams awarded at least 16 penalties against the New Zealanders for offside play and other breaches.[30] But much as the *Daily Mail* and several of its correspondents found fault with the referee, others were in no doubt that the visitors deserved their punishment. *The Field* declared that the penalties awarded to Surrey were hardly adequate compensation for the 'frequent disregard of the laws of the game' by the All Blacks:

> It was also seen that the wing-forward – if he is to be of any value to his side – must have great difficulty in observing the rule which forbids a player to remain in front of the ball while it is in the scrummage and he himself is not, while he is also liable to the charge of active or passive obstruction. The New Zealand team is so strong that it could well afford to restrict itself scrupulously to the orthodox interpretation of the laws instead of throwing the responsibility entirely on the referee.[31]

Even critics such as E. H. D. Sewell and Major Philip Trevor, who generally defended the methods of the All Blacks throughout the tour, felt that their conduct, and their challenging of refereeing decisions, was pushing the boundaries of acceptable sportsmanship.[32] Although there was some complaint about spectators who were 'quite obnoxious' by their continued calling of 'Play the game, Gallaher', there was equally no question that the New Zealand captain was very much the focal point for critics of the team as a whole.[33]

From start to finish, the staunchest critic of New Zealand methods was the ubiquitous Hamish Stuart, who maintained that they were deliberately following the letter of the law at the expense of the spirit of the game. Following the international against Scotland, he provided the *Athletic News* with a lengthy account of what he saw as the dilemma facing critics of the All Blacks – in that constant criticisms of a winning team could raise accusations that the vanquished were merely bad losers. Yet Stuart insisted that his criticisms were much more than the 'malevolent petty chagrin of defeat'. Rather, they were dictated by a conscientious conviction that 'the success of the victors was largely, though not wholly, due to their playing football which suggests a most careful study of the letter of the law, of the penalties attending to breaches, and of the advantages to be gained by scientific evasion thereof'. The Scots, he argued, never complained about opposition methods when defeated by England or Ireland. But they found much to object to in those used by the Welsh and the All Blacks:

> After closely watching the New Zealanders, I have no hesitation in saying that an aggravated and wholly unconscionable adherence to the principle 'play to the whistle' is the ruling motive of their game. This may not, and indeed does not, represent a very high ethical ideal, but there can be no question that all sides who play on this principle are bound to be successful. The degree of their success will of course depend upon their speed, skill, stamina and so forth, upon their ability, that is to say, to give physical expression to the principle, but other things being equal, the prudent 'punter' will put his money on a side playing on this plan.

While it was probable that the overly complex laws of rugby had 'killed off the true spirit' of the game, Stuart nevertheless saw no excuse for foul play and the evident tendency of the All Blacks to 'forget themselves' when under pressure against Scotland. He insisted that his criticism of New Zealand methods would have been much stronger had they lost – presumably implying that he would not have been constrained by the requirement of a sportsman to accept defeat with good grace.[34] Indeed, we shall see in the next chapter that attacks on Gallaher became most intense in Wales, where his team generally struggled. Shortly after the Newport match, Stuart outlined a further distinction between that which was merely 'illegal' under the laws of rugby and that which was 'unfair' within the spirit of sport. With specific reference to Gallaher's play as wing-forward, he concluded that 'habitual illegality is unfairness'.[35]

If Gallaher was the obvious target, he was not the only one. As the encounter with Surrey revealed, the tendency of some of the All Blacks to remonstrate with referees was not considered good sportsmanship. There were also suggestions that their play was unnecessarily rough. On this point, F. H. R. Alderson, an England international of the early 1890s, was scathing in his assessment of the hard-fought victory over Durham on 7 October:

> There was nothing very finished about their play and many of their methods are open to severe censure. One likes to see good, hard tackling, but there is no need to throw your man violently to the ground after he has parted with the ball. The finished way in which the New Zealanders obstructed their opponents reminded one of the Yorkshire tactics some ten or twenty years ago. It is a pity our visitors have so soon learned these sharp practices and a greater pity if they leave the country without being told we do not admire these tactics and without being taught to play differently.[36]

Other observers hinted at roughness by the Durham players and rebuked Alderson for wiring his comments to the London press,[37] but we shall see in the next chapter that the international fixtures later in the tour prompted similar complaints from a number of observers.

Some prominent followers of the game, although not necessarily liking the wing-forward, were less willing to condemn the All Blacks for using it and more inclined to defend them against the venom of their critics. Major Philip Trevor felt that the presence of a wing-forward was more likely to lead to the possibility of offside and other infringements, but the All Blacks were not an unfair team and merely played the game 'as refined by our existing laws and I trust that their visit will be a fresh inducement to our referees to administer the game most strictly'.[38] 'Judex' in the *Sporting Life* saw nothing to warrant condemnation of the wing-forward or to support accusations of rough play.

> I have seen the New Zealanders play a good number of times and I have never noticed any roughness in their play. I am quite prepared to admit that if their opponents tried that sort of game out, our colonial friends would be very well able to take care of themselves, and no small blame to them.[39]

The following year, after watching the South Africans, he concluded that the All Blacks would have won just as many matches without a wing-forward 'and they would have thus stopped a lot of contentious talking and writing'.[40] Former England international Harry Alexander was one of many who objected to the wing-forward only insofar as he obstructed the opposition halfback by shielding his own. But, as Alexander stressed,

> We in England do not, and never have, regarded such methods as conformant to the spirit of the game, and to state that the New Zealanders do so regard them is no reflection on the spirit in which they play, but merely a statement that in the Colony a very different view of the matter is evidently taken.[41]

After the tour, E. H. D. Sewell argued that although the wing-forward should have been penalised more, the New Zealanders believed they were playing within the laws. 'And I do not see why any particular move in their game, because it does not coincide with our views on the same subject, should necessarily be unfair or even illegal. May not our methods perhaps be the illegal ones?'[42] He also felt that many of the accusations and insinuations of rough play against the All Blacks had come from writers who 'endeavoured in the strongest and bitterest terms to make them out by inference to be a successful side because of their unfair and illegal tactics'. This approach, argued Sewell, was particularly harmful with regard to 'lesser educated' members of the sporting public who were not able to draw their own conclusions and distinguish properly between rough play and hard play. A 'varsity man' was able to make such distinctions and accordingly should find few grounds to criticise the visitors.[43]

From the distance of a century, and without a substantial amount of film footage, it is futile to relitigate the rights and wrongs of the wing-forward and other New Zealand tactics. But it is notable, as Caroline Daley points out, that the All Blacks did not adapt their play or make any concession to the controversial environment in which they found themselves. Nor have historical accounts of the tour shown any indication that perhaps the British critics had a point. To do so would erode the popular mythology that later enveloped Gallaher in particular and the team in general. In early October, Dixon gave a rare press interview in which he attempted to defend the general principle of wing-forward play:

> It is conceivable that under any system men can make things unpleasant. But the rough, unpleasant play does not arise from the system, the individuals are to blame. If a man chooses, he can play any system without getting vicious. We find no difficulty arises from wing-forwardism as we play it.[44]

At the end of the tour, Gallaher and Stead insisted that the wing-forward was basically a back and that if the position had been called 'halfback' there would have been no objection in Britain. As Gallaher mused, 'I have been jeered and hooted at over and over again for doing that which every other half in the country does every day'.[45] Moreover, British halfbacks infringed as frequently as New Zealand wing-forwards and a number of their opponents had conceded the merits of the position by using it against the All Blacks – but calling it a 'half' or a 'rover'. Gallaher also offered the intriguing suggestion that he attracted attention because he was the only player to wear shin guards outside his socks. Hence spectators thought that he was the only player in the team who wore them, and only did so because of the doubtful nature of his play in that his obstructive methods apparently attracted 'attention' from opponents. In fact every member of the team wore shin guards.[46] Of course these arguments conveniently ignore the various objections to the wing-forward within New Zealand rugby prior to the tour.

Controversy over the wing-forward did not end with the departure of the All Blacks from Britain. The subsequent history of the position is worth considering for the way in which it strained the fabric of international rugby during the first third of the twentieth century, thereby further undermining the claims of those who have derived a strand of New Zealand's national identity from a supposed admiration for its rugby players. Equally important is the way in which the wing-forward symbolises a broader struggle for control of the international game.

Certain vindication for the wing-forward can be seen in the efforts of a normally conservative British game to experiment with New Zealand tactics in the seasons immediately after the tour. While Blackheath was apparently the only prominent club to consistently adopt the New Zealand scrum formation and wing-forward during the 1906–07 season,[47] there were more obvious signs of it at international level. Both Wales and Ireland used seven forwards and a 'rover' or 'flyer' against England in 1906. Wales then struggled to victory over Scotland with the same formation before returning to its old style and losing to Ireland.[48] In 1910 Alan Adams, a former Otago player now in the London Hospital side, wrote to the *Otago Witness* that it was 'rather amusing to see the way the home unions have taken to the wing-forward game after all the adverse criticism of Gallaher'. The English selectors had used the position throughout the 1909–10 season, and 'much of England's success against Wales was due to the winger bustling the Welsh half-backs off their game'. Adams also noted that the Irish and Scottish forwards were rough with their feet, 'But this is called hard play here and is not stopped'.[49]

Perhaps at issue was the definition of a wing-forward as opposed to a halfback or a loose forward who was in some way bound to the scrum, for it is clear that most of those who expressed an opinion on New Zealand wing-forward play during this period were implacably hostile. In 1907 famed Welsh player Arthur Gould described wing-forward play as 'absolutely the most objectionable feature which has come under notice during the last twenty years. Gallaher's play was often deliberately obstructive and absolutely opposed to the spirit of Rugby football as we understand it in this country.' But Gould also concluded that New Zealand's success had been due not to its scrum formation and wing-forward, but because the All Blacks were individually great players.[50] The following year, in his account of the rather fraught 1908 Anglo-Welsh tour of New Zealand, to be discussed in Chapter Nine, R. A. Barr wrote that the wing-forward had been largely unknown in England prior to 1905,

> but from the time of making his acquaintance we have always considered – and still continue to do so – that he is responsible for spoiling much open play after possession has been fairly gained by his opposing forwards, and when defending he is breaking the rule governing obstruction on

the field by deliberately preventing the opposing half getting round the scrummage'. Every important Rugby man here seems to be anxious to make the wing-forward position, a thing of the past – admitting that it is harmful for the game – yet, funnily enough, they look to the English Union to take action, when at the same time they know that the position only exists in New Zealand.[51]

For New Zealand administrators it was perhaps a matter of balancing the desire to curb or abolish the wing-forward with the realisation that doing so could greatly reduce the effectiveness of the overall New Zealand playing style.

Nor were the 1924 'Invincible' All Blacks immune from criticism. Certainly, New Zealand's achievements in the Great War, and a greater consciousness of the need for imperial unity immediately afterwards, seem to have produced less hostility towards the tourists than in 1905. But there was nevertheless a noticeable undercurrent of criticism against the continued use of the wing-forward – a position once again occupied by the tour captain, Cliff Porter. As the *Morning Post* put it after the victory against London Counties on 15 November 1924: 'Their methods were not exactly popular with the crowd and seldom has victory in a big match been received with less enthusiasm . . . Though they were frequently penalised, they escaped on too many occasions.'[52] *The Field* added that it was a pity the New Zealanders jeopardised their popularity 'by methods which, if they do not always actually break a law, are designed to gain an advantage in a way that is generally regarded as contrary to the spirit of the game'.[53] Even some New Zealand commentators were moved to wonder whether credit ought to be given to victories apparently obtained by dubious and aggressive methods. As the *New Zealand Herald* put it after the victory over Wales:

> Spoiling tactics tarnished its brilliance. There was needless physical mauling. 'Playing the man' – instead of the ball – was regrettably prevalent . . . That a struggle of 'international' importance should be so marred robs the victory of its full satisfaction.[54]

Matters came to a head in May 1930 when a fully representative British Isles team arrived in New Zealand under the management of James 'Bim' Baxter – former English international player and referee, member of the RFU committee and of the International Board. At a dinner following the opening tour match at Wanganui, Baxter revealed rather less diplomacy than most who occupy such a managerial position:

> I do not like, I distinctly dislike your wing-forward. I am sure the gentleman

who had the misfortune to play there today does not like it himself because he knows that it is not near the border line but over the border line. He must be discouraged. I say, he must not only be discouraged but that he must be stopped. The wing forward is an irritation to both sets of forwards and he is contrary to the spirit of rugby football.[55]

Following the match against Taranaki, Baxter urged local club committees to take a firm stand in discouraging the wing-forward. 'The ordinary man who tries to play wing forward is nothing more nor less than a cheat. He is deliberately trying to beat the referee by unfair tactics.' Although he did not specifically want to criticise New Zealand, Baxter said he did want a standardisation of rugby laws throughout the British Empire.[56]

Given his intemperate tone, the response to Baxter was surprisingly conciliatory. Although some felt his remarks were too strong, there was general acknowledgment that New Zealand opinions on the wing-forward, a position not used in any other country, were mixed and that the game generally needed to be reformed and 'brightened up' to retain public support. Others felt that, having seen the limits of the 2-3-2 scrum badly exposed by powerful scrummaging during the All Blacks tour of South Africa in 1928, it was time to adopt the standard international formation of a three-man front row and in which all eight forwards committed their weight.[57] But one observer not entirely sympathetic to Baxter was former All Black G. T. Alley. In his book on the 1930 tour he pointed out that although the British insisted that all matches had to be played under the international laws, there was still no law regarding the distribution and formation of players in the scrum.[58]

There can be no mistaking the fact that Baxter's notion of standardising rugby laws for the British Empire meant doing so entirely on British terms. In respect of the wing-forward, this was perhaps understandable in that New Zealand was the only country to use the position consistently. But in other areas this stance highlights one of the enduring tensions of international rugby during the first half of the twentieth century – the refusal of the British unions to concede any real authority in the administration of the game. Shortly after the defeat of the 1905 All Blacks by Wales in a match that, as we shall see shortly, highlighted a number of differing interpretations of the laws between Britain and New Zealand, an otherwise unidentified 'Anglo-New Zealander' voiced the opinion of many that such matters should be resolved by the International Board:

> But the representation on the Board must be far wider than the four home unions. New Zealand has more players than Ireland, Scotland or

even Wales. They have a right to voice their views, which are not on the lines of the Welsh match rulings. New South Wales and Queensland have equal claims to representation. They may before long send over a team that will take a lot of beating. South Africa has claims. It will be disastrous if a home union denies them also their legal rights.[59]

We shall see in Chapter Nine that as the Northern Union game took root in Australasia after 1907, soon to be followed by calls for the reform of rugby union in New Zealand, proposals for colonial representation tended to be greeted with outright hostility by the authorities in Britain who regarded themselves as the guardians of the traditions of rugby. The legacy of 1905 was not a universal admiration for colonial men and methods from the leading judges of the game, but a lingering distrust and determined reluctance to acknowledge either the validity of their innovations or their claims to a stake in the administration of the game.

Although the NZRFU was able to make amendments to the laws for domestic games within New Zealand, and was given a seat on the RFU committee from 1920, the inter-war period brought no real say in the shaping of the international game. In December 1924, during the All Black tour of Britain, a conference of delegates from Britain, New Zealand, New South Wales and South Africa apparently decided to form an Imperial Advisory Board to act in an advisory capacity to the International Board. However, the New Zealand delegates, S. S. Dean and S. F. Wilson, were very disappointed to discover that the International Board shelved the proposal shortly after the meeting.[60] At the end of 1925, amid claims that the true status of the dominions was not being recognised, the NZRFU proposed that each country be given two delegates on the International Board and that, as its triennial conferences in London placed a considerable financial burden on the distant unions, such conferences should be rotated between Britain and each of the three southern hemisphere unions in turn. Further, the costs to delegates should be met by a levy on profits from international matches.[61] In what was surely a deliberately calculated snub, the existing International Board members – England, Ireland, Scotland and Wales – resolved in March 1926 that a conference should be held annually in November or December in London, that it was desirable that delegates should be living in the country they represented and that all costs were to be met by each governing body.[62]

Meanwhile, Baxter was true to his desire to stop the wing-forward. In late 1930, shortly after the British team returned home, the RFU informed the NZRFU that there would no longer be any local dispensations to amend the laws of the game and that all fixtures must be played under laws standardised by the International Board. In due course, changes to the scrum, hooking and offside laws made it impossible for the 2-3-2 scrum and the wing-forward position to continue.[63]

Naturally these moves caused some resentment. At the 1931 NZRFU AGM, the president, Dr G. J. Adams, said that a board that did not include representatives from the dominions was 'not worthy of the Empire'. On the other hand, he felt that by displaying loyalty to the game by adopting international laws, New Zealand may enhance its prospects for gaining representation. If this did not happen, then perhaps New Zealand, Australia and South Africa should give some thought to establishing their own administrative body.[64] This veiled threat failed to amount to anything. Although another international conference was held in 1935, New Zealand was not admitted to the International Board until 1948 – 40 years after first requesting membership. But it seems that retention of the wing-forward was no longer a cause for which many in the New Zealand game were willing to sacrifice international opportunities – and especially lucrative British tours.[65]

In the last chapter we saw a list of counter-arguments to the popular notion of admiration for the 1905 All Blacks as an embodiment of superior New Zealand manhood. To these can be added the not inconsiderable perception that they, and the wing-forward especially, were far from ideal sportsmen in the full sense of considering physical *and* moral attributes – with the result that their innovations were rejected rather than embraced by those who retained control of the game. As the next chapter reveals, the international and Welsh matches that dominated the last six weeks of the tour heightened these perceptions and produced a hostile environment a long way removed from the ideals of international sport.

CHAPTER SEVEN

Big Matches and Bigger Legends

MOST NEW ZEALANDERS remember only one aspect of the 1905 tour with 'certainty': Wales defeated the All Blacks 3–0 and Bob Deans was denied a potentially match-winning try owing to incompetent refereeing, cheating Welshmen, or both. Such was the apparent significance of the occasion that Keith Sinclair has claimed 'The Gallipoli of New Zealand sport was the famous game against Wales in 1905 – a defeat to be forever celebrated as, if not a kind of victory, at least a draw. It was a major episode in the mythology of New Zealandism.'[1] The struggle was not merely one between two societies in which rugby was the dominant sport, but in which the game has been commonly regarded as serving the wider causes of emergent national identity.

Certainly the four weeks from 18 November to 16 December, encompassing the four international fixtures, possessed an added significance to the sporting public. With few exceptions, international results rather than 'minor' fixtures attract the most media coverage and public expectation during any sports tour. While a national team playing together on tour should always be superior to local club or county combinations, meetings between representative national teams are never so straightforward. Even as the All Blacks swept all before them in September and October 1905, there were frequent claims that they would be 'found out' in the internationals against Scotland, Ireland, England and, especially, Wales. The Welsh record since the early 1890s dictated that long before the All Blacks left New Zealand it was anticipated that this fixture, and those against the Welsh clubs, would provide the stiffest challenge. More importantly for present purposes, the international fixtures also represent the double edge of the imperial touring network that is often forgotten by historians who emphasise the role of sport in creating continuity and understanding between the colonies and the Mother Country. There is as much evidence from the last half of the 1905 tour, and especially the fixtures against Scotland and Wales, to suggest that such meetings also provided an arena in which difference and dispute could flourish. As the last chapter shows, the growing controversy over the wing-forward inevitably carried over to the internationals, but other barbs were now pointed at the All Blacks – claims of rough play, illegal tactics and disputes with and about referees. While all of these had an immediate impact on the tour, they are also central to the strained relations that shaped Anglo-Australasian rugby for the next quarter century and to the different strands of nostalgia that have enveloped it since 1905. In all of this the exploits of Bob Deans were somewhat peripheral.

As the All Blacks' record developed during the first two months in Britain, New Zealand rugby followers began to express expectations of success in the international matches that had not been as evident at the start of the tour. At the end of October the Otago RFU recommended to the NZRFU that the fixtures before the Irish and English internationals be cancelled, as it was unwise to jeopardise the chance of victory by playing midweek games in which players may be injured. Strangely, no mention was made of the fixtures before the Scottish and Welsh internationals, although the *Otago Witness* later criticised the playing of a game against Yorkshire three days before meeting Wales, because it was 'vital' that the Welsh should be defeated. In early November, in response to a letter from George Dixon, the NZRFU granted him authority to drop some fixtures if this was considered desirable.[2] Meanwhile, reports began to reach New Zealand of a growing injury toll within the team. As Chapter Four explained, players such as Abbott, Harper, Johnston and Mackrell certainly missed significant portions of the tour with injuries, a situation that inevitably placed greater demands on those who were fit, but by December there were also claims that many of the team were stale from too much rugby. Reflecting on the tour shortly after the Scottish international, Dixon noted that 'The indications of staleness were increasing, we numbered a fair proportion of cripples in the team.' Later he remarked: 'In the matter of physical capacity, it was by no means the team that had set out on its victorious career in England ten weeks earlier.'[3] Moreover, as Caroline Daley points out, a number of historians have seized on this point to explain the struggle of the All Blacks in Wales.[4]

While Dixon made no move to alter the itinerary, the mere suggestion of it and the reports concerning the health of the team offer some interesting perspectives on the tour and the way it has been interpreted. In the first place, this does not sit comfortably with some of the grander claims for the physical prowess of the team, and the decadence of their opponents, examined in Chapter Five. Calls to reduce the itinerary are a clear contemporary acknowledgment that the All Blacks were fallible. Second, although the injury toll, especially among the backs, undoubtedly placed extra demands on some players, claims of staleness are hard to justify when set against the demands placed on leading Northern Union players, who appeared in as many as 40 matches each season. In addition to the regular league competition there was a Challenge Cup and the Lancashire or Yorkshire Cup. Representative players also appeared in trial matches, two county fixtures and an England versus 'Other Nationalities' international.[5] Not only were the All Blacks frequently opposed to less physically combative opposition than in the north of England, they did not have to contend with the second half of the season. Finally, as Chapter Four suggested, even if some players were stale, it was possibly due to a reluctance to spread the weight of selections evenly and a determination to put the strongest team in the field on a regular basis. Apparently fit players such as Corbett and Glenn were underutilised, while others, such as Casey, Glasgow, Roberts and Stead, carried a much heavier load. When significant changes were made to the New Zealand team, such as for the match against Somerset on 21 October, the performance was notably less convincing. It seems that even the tour selectors held reservations about the depth of their party.

The first of the international fixtures, against Scotland at Inverleith, Edinburgh, on 18 November, was to cast a long shadow over Anglo-Australasian rugby relations – and little of it to do with events on the field. The nub of the subsequent difficulties was the very conservative Scottish Football Union and especially its long-serving secretary James Aikman Smith, who strenuously opposed any legislation designed to speed up or popularise a game that ought to be for players rather than spectators. Perhaps the most symbolic stance in this regard was the refusal of the Scots to put numbers on their jerseys until 1936, and Aikman Smith's reported rebuke to George V that 'this is a rugby match not a cattle sale' when the king asked why they did not.[6]

There is ample evidence that the immense public interest in the All Blacks did not sit easily with the Scots, but it is debatable whether they are guilty of all that was charged against them – and especially over the financial arrangements for the international. As Chapter Two explained, Scotland informed the NZRFU in 1904 that owing to its £6,600 debt for developing the Inverleith ground, it could not guarantee £500 for an international fixture but would instead give the entire gate, less expenses, to the tourists. These terms were entirely acceptable to the NZRFU and prompted no comment at the time. Yet, as it became clear that the tour was extraordinarily popular, there was speculation that the SFU would have cause to regret its decision in that, unlike the other unions who retained 30 per cent of the gate, it stood to gain nothing from the fixture. As Hamish Stuart observed on 6 November, 'If it be true, as most Englishmen appear to believe, that the "banging of a sixpence" shakes a Scot to the very foundation of his being, then the loss of sixty thousand sixpences ought to exterminate the race by a sort of financial syncope.'[7] Similarly, the *Yorkshire Post* felt the Scots would regret their decision, 'but, of course, a bargain is a bargain and a Scotsman's word is as good as his bond'.[8] After expenses, Scotland handed over £1,702,10s,6d to the NZRFU – at least £500 of which could have remained in its own coffers had it reached the same agreement as the other unions.[9]

There is an enduring belief that this financial 'blunder' by the SFU cultivated an animosity in Scotland that culminated in their refusal to play against the 1924 All Blacks.[10] However, at the annual general meeting of the union in 1906 it was reiterated that the business decision to offer all receipts to the touring team always raised the possibility that this could be more than the £500 guarantee. Yet this was regarded as the most prudent course of action for a debt-laden body, and exactly the same terms were offered to the South Africans for the following season.[11] As for the refusal to play the All Blacks in 1924, this stemmed directly from a belief that the RFU had breached a 1911 agreement of the International Board that tours would be organised by it rather than individual unions. When, without consultation, the RFU issued an invitation to New Zealand in 1923, the highly principled SFU refused to become involved.[12]

What can not be denied, however, is the existence of a widespread perception that the Scots reacted with petulance to their lost opportunity and exacted 'revenge' on the All Blacks in other ways. As one former Scottish player wrote to the *Stirling Journal* after the tour:

> One thing we must very bitterly regret . . . is the reception the Scots union gave to our visitors. They never welcomed them, never dined them, never took any notice whatever of them except while they were on the field. In Ireland, England and Wales they were cordially and warmly entertained. In Scotland, the union made a bad bargain about the gate money and then sulked.[13]

Certainly there is a suggestion that the reason the SFU did not entertain their visitors was in response to a letter prior to the tour from C. Wray Palliser stating that the New Zealanders did not want to be entertained after matches. They had also declined an offer of theatre tickets on the night before the match.[14] Yet nowhere else in Britain was such a literal interpretation taken of Dixon's determination to avoid excessive social demands. Moreover, the SFU had already shown its hand by announcing that its players would not be awarded international caps for the fixture – a 'display of parsimony' that, according to the *Daily Mail*, attracted much adverse comment in and beyond Scotland. Further Scottish ambivalence, if not antagonism, can be seen in the original intention to exclude all 'Anglo-Scots' from the team – a stance that was only reversed after good performances by those in the Cambridge University team.[15] Some conspirators also detect another sign of SFU hostility towards New Zealand in that, shortly before the match, a New Zealand medical student, Nolan Fell, withdrew from the Scottish team, stating that he was unwilling to play against his fellow countrymen. Having won seven caps for Scotland in 1901 and 1903, Fell was never selected again.[16]

The match itself, the most intensely contested so far on tour, was nearly abandoned because the ground was frozen solid three hours before play. Further compounding difficulties for the players was a ball of a long torpedo shape that was not properly inflated. As Dixon noted, 'I never saw a ball cut such extraordinary antics in my life + having regard to the slippery football it is wonderful that the players of both sides caught + fielded it as well as they did.'[17] For the first 10 minutes it seemed the All Blacks would dominate the whole game. Billy Wallace and George Smith were recalled for forward passes when tries were likely. The visitors were also awarded several penalties, but the ground was too hard to kick goals, even with Gallaher holding the ball for Wallace. Scotland took the lead with a dropped goal to Ernest Simson, shortly after which Frank Glasgow scored for the All Blacks when Bronco Seeling broke away after a long lineout throw. Jimmy Hunter then scored in the corner after a break from George Smith. But Scotland went ahead on halftime after a try from Jock MacCullum. The score remained at 7–6 to Scotland until, with only four minutes remaining, Smith scored in the corner after a break by Fred Roberts at halfway and a pass to Deans. Finally, Bill Cunningham scored on fulltime after a high kick from Billy Stead.[18]

As with everything achieved by the All Blacks, the verdict on their 12–7 victory was decidedly mixed. The *Glasgow Herald* claimed that although individual Scottish players possessed the same skills as their opponents, they lacked time together to develop combination and efficiency.[19] Hamish Stuart felt that although New Zealand's success would 'doubtless be characterised as a "triumph of brains over brute strength"', this 'time-worn platitude' gave no credit to a Scottish team that had deliberately adapted its game and almost been successful.[20] *The Scotsman* reported that the All Blacks 'blundered over and over again' with forward passes, knock-ons and fumbling in the backs and had become 'flurried and excited' as the prospect of defeat loomed.[21] But the *Yorkshire Post* rejected any contention that the home team should have won: 'A victory for Scotland would have been a triumph of dash, pluck and endurance, but it would not have been in keeping either with the run of the play or the comparative skill of the combatants.'[22] *The Field*, however, was less charitable: 'That the better side won is unquestionable, but some of their tactics were, to say the least, illegitimate, and but for illegal obstruction, which the referee unfortunately did not see, the try, on the call of time, would certainly not have been gained.'[23] Others, Hamish Stuart included, felt that both of the All Blacks second-half tries were illegal.[24]

While the All Blacks particularly enjoyed an evening reception by the Australasian Club of Edinburgh, Dixon recalled in his book that 'It was the general feeling that the Scottish team did not take their defeat well, and we saw nothing of them after the match, which was an unusual circumstance in our experience of British footballers'.[25] Beyond this, both manager and players declined to comment on various press reports concerning the discourtesy of the SFU.[26]

Four days later, when the All Blacks defeated West of Scotland 22–0, their methods were again under scrutiny. As *The Scotsman* put it:

> Hissing from spectators is not common on the rugby field. There was a good deal of hissing at Edinburgh on Saturday, there was much more at Glasgow, and matters reached a climax when the referee had to speak to one of the colonial forwards for the manner in which he rushed at a Glasgow man.

To this the *Athletic News* added that rugby had to be very rough before a Glasgow crowd was prompted to hiss.[27] But Major Philip Trevor took a contrary view: 'There is no one who has a greater admiration of the Scotch game than I have, but at the same time I would be the last to say that the Scotch style savours of drawing-room methods.'[28] On this note the 1905 All Blacks departed Scotland with their unbeaten record secure. But we shall see in Chapter Nine that the Scots were soon to become a significant thorn in the side of the All Blacks and Australasian rugby generally in other ways.

The undercurrent of hostility from the Scots was reinforced by the contrasting spirit and hospitality experienced from an equally conservative and avowedly amateur Irish rugby culture. As Dixon rather evasively remarked, 'The generous spirit displayed by the Irishmen, and the good feeling between the two teams, were in marked contrast to our experience in one or two other notable matches.'[29] On the Thursday night before the match, the two teams attended the theatre together and were seated alternately to enable them to mix They also dined together as guests of the Irish Rugby Union on the Saturday night after the match.

The match itself, at Lansdowne Road, Dublin, was completely sold out.[30] The All Blacks, without David Gallaher, who had injured a leg against Scotland, began energetically but were soon contained by strong Irish tackling and only led 5-0 at halftime, through a try by Bob Deans and conversion by Billy Wallace. Soon after the start of the second half Deans secured another converted try. Smith then lost the ball over the line with a try beckoning. Halfway through the second half, Alex McDonald scored from a scrum and Wallace landed his third conversion to complete the scoring at 15-0 in a fast, exciting and by no means one-sided game.[31] The *Irish Times* enthused: 'A more perfect team has never been seen in this country and the match at Lansdowne Rd will live long in the memory of those who were fortunate enough to see it.'[32] Others noted that more penalties were awarded against Ireland than New Zealand, and declared themselves surprised at the good spirit in which the game was played.[33] As the *Sporting Life* put it:

> The Irishmen were quite prepared, in view of the erroneous and wilfully untrue statements that had been circulating about the New Zealanders methods of play, to have to play in their international a team who played rough, but a few minutes of play was sufficient to prove to them that their surmise about what to expect from their colonial friends was wrong.[34]

Predictably, only Hamish Stuart seemed to find fault with the match, suggesting that the Irish forwards had exposed weaknesses in the All Blacks and that the Welsh backs would exploit opportunities far better than their Irish counterparts had done.[35]

Following a 33-0 victory over Munster in very wet weather and in front of the smallest crowd of the tour (4,000),[36] the All Blacks returned to England for their third international in as many weeks. Unprecedented demand for tickets and reports of very high prices being offered on the black market prompted the RFU to shift the match from Blackheath to Crystal Palace.[37]

Although played in good spirit, the match against England, witnessed by a crowd variously estimated at 45,000 to 70,000, did not provide a memorable sporting spectacle. Very wet weather produced a sodden ground to which both teams largely failed to adapt. Five minutes after kick-off, Duncan McGregor scored in the corner from a pass by Roberts. Ten minutes later a break by Stead sent the ball along the line to McGregor for another try. McGregor's third try came just before halftime from a short-side break by Roberts and Stead. Wallace was again unable to succeed with the conversion, owing to the heavy ball. In a more evenly contested second half, Fred Newton scored from loose play with 10 minutes remaining, and McGregor secured a 15–0 victory by adding another try in the corner just before fulltime. His record of four tries in an international was not to be equalled for the All Blacks until 1987.[38]

Again Hamish Stuart was not impressed, describing the match as very disappointing, especially in back play, compared with other internationals:

> The New Zealand backs were very moderate in attack against an in-different and disintegrated defence. Much of the passing was wild, while the wings often dropped the ball without any apparent reason. Scotland and Ireland would not have defeats to mourn if New Zealand had played as they did at the Palace.[39]

The *Yorkshire Post* added, 'There was a great deal too much of the scrambling and rushing element in the match for it to be considered a characteristic exhibition of New Zealand football.'[40] Others, however, were more inclined to criticise the English team for adopting a very defensive attitude, not least in its back formation of five three-quarters, and its failure to mount any convincing attack. As *The Field* lamented:

> The manner in which rugby football has recently been cultivated in England is not calculated to produce players with the skill or confidence to make their own openings in attack, or even to leave their colleagues to do each his own proper share of the work of defence. As it happened, the England fifteen conclusively proved itself weaker for both purposes than many leading club teams would be at this stage of the season, and its resistance compared badly with that made by Richmond a few weeks back.[41]

Even Dixon, usually the most enthusiastic advocate for his team, described this match as tame and lacking in excitement, and devoted less space to it in his book than to many fixtures of apparently lesser importance.[42] In short, what should have been one of the most important fixtures of the tour against the full strength of English rugby was an anticlimax that embodied none of the intensity to be found in the columns of the *Daily Mail* and other sources during the first month of the tour.

Aside from their opponents, and those spectators who were seeing the All Blacks for the first time, there is a sense in which the next three matches became something of a distraction to the looming challenge against Wales. Yet two of them provide an important reminder of the state of English rugby and the calibre of opposition encountered by the All Blacks for much of their tour. After defeating Cheltenham Club 18–0, the team travelled north to register 10 tries each against Cheshire and Yorkshire.[43] Such margins of victory would have been unthinkable in English rugby a decade earlier, and there were perhaps good grounds for the claim by a Northern Union commentator, F. W. Cooper, that 'Yorkshire played like a lot of schoolboys and would not have extended some Northern Union reserve teams'.[44] In sum, such feeble opposition was not ideal preparation for a meeting with the might of the Welsh.

No other aspect of New Zealand or Welsh rugby has been as intensively chronicled as the first meeting between the two national teams in 1905, but it is important to distinguish the intensity of expectations for the game and immediate reactions to it from the debates and nostalgia that soon enveloped it. As with the accounts by some New Zealand historians, Gareth Williams presents the match very much in national terms:

> It was that both XV's were directly representative of a manner of life as much as a style of play, of a social philosophy as well as of rugby thinking, a classic example of the permeation of a game through the interstices of their respective societies so that it was far more than a game, but a factor defining national existence.[45]

According to Williams, both societies had a desire to define themselves – the Welsh against the dominance of neighbouring England, and New Zealand within the wider British Empire. For Wales, sporting success was confirmation of an economic and cultural revival, industrial growth and popular notions of Welsh racial superiority that had been underway since the mid-nineteenth century. By its victory in this match Wales not only enhanced its own prestige, but redeemed that of Britain as a whole and asserted its loyalty within the Empire. At the same time, Williams suggests that success in rugby enabled the Welsh to adopt as their own a game that was a recent English import. While a number of Welsh players were born outside the principality, the game they excelled at was shaped by the particular circumstances of Welsh society and in turn helped to bring continuity to an environment that had experienced dramatic change owing to immigration and economic growth.[46]

Given the success of Welsh rugby since the 1890s, reflected in the fact that Wales had won two-thirds of its international matches in the decade since 1895, it makes sense to see 1905 as confirmation of a growing momentum and, at the same time, the launching pad for a new wave of euphoria in which rugby success epitomised all things Welsh. But whether such a national narrative holds true for New Zealand as it approached 16 December 1905 is highly debatable. As previous chapters have shown, there is little evidence for the rhetoric linking rugby to the supposed national characteristics of a rural, pioneering New Zealand society and, with the exception of a few contributions to the *Daily Mail* debates, such themes are similarly absent from New Zealand and British press comment during the tour. Nor did the genesis of the tour reveal a great deal of consensus and unrestrained national support for the team. Further, as Chapter Three explained, there was a degree of scepticism at efforts to link it with broader imperial themes. We shall also see in the next chapter that efforts by Richard Seddon in particular to exploit the All Blacks for national purposes were less than popular. Rather than 'a factor defining national existence', the immediate significance for New Zealand of the encounter with Wales should be seen purely in terms of the All Blacks' unbeaten record in Britain. Moreover, the New Zealand experience on the day was one dominated by antagonism and failure. For a variety of reasons to be discussed shortly, the wider meaning of the occasion only gradually emerged after the end of the tour, and perhaps not until after the Great War.

By the time the All Blacks arrived in Cardiff, the tour points tally stood at 801–22 from 27 matches. As with Scotland and Ireland, the international fixture was played before those against local clubs. Consequently, as we have seen already, Welsh observers were closely watching the All Blacks from the beginning of the tour amid considerable debate about the best way to beat them and whether or not to adopt the New Zealand scrum and back formation. Similarly, Gallaher, Stead and Wallace conducted their own reconnaissance by attending the match between Swansea and London Welsh in mid-November.[47] There is no sense that the Welsh were overawed by the task at hand, and some were openly confident. As early as 25 October, many who made the journey to see the All Blacks defeat Somerset 23–0 predicted a Welsh victory based on present New Zealand form.[48] After the England international, 'Forward' of the Cardiff *Western Mail* told his readers the New Zealanders would have to play a far better game to trouble Wales.[49] On the morning of the match the same paper had no doubt that the Welsh team would approach its work with much greater confidence than many previous opponents of the All Blacks: 'Most of them have gone on the field of play with the expectation of defeat, only hoping to keep the score down to modest figures. But the Welsh team will go on the field today with full confidence in their powers derived from the splendid record of their past achievements.'[50] Others, however, were more circumspect. As the *Cambria Daily Leader* observed, 'Ordinarily, the sanguine Welsh temperament produces a feeling of self-confidence, but the general disposition is to regard the result with anxiety rather than hope.'[51] Gil Evans, who had refereed the England international, declared: 'He would indeed be a prophet who would venture to forecast the result of what will undoubtedly be the game of the century.' Questioned about New Zealand tactics, he added, 'My experience of their tactics is that they go in for an absolutely fair game, yet as keen and vigorous as needs demand. They have but one captain, and he the most thorough sportsman whose word on the field is law.'[52] We shall see shortly that many fellow Welshmen and another referee begged to differ.

When the All Blacks arrived in Cardiff on Thursday, 14 December, they were met by vast crowds at the station and in the streets on the way to their hotel. As Dixon recalled, 'It was a somewhat embarrassing and novel experience to be made participants in such a royal progress, but certainly the welcome to Wales will live long in the memory of every member of the team.'[53] The following day and on the morning of the match the Great Western Railway provided 30 excursion trains from all parts of Wales, and the largest press attendance for any international also found its way to Cardiff. When the gates opened at 11 a.m. on Saturday the ground quickly filled to an estimated 50,000. An hour before kick-off, the gates were closed, denying entry to thousands more.[54] Meanwhile in New Zealand, arrangements were being made to convey the score as quickly as possible. In Wellington it was announced that flags would be flown from the town hall – the New Zealand ensign for an All Black victory, the Union Jack for Wales and a white flag with a red centre for a draw. Telegraph offices were also to open at 9 a.m. on Sunday morning instead of 9.30.[55]

The Welsh team that so many pinned their hopes on was very experienced

– including some of the great players of Welsh rugby history such as Teddy Morgan, Gwyn Nicholls, Dicky Owen and Charlie Pritchard. Moreover, alone of the national sides faced by the All Blacks, only the Welsh could truly be said to represent a cross-section of society, being a cross-class rather than a middle-class side. Included were a doctor, two schoolteachers, two miners, a docker, a steelworker, an undertaker and several small-business owners.[56] Although many leading players had been unavailable for the two Welsh trial matches, the team eventually selected came together as early as 7 December to engage in lengthy practices and careful tactical analysis. The only new cap was Percy Bush, but he, along with four others, had toured New Zealand in 1904.[57] By contrast, all was not so well with the All Blacks. George Smith was injured and could not take his rightful place on the left wing. Also missing was Bill Cunningham, the lock who had been added to the touring party at the last minute and quickly became the vital pivot holding the scrum together. But the most serious loss was Billy Stead, the Southland five-eighth who had set the backline alight brilliantly throughout the tour. In the first of many mysteries surrounding this match, his absence has been attributed variously to dysentery, boils, a heavy cold and an unlikely claim that he withdrew after Simon Mynott expressed disappointment at not being selected. Whatever the case, Stead was fit enough to act as a touch judge. But his absence from the field was compounded by a particularly inept performance from Mynott.[58] As Dixon recalled, 'The team chosen, the best we could put in the field at the moment, was neither our best nor was it in anything like the physical condition of the earlier part of the tour.'[59]

To counter the All Black haka, Tom Williams, an influential Welsh selector, suggested the singing of 'Hen wlad fy Nhadau' (Land of my Fathers) by the vast crowd. So began the tradition of singing anthems before international fixtures. But more immediately, according to some observers, it had the effect of unnerving the All Blacks and putting them off their game.[60] Another factor that soon unnerved them was the referee. After Dixon had rejected four Welsh choices for the task, the Welsh in turn rejected his choices. Under the laws of the International Board, a neutral country, in this case Scotland, was asked to appoint the referee. Their choice was John Dallas, a 27-year-old who had played for Scotland in 1903. Four years younger than both captains, he was in only his second season of refereeing.[61]

Little of what followed is beyond dispute. The leading New Zealand rugby historians Rod Chester and Neville McMillan claim, probably based on reminiscences from George Nicholson or Billy Wallace, that every time Gallaher fed the scrum the referee penalised him for not putting the ball in straight. Eventually Gallaher instructed his hookers not to contest. Hence the All Blacks secured no ball from the scrums and were only able to obtain it from loose play. With so much possession, the Welsh were constantly on attack and had several chances to score during the first half.[62] Contemporary accounts, however, make it clear that although Gallaher was regularly penalised, the All Blacks also secured scrum ball throughout the game. Moreover, Dixon makes no mention of any instruction from Gallaher.[63] Either way, the Welsh dominated play for the first half-hour – not least because they reduced the effectiveness of the 2-3-2 scrum by using seven forwards and a 'rover' themselves and packing their front row as late as possible with extra men at each scrum to ensure that they always had the loosehead. Winfield, at fullback, was also able to reply to rather aimless New Zealand kicking with very accurate punting to touch. Then, from a scrum on the New Zealand 25, Owen ran right and then turned left and threw a long pass to Cliff Pritchard, who passed to Gabe, who may or may not (depending on the source of the report) have passed to Bush before the ball reached Morgan, who ran for the corner and scored. Amid wild jubilation from the crowd, Winfield narrowly missed the conversion. After this the All Blacks were gradually able to assert themselves and were on attack when halftime was called – two minutes early according to Dixon.[64]

The second half began as a more even contest than the first. Again the Welsh had opportunities to score through dropped-goal attempts from Bush and dropped passes by Morgan and Harding when tries seemed likely. Finally, after 17 minutes (or with 10 minutes to go or 'very close to the end', depending on the chosen source) the All Blacks had their first real opportunity.[65] From a lineout inside New Zealand's half, Wallace gathered a Welsh kick and embarked on a long run before, approaching the Welsh fullback, he passed to Deans. For the moment it is only necessary to say that Deans was tackled on or near the line and that the referee awarded a five-yard scrum from which the Welsh were able to clear the ball. Later in the game the All Blacks had further opportunities to score when Mynott was held up over the line, Deans made another break but was brought down by determined Welsh defence, and McGregor touched down in the corner but was called back for a forward pass from Roberts. When fulltime arrived, the All Blacks had been defeated 3–0.[66]

The hundreds of reports and editorials appearing during the next few days were almost unanimous that this had been the most dramatic and intense international fixture played since these had begun in 1871. As *The Sportsman* enthused:

> For sheer hard fighting, dogged, grim determination and splendid defence on the part of both victor and vanquished, Saturday's game has never been surpassed. The New Zealanders took their beating . . . like the splendid sportsmen they are. Good winners, they are also good losers.[67]

But there was a much wider spectrum of opinion as to what had determined the outcome – the superiority of the Welsh or the weakness of the All Blacks. Moreover, there were many who did not share the conviction that the All Blacks, and Gallaher especially, were good sportsmen.

The euphoria of the *Western Mail* is typical of reactions in Wales:

> On a fair trial the Welsh players have proved the superior exponents of the new system, as of the old, in the whole British Empire. It is for them to develop it, and in time, given a succession of such great players as those who wore the Welsh colours on Saturday, Wales will out-distance the New Zealanders perhaps as much as the latter out-distanced the laggards across the border.[68]

In similar terms, the *Cambria Daily Leader* felt that

> Even those who say that the cult of athleticism is pushed to excess could not have repressed a feeling of pride at the knowledge that where England had failed lamentably, where Ireland had been badly beaten, and where Scotland also had been compelled to bite the dust, the representatives of the Principality had triumphed in the most signal fashion.[69]

With more measured tones, its weekly counterpart observed that the 'isolated views' of some who felt that a draw would have been a better outcome were probably derived more from sympathy for the New Zealanders than any reflection on the play. 'What appears to be the general concession is that the Welsh Union have for once risen to the occasion and the team fully justified its selection.'[70] In one of the stranger analogies to be found, the *Sunday Observer* declared that 'Our honour as an athletic nation is restored; the panache of our football fez once more floats proudly in the wind'.[71]

Outside Wales, many were more inclined to see the result in terms of a failure by the All Blacks. According to the *Daily Express*, 'The New Zealanders' passing was at times puerile, though it must be admitted very little went right with them.' The *Daily Chronicle* was similarly blunt: 'For a team with acknowledged scoring powers the All Blacks combination was too execrable, the failure too obviously caused by themselves to reflect corresponding credit on the Welsh. The general play of the New Zealanders reflected emphatically and unerringly the dullness which comes of too much football.'[72] The most savage verdict was reserved for Mynott. As a *Daily Mail* critic wrote, 'Though a player of great dash and speed, he was never Stead's equal for cleverness or judgement. But on Saturday he seemed to lose his head entirely. Times innumerable he mulled Roberts's passes, either dropping or knocking them on or passing them forward in the most juvenile fashion.'[73]

With an eye to the future of British rugby, *The Field* felt a sense of regret at the loss to Wales and the lessons that would be taken from it:

> To argue from results is generally fallacious, and in such a case it is ridiculously absurd that a tiny stroke of luck should be held to demonstrate that Great Britain is or is not lamentably inferior in football to one of the colonies. But inasmuch as results are the most impressive and permanent portion of sporting records it would have been better if the New Zealanders had not been condemned to possible misappreciation by posterity. They now occupy the position of the cricketer who misses a niche in the temple of fame by making a technically perfect score of ninety nine runs.[74]

By contrast, the *Birmingham Post* implied that there was little to learn from the tourists:

> The New Zealanders' play proved what the best judges of rugby football have advanced from the outset, that their success is not attributable to their formation or any system that they practise . . . Their combination is not the equal to Welsh clubs at their best.[75]

But the most revealing feature of reactions to the match was the unwillingness of the Welsh and their supporters to rest on the laurels of victory. Instead, many critics launched trenchant attacks on the All Blacks, and Gallaher especially – as much for his wing-forward play as for allegedly putting 'bias' on the ball when feeding the scrum. The *Newport Argus* informed its readers that the encounter was rough rather than vigorous and that Gallaher was 'both rough and tricky'. Further, the New Zealand determination to win embodied an idea of sportsmanship, or lack of it, that was not familiar to the Welsh.[76] James Livingstone, a former vice-president of the Welsh Rugby Union, claimed that the New Zealand team played 'an unscientific and brutal game, and especially the man Gallaher. Every time he put the ball into the scrum he twisted it under his own men's legs and he ought to have been penalised. There is no doubt they are a dirty team. That is a strong statement to make, but it is true.'[77] These sentiments were echoed by the *Glasgow Herald*, which described the game as 'disagreeably rough... For the roughness the New Zealanders were primarily responsible. Neither showed scrupulous regard for the rules, although in this respect Gallaher was the chief sinner, hardly ever putting the ball in fairly.'[78] In his obligatory contribution to such a discussion, Hamish Stuart pondered why such a fine person as Gallaher indulged in illegal methods: 'If Gallaher is suffered in New Zealand to do what he did on Saturday, so much the worse for the moral tone of New Zealand football. The laws may be arbitrary, but so long as they are what they are, putting the ball in in the way the New Zealand captain did is neither fair nor legal.'[79]

The ferocity of the Welsh attack on Gallaher is amply demonstrated by some of those who came to his defence. English critic E. H. D. Sewell was one among many who felt that the Welsh public and press had a preconceived notion of his methods and were prepared to criticise from the outset rather than evaluating what they saw on its merits. '[T]he numerous tirades not only in the Welsh press, against Gallaher, which appeared after the Welsh match constituted just the worst possible sort of literature to disseminate on such an occasion. They were mostly immoderately worded and of an inflammatory nature.' Important lessons for the future of British rugby could be lost if too much credence was given to such writings.[80] The apparently preconceived views of Welsh spectators are echoed in a story that circulated in the British press:

> First Welsh Spectator: 'Why doesn't the referee penalise Gallaher for unfair play?'
> Second Welsh Spectator: 'Yes, why doesn't he?'
> First Welsh Spectator: 'By the way, which is Gallaher?'[81]

According to the *Daily Mail*, Gallaher 'was subjected to a pitiless fusillade of epithets which, to anyone save a man who, like Gallaher, has had the hardening experience of actual warfare . . . must have been disconcerting too a degree.' While the wing-forward game may not have been palatable to those who did not know how to play it effectively, it was entirely within the laws of the game and, like any innovation, ought to be criticised on its own merits 'and not as something to be killed by prejudiced clamour.'[82] Another correspondent to the *Mail* reflected that in 20 years of watching representative rugby he could not remember an occasion 'on which one side was so heavily handicapped by a hostile crowd' as the All Blacks had been:

The unwarranted aspersions cast on Gallaher's play by contributors to Welsh football journalism had produced a general distrust in the colonial captain's fairness. More than 75 per cent of the huge assembly took it for granted that Gallaher's main object was to obtain an advantage by means that were opposed to the spirit as well as the letter of the law. The result was a continuous flow of barracking that completely unnerved the colonial players and enabled Wales to achieve a success which I for one think would not be repeated if the sides met 100 times on neutral ground.[83]

Here the final word belongs to Gallaher, who recalled in *Why the All Blacks Triumphed* that although there was strong criticism of his play throughout the tour, 'on our arrival in South Wales it seemed as if the pent-up indignation of the race for years had been let loose on us, and on me particularly'.[84] Any assumption that the more egalitarian Welsh rugby culture ought to have been tolerant of New Zealand methods, as many northerners had been of the Native team, was entirely offset by the intensity of the occasion and the pressure that fell on Wales to redeem the honour of British rugby.

When reports of the match reached New Zealand on 18 December, the result produced equal measures of disappointment and pride. 'There will be hardly a devotee of the winter pastime in the colony,' claimed the *Otago Witness*, 'who will not feel to-day that a personal injury has been done him.' The phenomenal success of the tour had begun to produce an expectation that it could be completed without defeat. On the other hand, 'it was never anticipated by the experts that the team would encounter as feeble opposition when it reached Wales as has been opposed to it in the great majority of the 27 matches it had played before last Saturday'. Even with one defeat, it remained the fact that the extraordinary achievements of the team had surpassed even the most optimistic predictions at the start of the tour.[85] In similar terms, the *Waikato Times* declared 'They have advertised New Zealand and her people in a special way that nothing else could, and we our proud of them – as proud of them in their hour of defeat as in that of highest victory.' So determined was this editor to make his point, he claimed that not a single British newspaper had accused the team of rough or ungentlemanly play.[86] In Christchurch, *The Press* described the gathering at the post office on Sunday morning to await the cabled score:

Before one reached the place where week after week one had read the news of victory, prescience of disaster fell upon the mind. Little groups stood about, talking in subdued tones, as if they were discussing some dire tragedy. Some of the most optimistic tried to convince themselves and others that the message was wrong. The blow would have been less severely felt if it had happened earlier in the tour, but the truth is that the continued success of the New Zealand team had led us all to gradually set for it a standard of absolute invincibility. When, therefore, defeat did occur, New Zealand was quite unprepared for the shock and suffered accordingly.[87]

Later in the day, when the SS *Rotomahana* arrived in Lyttelton with various members of the government on board, they immediately asked for the score. 'Gradually the sad conviction of defeat sank into their souls, especially when they looked at Mr Seddon and saw dejection writ large on his usually radiant countenance.'[88]

From late January, New Zealanders were able to read the full and lengthy range of reactions, both positive and negative, from the British press. From these the dominant impressions were that the Welsh had been thoroughly prepared and committed, that the All Blacks had played far below their best form and that Gallaher had met the wrath of both the referee and the crowd at every turn.[89]

Only now can we turn to what has become the most enduring controversy in rugby history. On 16 December 1905 the Deans 'try' was only one among a number of incidents within the Cardiff cauldron. Only later was it to assume its mythical proportions, or as Smith and Williams put it, 'The Deans "try" was the grit in the oyster that produced a black pearl for future generations.'[90]

To say the least the account is complicated and contradictory. In the version presented by Billy Wallace in various reminiscences during the 1930s, he gained the ball from a Welsh kick, ran diagonally, sidestepped Nicholls and beat Gabe. With a clear run to Winfield, the Welsh fullback, he debated whether to kick over his head, but heard Deans calling for the ball and sent him a long pass. Deans then veered towards the posts but altered course again towards the corner and grounded the ball six inches over the line as Teddy Morgan tackled him. The All Blacks had no doubt that Deans had scored, but as he got up off the ball Owen picked it up and placed it short of the line. When the referee arrived, having been a long way behind the play, he awarded a five-yard scrum to Wales. Wallace claimed that the silence of the crowd confirmed the try. But he also suggested that Deans had made two mistakes – the first in changing direction when he

135

could have beaten Morgan to the line without doing so, and the second in getting up off the ball after he had scored.[91]

It is hard to believe that Owen acted in the manner alleged by Wallace. Moreover, Willie Llewellyn claimed that he tackled and grounded Wallace, who was therefore in no position to clearly see what followed. Nor is it likely that many in the crowd would have had a clear enough view of proceedings to form an opinion. Morgan, however, sometimes supported the contention that Deans had scored. Having written in 1921 that he had tackled and held Deans short of the line, he then appeared to change his mind in a note to Wallace written on the dinner menu of the All Black captain Cliff Porter after the 1924 All Blacks had comprehensively avenged the earlier defeat. Naturally this became the vital piece of evidence for New Zealanders. Morgan then repeated his view in a 1935 radio discussion. But at the same time he did not contradict Rhys Gabe, who, with support from Cliff Pritchard and Gwyn Nicholls, claimed that he, not Morgan, had tackled Deans. Perhaps, as Smith and Williams suggest, the confusion lies in Morgan only partially tackling Deans, and Gabe finishing the task. Gabe, after realising that Deans was not over the line but was trying to wriggle forward, claimed to have pulled him back – after which Dallas awarded the scrum to Wales. Dallas echoed this version in a letter to the Welsh rugby union during the 1930s in which he stated that he first blew his whistle for a scrum as he ran between the posts, before running across to where Deans was lying on the ground.[92] Implicit in this recollection is that Dallas was parallel with the play, not many yards behind it as New Zealanders have consistently claimed.

On the Sunday morning after the match, Deans sent the following pre-paid telegram in response to a request from the *Daily Mail*: 'Grounded ball 6 inches over line some of the Welsh players admit try. Hunter and Glasgow can confirm was pulled back by Welshman before referee arrived.'[93] Given its fascination with the tour, it is hardly surprising that the *Daily Mail* had a role to play. Smith and Williams suggest that Deans was part of a *Daily Mail* 'stunt',[94] and one wonders whether, if the Deans opportunity had not presented itself, the newspaper might have latched on to another incident – such as whether the pass Roberts delivered to McGregor was really forward. On the other hand, Deans, a very religious teetotaller renowned for his integrity and humility, could be regarded as the team member least likely to embellish his reply.[95] The entry by Dixon in his private diary on the night of the match is also likely to be without exaggeration:

Wallace picking up in the loose on his own side of 1/2 way made a brilliant

> run & right on the line passed to Deans who dived over & grounded the ball well over the line. He was at once dragged ball & all back into play & when the referee, who was fully 40 yards away at the time, came up, he gave a scrum 5 yards out. That this was an absolutely fair try, there is overwhelming evidence, including Gabe who tackled Deans as he was falling & pulled him back into play, and Llewellyn the Welsh line-umpire.

Surely, even if Dixon had not seen the incident clearly, he is likely to have discussed it with his players. Yet he claims that Wallace passed 'right on the line' when it is clear that he passed earlier. He also attributes the tackle to Gabe and not Morgan, but oddly omitted any reference to the tackler when this account appeared in his tour book in 1906.[96]

The first reports of the match to reach the New Zealand press and Premier Richard Seddon on 18 December make no mention of a disputed try, merely stating that 'The ill luck of the New Zealanders pursued them to the end, Deans spoiling a fine chance to score by passing forward'.[97] *The Press* noted that the All Blacks missed two very close attempts to score.[98] In these accounts, Gallaher was by far the most-mentioned All Black. But in the fortnight after the match, reports began to emerge in Britain and eventually filter through to New Zealand suggesting that the All Blacks may have scored. On 3 January the *Otago Witness* asked whether any of its readers could confirm rumours of a private cable to New Zealand stating: 'Robbed of the match'.[99] Four weeks later, in its first comprehensive match reports, the *Witness* alerted readers to both the growing British debate about whether a try had been scored and which player was involved. Some said Deans; others Wallace; one report refereed to a 'New Zealander' and Jimmy Duncan insisted it was Hunter.[100] A week later the *Auckland Weekly News* noted that although it was generally agreed that the better team had won on the day, several leading British writers, along with P. A. Vaile, who had also witnessed the match, were in no doubt that New Zealand had scored.[101] By the end of February the general consensus was that Deans had scored the try.[102]

When the All Blacks returned to Auckland on 6 March, the certainty of the try was enshrined in reports of Richard Seddon's speech of welcome to the team:

> In the Welsh international the men had gallantly fought an uphill game to the finish. They had not questioned the result, but in their hearts and in the opinion of most people it was recognised that morally this was not a

defeat but a try to a try. He believed that the New Zealanders had desired to be generous. Nothing in Wales had happened for years that had brought it into such prominence as the try against the New Zealanders.[103]

Here, as Caroline Daley emphasises, Seddon was more interested in the political capital to be made from the situation than in what actually happened on the field. As with his cable to the *Daily Mail* in October, there was kudos to be gained from association with such a successful team. Moreover, numerous historians have seized on Seddon's sentiments as an illustration of the shock that apparently gripped New Zealand after the defeat, and the growing indignation once the circumstances became known.[104]

The appearance of Dixon's tour book in June 1906, with its numerous claims that Deans had scored, no doubt sustained the debate, but it also contains an extract from the *Yorkshire Post* that puts the matter firmly in perspective:

> The experience of the Colonials in having a try disallowed is, of course, merely the luck of the game – like an umpire's decision in cricket, or a rub of the green in golf. It has to be borne cheerfully. But when men are charged with trickery and unfairness something forcible may be said, and this is just where the Colonials have cause for complaint.[105]

Yet it is the Deans 'try', not Gallaher's methods, that became central to the collective memory of the Welsh defeat. Perhaps it is the case that a try, and especially one shrouded in contradictions, is a moment that fits more easily into popular imagination than debates about playing methods such as those surrounding Gallaher. Perhaps also, as we have seen already, the mixed reception for the wing-forward even in New Zealand lessened Gallaher's appeal as a victim of a rugby injustice.

The early death of Deans following an appendix operation in September 1908, and that of Gallaher at Passchendaele in October 1917, combined with the fact that the dispute over the 'try' can never be resolved, no doubt added to the mythology of the Welsh loss. By the time the 1924 All Blacks toured Britain amid the heightened imperial sentiment and developing New Zealand nationalism following the Great War, there was an evident sense of a defeat that needed to be avenged – not merely because it was the only one of the tour, but because it had not been deserved. All Black lock Read Masters recalled the challenge facing his team: 'Knowing that New Zealanders were looking to us to avenge the defeat of 1905, we realised we must "do or die".'[106] Wales was duly defeated 19-0 – supposedly one point for each year since 1905. But as time moved on and the All Blacks suffered further losses to Wales in 1935 and 1953, historians of New Zealand rugby shaped an image wherein their team of unheralded gentlemanly pioneers, and especially the humble and virtuous Bob Deans, had been denied the glory that was rightfully theirs.[107]

We have seen in this and previous chapters, however, that many observers were highly critical of New Zealand methods and consequently would more than likely have regarded an All Black victory as a travesty on the game. Given the vitriol that accompanied many accounts of the Welsh victory, one can only imagine what would have greeted their defeat – even allowing that some would have felt constrained by the diplomacy of sportsmanship in their hour of disappointment. It is equally important to remember that the All Blacks themselves did not begrudge Wales its success. Gallaher and Stead felt that too much anticipation of the match had produced nervousness and bad play among the All Blacks: 'Our usual coolness vanished, and if not the whole of our machinery, the biggest part of it was thrown very badly out of gear.'[108] Likewise, Dixon, although in no doubt that Deans had scored, said that the Welsh had played a better game and deserved to win. As he summarised the game in his dairy:

> The N.Z. forwards played a grand game under trying circumstances. Bearing in mind the indifferent play of the backs & the amount of unnecessary running about in consequence thereof, it is marvellous that they should have played the game out to the bitter end as they did . . . behind the scrummage our play was disappointing in the extreme. Bar Roberts & possibly Deans there was not a back who did not play miles below his fine form. There can be no doubt that staleness is beginning to manifest itself, but staleness alone wd. not account for the frequent muffing of good passes, indifferent fielding and faulty kicking. Nerves had something to do with it – a record such as the team possess is a big load to carry & any over anxiety from this cause was doubtless accentuated by the intense excitement prevailing amongst the big crowd & the extremely hostile attitude adopted by the greater portion of it.[109]

Dixon was also highly critical of the performance of John Dallas as referee – claming that he was frequently 30 or 40 yards behind the play and refereed such an important fixture wearing ordinary walking boots and clothing, including a stiff high collar.[110] Yet there is no sign in contemporary accounts that the refereeing was used by Dixon or anyone else as an excuse for the loss. While it is understandable, given the importance of the occasion, that debate surrounds the Deans 'try', its longer-term significance is not justified in relation to other events and contemporary reactions.

The four weeks of the tour in which the international matches were played set some limits on perceptions of the All Blacks that had not been apparent during October. Scotland showed them to be vulnerable, and Wales showed them to be fallible. Of equal significance, the weight of controversy and animosity accompanying these fixtures, and the setting of the Deans incident in its proper context, provides further balance to standard interpretations of the tour. What was to follow, in Wales and in North America, embodies further aspects of this contested environment.

CHAPTER EIGHT

Serving the Minister for Football

IF NEW ZEALAND'S 1905 tour itinerary had been designed by anyone with an eye for the dramatic, it would have concluded with the international against Wales. But having fallen at that much-anticipated hurdle, the All Blacks now faced four more demanding fixtures against Welsh clubs. After these they met France in its first rugby international. And then the United States beckoned for a short tour. All of these aspects need to be considered: the Welsh because they provide yet more challenges to the euphoria that too many historians have derived from the early weeks of the tour; the French for an international that would later become enshrined with the symbolism of the Great War; and North America for a tour that briefly threatened to change the course of American football history but ultimately revealed how much British sporting traditions had been altered as they were transplanted to the United States.

Meanwhile, lurking rather obtrusively behind these final stages was Premier Richard Seddon, determined, as some historians have frequently reminded us, to exploit the fame of the All Blacks for national purposes and his own brand of political populism. But here again we will see that the 'Minister for Football' was rather less successful in exploiting the tour than many have imagined.

For a time it seemed that the tour may indeed have ended after the loss to Wales. Prior to the next fixture, against Glamorgan, Dixon, with full support from the NZRFU, threatened to cancel the remaining matches unless the Welsh Rugby Union allowed him a say in the appointment of the referee, as had been customary throughout the tour.[1] On 20 December, Dixon also broke with his customary diplomacy and wrote directly to the press about the difficulties and hostility encountered in Wales:

> A great many untrue, unfair and unsportsmanlike statements have been made in various newspapers alleging amongst other things that the New Zealanders put the ball unfairly into the scrum. I have suggested to the

> Welsh football union that in any or all of our future matches in Wales the referee be asked to put the ball into the scrum on every occasion. If this is done, the public will be able to judge by results which side has been the greatest offender in this respect ... I desire also to correct statements made regarding the appointment of referee for the Glamorgan match. All that we have ever asked, and still insist upon, is that we should be allowed a voice in the appointment, in other words, that the referee should be mutually agreed upon as provided in the laws of the game.[2]

Eventually, 'very reluctantly & with much hesitation' so as not to disappoint an expectant public, Dixon conceded the point and the Glamorgan match was satisfactorily refereed by the appropriately named James Games – who did not feed the scrum.[3] But the issue was kept alive by Hamish Stuart, who claimed that the New Zealanders were very aware of different referees and tried to secure those who were less strict over their numerous breaches of the laws. Further, he maintained that they would have beaten Wales if allowed a free choice of referee.[4] In retort, London's *Truth* expressed some sympathy for Dixon's position: 'The attitude which was adopted by the Welsh Union seriously suggests that they regard the referee as a determining factor in the game. There are referees with pig-headed notions and racial bias. These last few matches are likely to have an unpleasant flavour.'[5]

The sentiments surrounding these last Welsh matches were at a polar opposite to those of mid-September. Having averaged nearly 30 points and more than seven tries in each of their 27 matches before arriving in Wales, the ledger for the final five matches was 29 (six tries) to 17 (four tries). Such was the need for points that Wallace also added only his third penalty goal and second dropped goal of the tour, having previously eschewed many such opportunities. Against Glamorgan, the All Blacks scored two of their three tries with only minutes remaining. Dixon observed that 'there scarcely appeared to be much difference between the teams as the scores would indicate. The New Zealand forwards lacked some of their accustomed dash, and displayed evident staleness, but stuck grimly to their work, and finally outstayed their opponents.'[6] Two days later, after only one try was scored in the 6–3 defeat of Newport, the *Yorkshire Post* pondered the reasons for the evident decline:

> The New Zealanders have lost their scoring form and the question is whether it is due to staleness or the meeting with clubs who know the best points of the game. The Welsh idea is that they play as well as they

are allowed to, and that it is a far different thing to meet a team who are beaten before they go on to the field than a team who are determined to try and win.⁷

Similarly, the *South Wales Daily Post* wondered at the long list of victories obtained by the All Blacks: 'They must at the present moment either be playing under form or are a greatly over-rated side. The impression is that had they played a Welsh club at the commencement of their tour, they would have been defeated.' It was also argued that staleness could hardly be an excuse given that they had the greater part of two teams to choose from.⁸

The match against Cardiff on 26 December became, for some, a vindication of New Zealand methods. During the first half Jimmy O'Sullivan left the field with a broken collarbone, and Gallaher was forced to take his place in the scrum. Without a wing-forward, and without any way of feeding the scrum, the All Blacks were obliged to give their feed to the Cardiff halfback. But as Dixon mused, 'The scribes who in previous games made such wild statements regarding unfair putting in, never commented on this phase of the game.'⁹ Likewise, E. H. D. Sewell felt that an important point was raised by Gallaher's enforced move:

> Despite the absence of Gallaher's alleged unfair tactics and his alleged insistent off-side and rough play as wing-forward, the New Zealanders – playing all the time one short – won the match against the leading and unbeaten Welsh club. This in itself gives the lie direct to all the baseless charges made against the New Zealand captain who, by the result of the Cardiff match, stands completely vindicated.¹⁰

Of course, the Welsh were not so easily impressed, preferring instead to dwell on a mistake by Percy Bush that led to the second New Zealand try and on Winfield's failed conversion attempt on fulltime that would have drawn the game. As 'Pendragon' informed the *Western Mail*: 'The New Zealanders ought to consider themselves the luckiest side that ever played football. They have played four games in Wales, lost one, and won the other three with pure, unadulterated luck.'¹¹ The *South Wales Echo* was no more enthusiastic, claiming that the All Blacks 'reached a high standard of club football', but showed nothing to justify the contention that they were able to field two sides of international strength.¹²

Finally, as far as the British section of the tour was concerned, on 30 December the All Blacks met Swansea in a match marked by indifferent play on both sides and a strong wind that dictated attacking opportunities.

Swansea scored a try in the first half and led 3–0 until 10 minutes from the end, when Wallace landed a left-foot dropped goal from a difficult angle to secure a 4–3 victory. Immediately the *South Wales Echo* took the higher moral ground, declaring that 'we in Wales will always regard a try as beating a dropped goal in merit' and then proceeding to lambaste the All Blacks for 'fouling of a worse nature than anything seen in any of the other matches on their tour in the Principality'.[13] Even Dixon could not bring himself to disagree with the numerous Welsh critics who felt that Swansea deserved to win: 'This was the only game of the series of which it may be said that the victory was a lucky one. Undoubtedly the team has got to the end of its tether & it is a great relief to all concerned that the serious business of the tour is at an end.'[14] All things considered, Jimmy Hunter's opening try against Devon on 16 September was now a distant memory.

Shortly after the Swansea match the All Blacks departed for London amid enthusiastic cheering, repeated at every station at which their train stopped in Wales.[15] Perhaps they were inclined to ponder such a fickle farewell from many who had so enthusiastically condemned them during the previous fortnight, but they had little time for this or other reflections as they immediately embarked for France.

French rugby began during the 1870s in the aftermath of the Franco-Prussian war and collapse of the Second Empire. After its establishment by expatriate Britons in Paris, the game soon broadened its appeal to Frenchmen looking to counter the perceived physical and moral degeneration of a once powerful nation. As France embarked on a period of significant growth and restructuring, rugby took hold in a number of socially exclusive Parisian schools from the 1880s before gradually moving into the provinces during the last years of the nineteenth century.[16] Nevertheless, the team that was assembled for France's first international, against the All Blacks at the Parc des Princes, Paris, on 1 January 1906, was dominated by the two oldest and strongest Paris clubs: Racing Club de France and Stade Français, each with five players.[17]

The prospect of a visit to France had scarcely been mentioned before or during the British tour. On 25 October, Dixon recorded in his diary that he was visited by a gentleman seeking to arrange a match in Paris and 'extraordinarily determined to get us at any cost'. Thereafter it is uncertain how the arrangement came about, although it can be assumed that the RFU had some role to play because a number of English club teams had visited France during recent years. From a New Zealand perspective, the trip was viewed as a welcome relief after the strenuous fortnight in Wales, and it was amid something of a festive atmosphere that the All Blacks were accompanied to Paris by Cecil Wray Palliser and various other New Zealanders.[18]

The French were evidently determined to make an impression in their first international outing. In front of 9,000 enthusiastic spectators, they displayed 'dash and speed' to dominate the first 20 minutes, although lacking cohesion as a team. But despite numerous changes from what was considered to be the strongest XV, the superior 'training, stamina and collective play of the New Zealanders' soon began to take its toll. Eventually they accumulated 10 tries, including three to Wallace and two each to Abbott, Hunter and Harper. Glasgow was the only forward to score. But amid 'considerable delight' and the 'liveliest satisfaction', the French scored two tries of their own – a feat only matched by Cardiff during the serious portion of the tour and by British Columbia during an exhibition match.[19] As a special correspondent to the *Otago Witness* wrote: 'New Year's Day was a great day for football in France – perhaps the greatest day ever known, for France scored 8 points against New Zealand, and in the circumstances the New Zealanders' 38 points are relatively nothing to the French goal and try.' The suggestion from some critics that the All Blacks had 'allowed' France to score twice was strongly denied by Major Philip Trevor and others present.[20]

The goodwill of this international occasion was far removed from the mood at Cardiff on 16 December. Dixon recalled: 'If this game was not distinguished by first-class football, it was at any rate a fine sporting game, played in the best possible spirit, and witnessed by as impartial and enthusiastic a crowd of spectators as the heart of man could desire.'[21] Among French observers, *Les Sports* was clearly impressed by many, but not all, aspects of the visitors' performance:

> The New Zealanders played as only a team can play who have long since brought their game to the point of perfection . . . The war song of the New Zealanders is terrible, but as players they are the most courteous of adversaries.[22]

Even in defeat, the home team could claim something of a moral victory for equalling the highest score made against the All Blacks in Britain and showing considerable improvement over the earlier standard of French rugby. Immediately after the match a *Daily Telegraph* correspondent described a buoyant mood in the streets:

I came back from the game in a delirious crowd of young Frenchmen. They dreamed of the day when football shall become a national game in this country. They were intoxicated with triumph, measuring the distance between what France showed this afternoon she can do in the field and the miserable achievements of but half a dozen years ago . . . It was indeed a great day for football in France and all the greater because the French crowd appreciated thoroughly how great it was.[23]

As the teams dined and sang together, with the assistance of interpreters, on the evening after the match,[24] many undoubtedly felt that the French athletic reputation was well on the way to countering many long-held British stereotypes. From 1906 France began regular international fixtures with the British unions and achieved its first international victory, against Scotland, in 1911. French rugby showed further marked improvement during the 1920s, but by this time the game had also established a reputation for violence and not-so-veiled professionalism that sat more uncomfortably with the International Board than anything managed by the All Blacks. France was suspended from the Five Nations Championship in 1931 and not readmitted until after the Second World War.[25]

For New Zealand, the full significance of this first meeting with France would only emerge much later in the years after Dave Gallaher's death at Passchendaele in 1917. For many, he came to epitomise the type of courageous New Zealand manhood that was sacrificed in such large numbers on the battlefields of the Great War. Prior to their own encounter with France on 18 January 1925, the 'Invincible' All Blacks toured the French and Belgian battlefields and placed two wreaths on Gallaher's grave in the Nine Elms Cemetery, Poperinghe, Belgium – one from the team and another from his Ponsonby club in Auckland.[26] In subsequent years various New Zealand teams and many more of their supporters made the same pilgrimage. In 2000 the Dave Gallaher Trophy was inaugurated for internationals between the All Blacks and France. In 2004 the All Blacks wore a red poppy on their jerseys against France and the best-performed players in the touring party were honoured with training jerseys ingrained with a photograph of the 1924 All Blacks visiting Gallaher's grave.[27]

After three days spent sightseeing in Paris and Versailles, the touring party returned to London pending departure for New York on 20 January.[28] Although various correspondents to the press advocated a return match against Wales or a combined British team to provide a suitably dramatic finale to the tour, these proposals were not enthusiastically received by either the All Blacks, who were tired, or the various British unions, who could see no way of fitting it into the existing international schedule.[29] But three players – Mynott, Seeling and McGregor – had apparently not had their fill of rugby and appeared as guest players for Gloucester against Leicester in early January.[30] The tourists as a whole attended the match between England and Wales on 13 January, receiving a rousing ovation as they took their seats. Meanwhile, Gallaher and Stead worked rapidly to fulfil their book contract for the *Daily Mail* as other players used the time to visit friends and relations or to see the sights of London. However, Massa Johnston developed a serious throat infection that resulted in his being unable to travel, and it was decided that Bronco Seeling would remain with him in London until he was fit to leave. At the same time, for reasons unknown, Billy Glenn and Eric Harper decided to return directly to New Zealand via Suez.[31]

On the evening of Friday, 19 January the All Blacks were entertained by the London New Zealand Society. The following morning a large gathering including William Pember Reeves, Cecil Wray Palliser and various members of the RFU committee farewelled them as they departed Waterloo for Southampton. Dixon recalled the scene: 'The sea of upturned faces, the forest of outstretched hands, the enthusiasm, the good-fellowship, the unanimous expressions of good will – all these things are indelibly impressed upon the memory of each one of us.'[32] At Southampton another enthusiastic crowd gathered as the team embarked for the United States on the *New York*.[33]

Given the array of press coverage discussed already, there is nothing to be gained from dissecting the numerous assessments of the tour that accompanied the team's departure. Even after the loss to Wales, none of the leading critics, positive or negative, appears to have shifted from positions taken early in the tour. However, two themes that had marked the tour as a whole are worth reiterating as contrast to the prevailing tendency to interpret 1905 through a selective set of enthusiastic reactions during its first six weeks. First, no amount of fond farewells could remove Dixon's enduring frustration with those who refused to give credit to his team:

> Some of the critics who had shown prejudice against our team and its style of play at the outset, and who had exhausted every excuse to explain and lessen the credit for our victories, still persisted in their argument that the New Zealanders had shown no superior play, in the face of our record, and harped against unfairness in our methods, a charge that was not endorsed by any British player or authority of high standing.

147

Dixon was also unimpressed with critics who praised the Welsh while downplaying the staleness of his own players – pointing out that staleness had been used as an excuse for the poor form of the 1904 British team after only 13 matches in Australia and five in New Zealand.[34]

The second point to note is that critics who did meet Dixon's definition of 'high standing' – those who praised the All Blacks throughout the tour – claimed to see in the team's methods not a revolutionary new approach to the game but the return of an older style of British rugby. As A.W. Pullin, 'Old Ebor' of the *Yorkshire Post*, wrote to Dixon on 18 January 1906:

> I shall always remember your performances in England as being certainly the best seen since the early '80's, and consider your team have developed the style of those days more than the setting up of new methods of Rugby football. More than anything else have I admired the splendid way in which your fellows have borne themselves throughout the tour, and also the sportsmanlike manner in which they accepted the somewhat unlucky defeat at the hands of Wales. I think you have taught British footballers a good many lessons, not the least of which may be mentioned modesty in success, and sportsmanlike bearing under all circumstances.[35]

Similarly, Major Philip Trevor of *The Sportsman* felt that while the tour had created unprecedented interest in rugby, paradoxically the All Blacks had demonstrated nothing that was new. Rather, they had 'emphasised the real value of old lessons which we perhaps took it a little too much for granted that we knew already.'[36] The London *Referee* added that the tourists had encountered a lethargic British game in which 'the men had grown slack, and even the Internationals among the four unions had failed to rouse the clubs from their lethargy'. Rather than showing any revolutionary approach, 'The New Zealanders have shown us again the game roughly as we knew it in the eighties – the most glorious period of English rugby'.[37]

Of course, the claim that the All Blacks represented a return to an older style of rugby from the 1880s is nothing more than selective nostalgia that ignores the fact, as the Native team had discovered, that the British game of the 1880s was still dominated by prolonged scrummaging and limited back play. Perhaps the objective here was to associate the All Blacks with an era of 'traditional' and amateur British rugby that had existed before the rise of the north and the onset of the split in 1895. But, irrespective of the reasoning, it is notable that those who had sparked the *Daily Mail* debate in early October with claims of radical new methods derived from a unique colonial setting were simply not in evidence by the time the All Blacks departed in January 1906.

Finally, as the Native team had been the only basis for comparison and prediction before the All Blacks began their tour, the London correspondent for the *New Zealand Times* now suggested that the record in 1888–89 would have been even better had they encountered the circumstances of 1905.

> They had less men, more travelling and inferior board and lodgings than Mr Dixon's men, and for half a year they were called upon to play practically three times a week against teams which were on the whole vastly stronger than the club teams which the 'All Blacks' had to meet. I have no wish to detract from the merit of the performance of the present team, but the Maoris 'struck' England at a time when rugby football was taken a good deal more seriously here than it has been for the past ten or fifteen years, and had they not been a set of good players possessed of splendid constitutions, they could never have lasted through their long and trying tour as they did.[38]

In a similar context, it is easy to speculate, as many did, whether the All Blacks would have performed better in their Welsh matches and secured an unbeaten record if these had been played earlier in the tour. But this approach is problematic: if the Welsh had been met earlier, perhaps the tourists would have been more vulnerable to Scotland or Durham later on. More importantly, as previous chapters have suggested, if they had played against strong northern clubs, their record may have been considerably less impressive. Prior to 1895 the north had proved that it was the dominant force in English rugby. Moreover, only after 1906, when the Northern Union reduced its teams to 13 and adopted the play-the-ball rule for tackled players, did the northern game begin to diverge from rugby union to an extent that made comparison between the two codes difficult.[39] Certainly the All Blacks had done almost all that was asked of them in terms of winning their games, but it is important to remember that comparatively little was asked.

The selective focus on mainly positive assessments of the All Blacks produces a similarly distorted understanding of the final phase of the tour. It is commonly assumed that, having swept all before them in Britain, the team was now sent on a government-funded tour through the United States with the gratitude of their premier and fellow citizens ringing in their ears. Undoubtedly, as Jock Phillips acknowledges, there was some sniping at Seddon's political opportunism, but no one apparently could find fault with his ultimate cause in using the 1905 team to promote New Zealand on the world stage.⁴⁰ But such an interpretation of the North American 'picnic' greatly underestimates opposition to it and to Seddon's continued efforts to capitalise on the tour. Moreover, it ignores those in the United States and Canada who had their own reasons for wanting to see the All Blacks at close quarters.

The genesis of the American venture is rather obscure. Early in 1905 a rugby enthusiast in Vancouver wrote to the NZRFU asking whether the tourists could play British Columbia on their way home, but the union's management committee replied that the tour could not be extended. As we shall see shortly, it is likely that the next invitation to tour came from California. In early December a special correspondent for the *Evening Post* reported that the team was not looking forward to returning home via South Africa, implying that the NZRFU saw this as a possibility. The players wished to travel either via Suez or Canada, and were willing to play exhibition matches in British Columbia: 'This should be done as the team deserve the best treatment, and it is likely to do good in America. If the team are asked to return via Cape Town, I am afraid it will only be a part that will carry this part of the programme through.'⁴¹ In a cable to Dixon shortly before the Welsh international, the NZRFU Management Committee suggested that growing dissatisfaction with American football provided an ideal opportunity to play rugby in the United States. Dixon was therefore empowered to seek support from the RFU to recruit a number of British players to make up teams for exhibition matches.⁴² Within a week he replied that such a tour was not practical and that extra players could not be secured.⁴³ At the same time, the *Otago Daily Times* declared that the team deserved better from the NZRFU than a 'crazy proposal' to send them to the United States, where they may not be wanted.⁴⁴ Under these circumstances the tour was seemingly abandoned.

The tour proposal resurfaced with an announcement from the NZRFU, on 2 January 1906, accepting a government offer of funding to send the team via New York and San Francisco on its return to New Zealand.⁴⁵ How this was reconciled with the strenuous objections to proposals for government funding of the tour in 1904 is not recorded. Nor is it known whether the union approached the government or vice versa. But the key player here was undoubtedly Richard 'King Dick' Seddon. Ever the imperialist keen to exploit any opportunity to promote New Zealand interests within and beyond the British Empire, Seddon was also, by 1906, presiding over an increasingly unpopular government that was largely bankrupt of ideas and seemed to be pursuing a policy that amounted to little more than holding on to power. Thus, an association with the All Blacks was just the sort of populist position that would maintain support. Seddon was a renowned autocrat who exercised close control over all aspects of government and encountered little difficulty exerting his will over the mediocre officials and politicians with whom he surrounded himself, and there is little reason to suspect that his approach or response to the NZRFU was derived from any sort of consultation.[46] It was also helpful to this specific cause that Parliament was not in session during December and January.

Whatever the actual chain of events, the New Zealand press was clear that Seddon's offer represented both an unhealthy precedent and a distortion of national priorities. The *Evening Post* fumed at a premier who was clearly playing to the 'football gallery':

> Even if the state were not burdened with debt, the proposal would be open to serious objection, but with thousands of our settlers in the back blocks suffering the greatest hardship for want of proper access to their homes, and the many public works necessary to the settlement and development of a new country still in the making or waiting a beginning for lack of capital, the national picnic through North America seems to us a wicked waste of public money.

Certainly the team had brought honour to New Zealand with its success, but it had already secured a greater reward than most in seeing the 'Old World' under agreeable circumstances. Moreover, the All Blacks' success could only be taken so far:

> Even the threadbare argument of advertising the colony can not apply in this case, for by the wildest stretch of imagination it can not be contended that a victorious football team is representative of our 'staple industries' or even the 'magnificent scenic attractions of New Zealand'. It may be said that the proposed picnic will bring us into notoriety, but would it bring compensating 'business'.[47]

A century later there would be no such reticence in using the All Black 'brand' to market popular images of New Zealand. Meanwhile, the *Wairarapa Daily Times* was sure that the decision of the government would be popular, but the question of whether it was right was quite another matter: 'A generosity which gives away the money of the people without legal authority, or without the consent of the representatives of the people would not be tolerated in any country where constitutional government is respected.'[48] Likewise, *Truth* wondered 'What will the Seddonian politicians have to say about their chief's colossal impudence in thus applying the consolidated funds of this country? But R. J. Seddon knows no laws – he is a law unto himself.' Further, with reference to claims that had surfaced shortly after the All Blacks departed in August 1905, *Truth* pondered the legitimacy of such funding in terms of the rugby laws on professionalism. What, it asked, was the difference between a trip of this kind and a gold watch or a purse of sovereigns being presented to a player?[49]

Others directed barbs at the NZRFU for accepting Seddon's offer. From Christchurch, both *The Press* and *The Star* pointed out that the union had originally abandoned proposals for a tour, but was now happy to accept government money for costs that could easily have been met out of its own considerable profits from the British matches. At the very least, the government should only have paid any difference between the American tour and the original cost of returning the team directly to New Zealand. According to the *Otago Daily Times*, the failure of the NZRFU to spend its own profits now made it, rather than the team, the beneficiary of 'state benefaction'.[50] Only the *New Zealand Times* appeared to support government funding for the tour, arguing that these were exceptional circumstances and unlikely to be repeated. The tour was also a good advertisement for the colony, in that advertising could not always be assessed in cash terms and football interest could create other possibilities.[51]

In June 1906 it was reported that the government had contributed £1,963 to the tour – although nothing is revealed in the published tour accounts.[52] Given the eventual tour profit of £8,908 10s 4d, objection to the NZRFU's acceptance of the subsidy is understandable. Of course, we have no way of knowing whether the general public, let alone those devoted to rugby, entirely shared the complaints aired by various newspaper editors. However, from the lack of correspondence to the press opposing their stance, it seems that while many were proud of the All Blacks, adulation had its limits.

On 5 January 1906, Dixon wrote in his diary: 'This trip is a confounded nuisance. Would much rather have gone aboard the steamer to enjoy a six-week rest and immunity from letters, callers, newspapers and worries generally.' Whether the players shared his views, or anticipated a relaxing holiday at the expense of the taxpayer, is unknown. But for their American hosts it was increasingly important that the tour went ahead. The United States was in the midst of a 'football crisis' in which the brutality and intensity of American football, very largely an intercollegiate game, was now posing a very real threat to its future. As calls to modify or ban American football increased, rugby loomed as a possible alternative.

Ronald A. Smith, the leading historian of collegiate sport, argues that the growth of a distinct American football code mirrored the ideology of freedom and equality of opportunity that marked the emergence and growth of the United States as a whole.[53] Although Harvard, Yale and other colleges initially followed an Oxbridge sporting model, with an emphasis on virtue and amateurism, and while most American students came from a privileged background, a relative absence of English sporting traditions and rigid class distinctions soon dictated a willingness to embrace elements of professionalism and commercialism, a pronounced win-at-all-costs attitude, and amateurism in name only.[54] As new colleges challenged the dominance of the older institutions during the late nineteenth century, the securing of collegiate prestige by athletic success became increasingly important. Professional coaches, 'scientific' training and recruitment of athletic talent became common.[55]

As in Britain, difficulties and disagreements marked efforts to standardise the rules of the various local football codes.[56] In 1874 Harvard met McGill University of Canada at rugby. Yale and Princeton adopted the game within the next two years, and rugby became the dominant intercollegiate football code during the late 1870s. At the same time, however, Walter Camp began his career as the most influential innovator and strategist of a new game. As a player and then coach at Yale, Camp oversaw the Americanisation of rugby with such things as mass formations, interference plays and 'downs' to gain a set number of yards.[57] His emphasis was very much on football as a team game in which rationalisation and tactical development would instil in men the character essential for success in society. It was a game to be carefully orchestrated by coaches to eliminate risk and chance – a clear implication that the achievement of winning was more important than enjoyment of the game and that strategy, rather than the incidental brutality that arose from it, was the prime consideration.[58] As Smith sees it, there were strong parallels between the new game and Camp's own industrial career: 'Yale football and Walter Camp were much like the economic ideology of capitalistic America. Under that belief, the strong survived and prospered; the weak languished or perished.'[59] Perhaps then, to reconsider Smith's own interpretation, the regimented war of attrition that became American football was less a reflection of ideas of freedom than of capitalism. And the two are not the same.

As football experienced dramatic growth in popularity during the 1880s and 1890s, the intensity of its rivalries began to draw complaints of brutality – especially against the use of the flying wedge, in which players were propelled towards the opposing defence. To an extent these violent elements were justified as a part of the broader American embrace of manliness and virility as a counter to fears of degeneration in a rapidly urbanising society. But it is evident that increasing brutality, occasional deaths and the excesses of professionalism posed a real threat to football at the leading eastern colleges by 1905. Columbia banned the game, and Harvard nearly did so. The intervention of President Theodore Roosevelt, a strong supporter of the game and advocate of the 'strenuous life', with the football authorities of Harvard, Yale and Princeton led to a national conference and the establishment of the Intercollegiate Athletics Association.[60]

While the perceived problems with football were not as pronounced in California, in large part owing to more recent and less intense rivalries and a shorter playing season, the proposed solution was more dramatic. Although the presidents of the University of California, Berkeley, and Leland Stanford Junior University, Benjamin Ide Wheeler and David Starr Jordan, both possessed strong athletic interests, they nevertheless held significant objections to both the brutality of American football and the professional, commercial and unethical practices that had enveloped it. Accordingly, both engaged in an active campaign to convert local universities and secondary schools to another football code.[61] Among numerous articles and public pronouncements condemning the methods and excesses of football, Wheeler dispatched an 'Are You Ready to Have Football Abolished?' letter to college and university presidents throughout the United States in November 1905. Later, in an address to his student body, he blamed Walter Camp for destroying football and suggested that soccer might replace the American game.[62] On 29 November the University of California Academic Council declared its unwillingness to submit to a game governed by the established Football Rules Committee and urged either a new set of rules or the abandonment of football altogether. During December 1905 and January 1906 the two college presidents and their faculty athletic committees met to discuss new rules. Although soccer and Australian rules were mooted as possibilities, a motion was eventually moved to adopt rugby. As Roberta Park explains:

> Rugby was deemed the superior game for several reasons: it was not professional or commercial; it was 'a game' rather than a spectacle – a pastime rather than a vocation; it could be played by small and light men as well as by larger and heavier men; it did not lead to injuries like those which were incurred in the brutal American game; it did not necessitate enormous time for practice and interfere unduly with studies; it was

free from professional coaches, class teams as well as the varsity could play it; most importantly, it was presumed to be free from the 'immoral' influences of the American game.[63]

In late January, Norman L. Halcombe of Stanford wrote to the NZRFU requesting a book on rugby and copies of the rules,[64] but the difficulty facing Wheeler, Jordan and their committees was that few in California other than some expatriate Australians, Britons and New Zealanders had any first-hand experience of rugby. Moreover, the proposals drew a lukewarm response from students and the local press, and outright ridicule from many eastern devotees of American football.[65] In this context, the visit of the All Blacks after such a successful British tour was vital in 'selling' rugby. To this end, it is probable that the initial approach to the NZRFU came from Jordan and Wheeler.

On 1 February 1906, on a baseball ground in Brooklyn, an All Black team played an exhibition game against a New York combination bolstered by six other members of the touring party including Jimmy Duncan. Although the attendance was very small, it included a number of college professors with an interest in reforming the American game.[66] The team then travelled to California via brief sightseeing stops in Niagara Falls, Chicago and the Grand Canyon, arriving in San Francisco on 8 February. With a further meeting of the California and Stanford athletic committee scheduled for 17 February, the two matches in California were perceived very much as a trail of the merits of rugby laws that would have a strong influence on the future of football on the Pacific Coast.[67] As the Berkeley student newspaper, the *Daily Californian*, observed:

> The New Zealand team is probably as fine a body of players as could be brought together to give an exhibition of the rugby game. Now that the form of the football game that we are to play has been brought into question, everybody will be unusually interested in taking the measure of this older style of play.[68]

The 1,200 to 1,500 Californians who attended the first game, at Berkeley on 9 February, were not disappointed. Despite rain, a wet ball and a very muddy ground, the All Blacks were able to play fast, open rugby in winning 43–6 against a British Columbia team that had travelled down from Vancouver to oppose them. Writing in the *San Francisco Chronicle*, Waldemar Young gave fulsome praise to the 'old style' game:

> If a vote had been taken yesterday afternoon on the Berkeley campus, the majority of spectators would have been overwhelmingly in favour of the

original game of rugby from which our own game was evolved . . . Judging from yesterdays game, no contest played under the rugby rules by teams reasonably proficient can be otherwise than interesting. Compared to the American college game, the possibility for spectacular features is at a ratio of about 100 to 1 . . . Yes it is a great game is rugby. Fresh from my first view of it, I have no hesitation in saying that it is a far better game than the American college game as we have had it within the highly developed state within the past few years. There is not in rugby the same clash of beef, the steamy straining of two highly organised machines, but there is something far better and more inspiring. The open formation, the wonderful possibility for sensational plays – not one or two a game, but one or two almost every minute – make rugby just as interesting to the unpartisan observer as to the man whose college is represented on the field.[69]

Four days later, at Recreation Park in San Francisco, the All Blacks defeated the same opposition 65–6. Soon after, they embarked on the final stage of their journey to New Zealand via Honolulu and Pago Pago. Shortly before the party left San Francisco, however, Fred Roberts developed severe tonsillitis and the decision was made to leave him behind with Billy Wallace.[70]

Although many Californians were greatly impressed by the style of the All Blacks, debate continued for the next two months on the merits of the rugby game, but it was effectively stifled by the chaos and devastation of the San Francisco earthquake on 18 April 1906.[71] By the following football season, resentment among Californian players was gradually subsiding and concerted efforts were being made to acquire a full understanding of the new game. Although proposals for an American universities tour of New Zealand during 1907 did not amount to anything,[72] Jordan visited Australia and New Zealand to watch and discuss rugby. Interviewed in Christchurch, he took the opportunity to castigate Walter Camp and the strategy of 'mass plays': 'We do not object to hard play. But President Wheeler and myself did object to the infliction of unnecessary injury. Then again, there has been a tendency to introduce into the American game various irrelevancies such as the forward pass which, of course, necessitates somebody being there to profit by it.'[73] Over the next three years, as various Californian clubs and high schools embraced rugby, several coaches also visited British Columbia, Britain, Australia and New Zealand to acquire knowledge.[74] The Wallabies played in San Francisco on their way home from Britain in February 1909, an American universities team toured Australia and New Zealand in 1910, and California received full tours from an Australian team, designated the Waratahs, in 1912 and an All Black team the following year.[75]

Competitive Californian performances against the 1912 Australians generated considerable optimism for the future of rugby, though this was shattered as the All Blacks, under the captaincy of 1905 tourist Alex McDonald, totally demoralised their opposition by scoring 610 points to six in 13 matches. Such one-sided results confirmed for many Californians the difficulties of one country's attempting to artificially develop the established game of another. As the *San Francisco Post* lamented after the All Blacks defeated All America: 'The California players are the best we have developed in seven years of intercollegiate rugby – the very best. And the score against them was 51 to 3. The only conclusion is that we have not yet learned how to play rugby. It is still a foreign game.' While the players knew the laws, they lacked any 'sense' or 'instinct' for the game of the sort that had been gradually fashioned in New Zealand and could not hope to succeed until the game became 'indigenous' to California.[76] The tours also demonstrated that although California could change the type of its football, it could not so easily change the aggressive mindset that accompanied it. Both the Australians and New Zealanders were highly critical of rough tactics on the field and exaggerated fervour off it. No doubt some of the problems derived from a lack of familiarity with the laws and traditions of the game and a lack of suitably qualified coaches. Other aspects were clearly derived from the highly competitive sporting culture that had gripped intercollegiate sport, if not the country as a whole, from the 1890s. By late 1915, rugby was well on its way to oblivion in the United States, and the source of many of its best players, the University of California, had already abandoned it in favour of a return to American football and a reestablishment of important athletic connections with the eastern colleges. The last flourish of Californian rugby during this period was perhaps its most bizarre in that a United States team consisting largely of Stanford players defeated France in the only match for the Olympic rugby gold medal at Antwerp in 1920. Four years later, in Paris, with the addition of Romania to the competition, the Americans again defeated France in the final. Thereafter rugby ceased to be an Olympic sport.[77]

With Glenn, Harper, Johnston, Seeling, Roberts and Wallace making other arrangements, only 21 of the original 27 All Blacks reached Auckland on 6 March. Before leaving the ship they were welcomed by Seddon, who had journeyed from Wellington, A. E. G. Rhodes and Edgar Wylie, respectively president and secretary of the NZRFU, and C. E. MacCormick, secretary of the Auckland RFU. Once on shore they encountered a very large and enthusiastic crowd, estimated at up to 20,000, which cheered their every move. As the *Otago Witness* captured the moment: 'It was at once seen that the men were in fine health. Every man carried more weight than when he went away, and all looked fit and well. The players all expressed themselves as delighted with the trip, and equally delighted at returning home.'[78]

After a brief stop at their hotel, the All Blacks were driven to an official welcome in front of the Auckland Art Gallery. Here Seddon praised the overall achievement of the team and read from a letter by William Pember Reeves extolling the tourists' virtues both on and off the field. After insisting, as discussed in the previous chapter, that the Welsh international was a draw, Seddon optimistically predicted that 'in future their kindred in the Mother Country would in all their important matches have their wing-forward whom they would remember as one of many things taught by the All Blacks'. In reply, Dixon said that the team were honoured by the unexpected scale of their welcome. He also assured the audience that the All Blacks 'had played the game both on and off the field, had behaved as the people of New Zealand would have them behave, as men and gentlemen and as New Zealanders'. Gallaher, in a very short address, offered only one recommendation to the NZRFU for any future tour – that the Welsh matches be played first. With these formalities completed, the All Blacks responded to calls from the crowd with a vigorous haka. Later in the evening the touring party and 200 guests were entertained at a banquet hosted by the NZRFU. Seddon was again to the fore, proposing a toast to the All Blacks before being presented with a framed, autographed photograph of the team, Each player was then presented with a commemorative medal.[79]

Amid such enthusiasm, the *Evening Post* again found an opportunity to attack Seddon for his prominent role in proceedings:

> To many people it may seem a sufficient justification for the departure from all prime ministerial precedent; to the Premier, himself, apparently, his presence was not a matter of choice but of duty. We are all familiar with the Premier's singular interpretation of his responsibilities. But it would have been interesting if he had explained in what respect his obligations differ from those of the British Premier in these matters, or by what code a football function takes precedence over the state business which demands his presence at headquarters and demands it vainly as long as there are back blocks banquets and Maori weddings to lure him away. As Minister for football he has already exercised some of his

functions, financial and critical, and it would probably have been crude to rob him of this opportunity of appearing in the benedictory exercise of his new portfolio.

To conclude, the *Post* was equally critical of Seddon's lack of grace in describing the Welsh match as a moral draw.[80]

As the touring party dispersed, the enthusiastic receptions continued. On 9 March a 'considerable crowd' gathered to welcome the Wellington and South Island members of the team. At an official reception in the Wellington Town Hall, Billy Stead was moved to describe the team as 'a happy and a large family' and issued an emphatic denial of rumours of dissension. In Christchurch another reception was convened to welcome Deans and Newton, and in Dunedin the remaining players were escorted by the Kaikorai band to a reception at the Garrison Hall. On 12 March, 500 enthusiasts attended a reception for Stead in Invercargill.[81] A week later, Glenn and Harper were welcomed in Wellington by the NZRFU, to be followed by Roberts and Wallace on 26 March. Johnston and Seeling arrived a few days later.[82]

All of these receptions were very much about celebrating the successes of the tour. While its various controversies and debates continued to appear in the press, these were temporarily far from the minds of those who welcomed home a team that, by any estimation, possessed a remarkable record. Such a response from the New Zealand public was only natural, but again it is important not to be lulled, as some have been, into interpreting the euphoria of March 1906 as indicative of the tour as a whole. In many respects, this was a rare outbreak of goodwill in what was frequently a divided and somewhat antagonistic rugby world.

For 10 of the 1905 team, their international careers were over. Thirteen toured Australia under Jimmy Hunter's captaincy in 1907, and 10 appeared against the Anglo-Welsh the following year. Mynott and Roberts toured Australia again in 1910, and McDonald endured to lead the All Blacks to North America in 1913. In due course a number would make significant contributions to the game as coaches, selectors, administrators and journalists.[83] Others, as we shall see in the next chapter, were to play a significant role in exposing the contradictions and tensions that had long simmered below the surface of New Zealand rugby.

CHAPTER NINE

The Fabric Unravels

'Go WHERE YOU WILL in England in rugby circles, and you will find the New Zealand team of 1905 unpopular,' wrote Garnet V. Portus, an Australian Rhodes Scholar and recent England rugby international, to the Sydney *Referee* in June 1908. 'Men who played against them, men who watched them, and the proprietors of the hotels where they stayed, have all more of criticism than praise for the silver fern men of two years ago.' By contrast, there was nothing but praise for the South Africans who had toured Britain during the following season.[1]

While the All Blacks had completed a victorious tour from which a popular mythology would soon emerge, any assessment of their achievements in 1905 is incomplete without some consideration of what happened to New Zealand rugby, its relationship with Britain, and broader British perceptions of colonial rugby, in the years immediately afterwards. As Portus suggests, what followed were a number of controversies and comparisons that cast much light back on the events of the tour and provide another important context and corrective to those who have focused largely on the idealisation of the All Blacks. Failure to consider the 1905 tour in terms of what happened in Britain and Australasia very shortly after is rather akin to the historian of the Great War who stops at Christmas 1914 and leaves the reader to guess the outcome. We need to consider the rather different British responses to South African touring teams in 1906 and 1912; the implications of the tour of the Professional All Blacks and the emergence of the Northern Union game in Australasia in 1907; the decidedly fraught Anglo–Welsh tour of Australasia the following year; the equally acrimonious visit of the first Australian team to Britain at the end of 1908; and the retrospective campaign against the 1905 All Blacks conducted by Scotland during the early months of 1909. Collectively, these events triggered a collapse in Anglo–Australasian rugby relations that is entirely at odds with notions of imperial sporting unity and admiration for colonial manhood that have featured in many interpretations of the All Blacks' performance.

3 p.m. 'See the Conquering Hero comes!'

4.45 p.m. The Kiwi has developed into a Moa. The Lion is not so chirpy.

The rampant lion and the timid kiwi (left) are symbolic of many predictions before New Zealand met Great Britain at Athletic Park, Wellington, on 13 August 1904. After New Zealand's 9–3 victory, the kiwi transformed into a large and powerful moa.
New Zealand Free Lance, 15 August 1904. National Library

Duncan McGregor shows a clean pair of heels to the Britishers. No 'cold feet' on this occasion.

Duncan McGregor, the speedy winger who scored two tries against the 1904 British team and four against England in 1905.
New Zealand Free Lance, 15 August 1904. National Library

PARTING UNJUNCTIONS
Mother New Zealand (to N.Z. Rep. Team): 'Now then, yer poor, weak little shaver, play up and don't get any more doin's like Welly there give yer!'

This depiction of the touring team as a schoolboy player dwarfed by Mother New Zealand and the provincial teams emphasises the limited expectations that accompanied its departure on 30 July 1905.

Otago Witness, 9 August 1905. Hocken Library

The 1905 New Zealand team shortly after arrival in England.
Back row: J. Corbett, W. Johnston, W. Cunningham, F. Newton, G. Nicholson,
C. Seeling, J. O'Sullivan, A. McDonald, D. McGregor, J. Duncan.
Middle row: E. Harper, W. Wallace, W. Stead, G. Dixon, D. Gallaher,
J. Hunter, G. Gillett, F. Glasgow, W. Mackrell.
Front row: S. Casey, H. Abbott, G. Smith, F. Roberts, H. Thompson,
H. Mynott, E. Booth, G. Tyler, R. Deans. (Absent: W. Glenn.)
W. J. Wallace Collection, Alexander Turnbull Library

Members of the team dressed for practice at Newton Abbott, Devon,
during the early days of the tour.
W. J. Wallace Collection, Alexander Turnbull Library

Incidents from the All Blacks' 28–0 victory over Leicester on 30 September.
Athletic News, 2 October 1905. British Library Newspaper Library

A rather shambolic performance of the haka – a long way removed from the highly choreographed displays of the professional era.
New Zealand Rugby Museum

Left: *New Zealand as a precocious lion cub begins to impress English opponents during October 1905.*

Punch, 11 October 1905.
University of Canterbury Library

Below: *Torment for the British lion in 1905.*

Alexander Turnbull Library

THE UNLICKED CUB
The New Zealanders have met several of our best Rugby teams, and easily defeated them all.

Members of the team practising at West Ealing, London.
W. J. Wallace Collection, Alexander Turnbull Library

SEPTEMBER
'Well, my little man, want a game at football, do you? I daresay some of our boys will oblige you.'

DECEMBER
'My dear boy, we are delighted to have you with us. You have done us a world of good. Come again soon.'

Changing perceptions of the All Blacks as the tour progressed from September to December 1905.
Football News, from George Dixon, *The Triumphant Tour of the New Zealand Footballers*, 1906

Above: *Billy Wallace running in for a try during the 44–0 victory over Gloucester on 19 October.*
New Zealand Rugby Museum

Below: *Wallace preparing to kick for goal.*
W. J. Wallace Collection, Alexander Turnbull Library

Above: *A line-out during the 21–5 victory over Midland Counties on 28 October.*
Making New Zealand Collection, Alexander Turnbull Library

Below: *Incidents from the Midland Counties game.*
Athletic News, 30 October 1905. British Library Newspaper Library

A line-out (above) *and scrum* (below) *in fog and bitter cold during the All Blacks' 12–7 victory over Scotland on 18 November.*
New Zealand Rugby Museum
Canterbury Times, 24 January 1906. Bishop Collection, Canterbury Museum

SOUVENIR CARD OF THE 'INVINCIBLE' FOOTBALLERS, ISSUED AFTER THE MATCH NEW ZEALAND v. SCOTLAND

Depicting the All Blacks as the devil perhaps suggests the antagonism that surrounded their meeting with Scotland.

Otago Witness, 10 January 1906. Hocken Library

WALES: 'What a mighty grip un gives!'
JOHN BULL (mournfully): ''Tain't nuthin to 'is kicks, Leeks. Take my advice and wear a few more pillows.'

Although the All Blacks were accumulating huge victories, many felt that their methods and behaviour on the field were highly questionable – a view reinforced by the continued portrayal of the New Zealander as much smaller than his British counterparts.

Otago Witness, 13 December 1905. Hocken Library

Incidents from the 15–0 victory over England on 2 December.
Athletic News, 4 December 1905. British Library Newspaper Library

A 'loose rush' during the match against England.
New Zealand Rugby Museum

WANTED – A GIANT-KILLER

HUMPTY DUMPTY HAD A GREAT FALL!

Above: *Official programme for the Welsh match, 16 December 1905.*
Alexander Turnbull Library

Above left: *Where others had failed it was now hoped that little Wales would maintain the honour of the Mother Country against the rampa[nt] All Blacks.*
London Opinion, from George Dixon, *The Triumphant Tour of the New Zealand Footballers*

Left: *A predictable Welsh reaction [to] the defeat of the All Blacks.*
South Wales Daily News, 18 December 19[05], from George Dixon, *The Triumphant Tou[r] of the New Zealand Footballers*

Incidents from the 3–0 defeat to Wales on 16 December.
Athletic News, 18 December 1905. British Library Newspaper Library

The New Zealand team, again portrayed as an infant, taking its punishment after defeat by Wales, who occupies 'The Seat of Rugby'.
Otago Witness, 27 December 1905.
Hocken Library

The telegram sent by Bob Deans to the Daily Mail on the morning after the Welsh defeat. This facsimile was published in New Zealand immediately after the All Blacks 'revenge' against Wales in 1924.
The Dominion, 2 December 1924, National Library

A powerful moa and frazzled lion at the end of the tour.
Alexander Turnbull Library

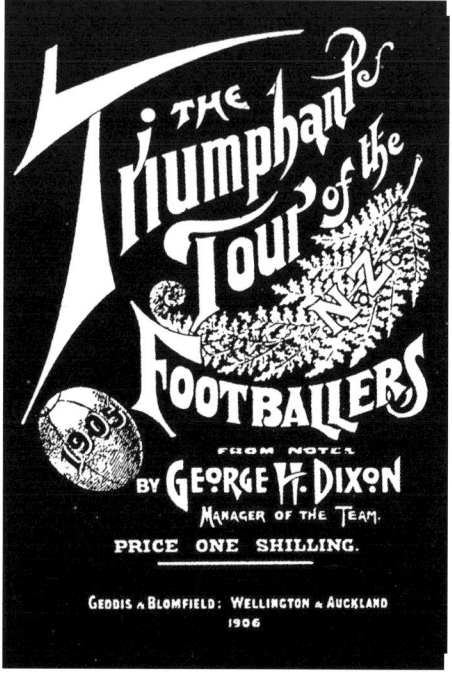

Left: *The cover of a book published by the* Daily Mail *at the end of the tour.*
Right: *An advertisement for George Dixon's book, published shortly after the team returned to New Zealand in March 1906.*
Wellington City Libraries / *New Zealand Free Lance*, 12 March 1906. National Library

The large public reception for the All Blacks when they returned to Auckland on 6 March 1906. Prime Minister Seddon at far right.
B. Basham Collection, Alexander Turnbull Library

OUR BOYS COME HOME TODAY
King Dick: 'Hip'ray! Kia ora! Ake ake! Welcome home! You have won the glory and will wear the laurel wreath.
The Moa: 'Well, Dick, I rather guess the world knows now where we roost'.

J. C. Blomfield cartoon from the New Zealand Free Lance, *12 March 1906.*
National Library

In certain respects it is difficult to draw comparisons between the All Blacks and the Springboks who followed them to Britain a year later. That the South Africans arrived less than five years after the end of the Anglo–South African War, and at a time when concerted efforts were being made to reconcile those of British and Afrikaner origin within South Africa, naturally gave the tour a vital political purpose that had not been possessed by the All Blacks. According to the *Yorkshire Post*, some believed that if the tour had taken place 10 years earlier, there would have been no war:

> This may perhaps be a far-fetched assumption, but the fact remains that the South African football team, by their clever, clean and honest football, and by their modest and sportsmanlike bearing, have done more for the promotion of a friendly parley, and for the development of the Imperial sentiment between two peoples, than all the polemics of Parliament and the platitudes of under-secretaries put together.

Similarly, the Springbok captain Paul Roos, reported after the drawn international with England, certainly felt that the result held significance far beyond sport:

> His team thoroughly represented South Africa; they were men of both races, of both parties; men who had fought on both sides. As in the game on that afternoon they had cried 'quits'; was it not a suggestion to cry 'quits' on far earlier questions? In this splendid game of football there was mutual respect. In South Africa the same mutual respect should prevail, and it would again be 'quits'.[2]

No doubt such considerations produced an element of diplomacy and generosity in assessments of the tourists. They also explain why a British team was sent to South Africa in 1903 and another would follow in 1910, the year in which the Union of South Africa was established.[3]

Yet even allowing for the particular circumstances of this tour, the tactics and demeanour of the Springboks prompted a number of comparisons that were not favourable to the 1905 All Blacks. Early in the tour *The Field* declared that Springbok successes derived not from radical tactics but 'by playing with considerable skill and exemplary vigour in the old-fashioned way'. Yet, with reference to both New Zealand and Welsh tactics, the writer wondered whether their 'chivalrous fairness' would prove a disadvantage when the South Africans met opponents 'who are trained to get on the windy side of the law whenever possible'.[4] *The Times* was more direct in its assessment:

> It is idle to deny the fact that some of the methods of the famous New Zealanders were, in the opinion of the strictest referees and the best judges of the game, distinctly questionable. Some referees held that they just kept within the bounds of the law, others held that they overstepped them. But all fair-minded rugby unionists were at least agreed that the obstruction practised by the man who was known as a wing forward was quite contrary to all the established ethics of football... The especially clean game which the South Africans play has, in consequence, been welcomed enthusiastically, but not more enthusiastically than it merits.[5]

At the end of the tour, in which the Springboks lost only two and drew one of their 29 matches and scored 606 points to 95, Hamish Stuart declared that 'A fairer side than the South Africans have never played rugby football' and that their success was due to 'conventional British' methods.[6]

> Happily, also, we shall not be called upon to discuss certain other, and far from agreeable, topics to which the play of the New Zealanders gave rise. Our old enemy, the wing-forward, has no place in South Africa, and generally speaking their play is so much above reproach that we will be saved all reference to foul or unfair play.[7]

Sporting Life added that although the tour was not quite as successful and had not produced the same spontaneous public enthusiasm as the All Blacks had in taking British rugby by surprise, the South Africans had won considerable admiration for their 'quiet style, their fairness in the field and their general bearing'.

> During the whole tour not as much as a single hiss was heard, and, great as the New Zealanders were, one cannot but remember that their methods in the international matches gave rise to much discussion. Not so the South Africans. They have passed through the fire and the excitement of their tour without a single blot on their escutcheon.[8]

Finally, in 1936, a number of Durham men who had played against the All Blacks, Springboks and Wallabies insisted that the South Africans were by far the finest team to play against: 'they gave a true interpretation of skilful Rugby which they played for the game's sake. Success came to these "admirable crichtons" by virtue of ability displayed in the correct interpretation of the fundamentals of the game.'[9] While such perceptions of Springbok chivalry would cause more than a little bemusement to many All Blacks who encountered these vigorous and uncompromising opponents later in the twentieth century, the fact remains that by comparison the 1906 tour served to reinforce a less than positive view of New Zealand rugby.

Even as the Springboks charmed Britain, plans were afoot that would do considerably more damage to the reputation of the All Blacks and the rugby culture they represented. At some point during 1906 it was decided, apparently at the instigation of a Wellington club player and postal clerk, Albert Baskerville, that a New Zealand team should embark on the challenge that had been denied the All Blacks: a meeting with the Northern Union.

When the All Blacks returned to New Zealand, a number of them confirmed widespread rumours that they had been approached by Northern Union agents in search of recruits.[10] Publicly at least, other players responded rather defensively to accusations against the team. In their tour book, Gallaher and Stead claimed that 'the arrangement made with the members of the team not only precluded any possibility of profit, but made it quite certain that, one and all, they would be out of pocket, in some cases very considerably'. Most had lost salaries or wages for the whole time they were on tour. Moreover, they were critical of the quality of professional sport, insisted that New Zealand rugby was entirely amateur and expressed strong support for the efforts of Rowland Hill and the RFU committee in promoting amateur rugby.[11] It would soon become evident, however, that other players did not share these sentiments.

We have seen already that many New Zealand followers of the 1905 tour were well aware that the real strength of English rugby resided in the north. Baskerville claimed that his specific inspiration was a letter from Northern Union critic F.W. Cooper to the *Daily Mail* indicating enthusiasm to play against New Zealand. Cooper wrote, 'The wearers of the silver fern may not have been defeated, but they have not played the cream of English football. Such men play under the banner of the Northern Union.'[12] Although Baskerville was not a provincial, let alone international, player, and along with almost all New Zealanders, had never witnessed the Northern Union game being played, he possessed a reputation as an innovative thinker and man of ambition. In 1907, at the age of only 24, he wrote a detailed rugby coaching book, *Modern Rugby Football: New Zealand Methods: points for the beginner, the player, the spectator*. As early as September 1906, Baskerville discussed tour prospects with George Smith and various other players. Smith apparently also made contact with acquaintances in Australia, although he did not visit Sydney on the way home from Britain in February 1906 as some have claimed. It is also hard to imagine that Baskerville did not talk to his Oriental clubmate and All Black halfback Fred Roberts. Whatever the exact chain of events, Baskerville soon became the public face and co-ordinating force for a wider network of interested parties in New Zealand and Australia who saw the same potential for a tour.

At this stage tour arrangements were conducted in considerable secrecy as players quite rightly feared that the penalty for any involvement with open professionalism was life disqualification by the NZRFU. Some also feared for their jobs because of close connections between rugby administrators and business interests.[13] By the time details of the proposed tour were made public in late April 1907, arrangements had already been made with the Northern Union committee and various clubs and recruitment of players was well in hand. Baskerville claimed that a public announcement would have been made much earlier, but dissatisfaction with the NZRFU was such that at least 160 players, including eighteen of the 1905 team, had applied for tour places. It was therefore necessary to form a selection committee with representatives from the four main centres and to confirm the team without jeopardising the playing future of many who had expressed an interest but had not been selected.[14]

As the Northern Union gained momentum in Australasia over the next few years, two All Blacks were prominent among those who suggested that very real objections to the administration of the game in general, and that of the NZRFU in particular, were at the heart of both the decision to tour and the subsequent growth of the game. In a lengthy contribution to the *Yorkshire Post* in November 1908, an 'ordinary All Black' (almost certainly E. E. Booth, who was then touring as a journalist with the Wallabies) claimed that there was a widespread desire for change to the amateur regulations in New Zealand. It was suggested that a professional team would not have been assembled if the 1905 All Blacks had been adequately compensated for their efforts. It was widely known that they 'could scarcely raise £10 in the team on their return passage home to New Zealand' and had not been well treated by a governing body that profited considerably from the tour while displaying 'meanness' towards players who were largely from working-class backgrounds.

> What is wanted, besides improving the game, is a readjustment of the laws of professionalism to make them harmonise more with Colonial ideas as to what is equitable to the player. Thus it is demanded that players representing clubs, provinces and states should receive an allowance for loss of time and wages as well as travelling expenses and hotel tariff.

That is to say, a player leaving his billet for a fortnight or a month should receive his usual wages. Also reasonable men recognise that the present 3s a day allowance for pocket money is a farce and that it is anything but justice to a player not well situated in life to be so seriously out of pocket. The leisure class footballer is decidedly the exception 'down under'.

Although the New Zealand public would not apparently tolerate full professionalism wherein players obtained their entire livelihood from the game, there were growing calls for substantial reform and some sort of broken-time payment. At the same time, the public also wanted a more spectacular game with less complex rules and 'a restriction of the referee's present powers of continuous interference through endless petty causes'. If the International Board failed to respond to these demands, it was predicted that the colonial unions would eventually have to take matters into their own hands and secede in order to save the game.[15]

Interviewed in December 1911 while touring Britain with an Australasian Northern Union team, another 1905 All Black, George Gillett, predicted that the game would soon become the most popular rugby code in New Zealand, owing to the 'rampant dissatisfaction' of players at the treatment they received from the NZRFU:

> [T]he management have horded up money which they are putting to no useful purpose. The All Blacks came back to New Zealand with a profit of £9500. The whole of that sum is lying dormant. It has neither been used for buying grounds or developing the game in any shape or form. Withal the management are niggardly to a degree. When a player is laid up, it is the most difficult thing to get a little drop of medicine or medical attention for him ... No one can understand why the rugby union should be so mean. They hold their thousands of pounds in the bank, where they are doing the game nor the individual player any good.

In this light, Gillett stated that his reason for switching to Northern Union was not for money but to 'show how much I protested against the Rugby Union's way of conducting affairs'.[16]

It is misleading, however, to characterise the genesis of the tour as a concerted working-class revolt against the NZRFU. As Jo Smith reveals, there were more white-collar players in the professional team than in 1905, in part because only those with some financial means could afford the £50 deposit required of each player before the tour. Evidently a number of prospective players pulled out owing to their inability to meet the deposit, which may explain why only four of the 1905 All Blacks eventually joined the team. It seems that those who did make the investment to play a game with which they were entirely unfamiliar were motivated by an entrepreneurial adventure from which they would receive a share of the profits.[17] And they could be in no doubt after the published accounts of the 1905 tour revealed a considerable profit that rugby could be a very lucrative business.

The immediate response from the NZRFU when reports of a professional team surfaced in April 1907 was utterly uncompromising. Earlier chapters have noted the tendency of some New Zealand administrators to pursue a liberal interpretation of the amateur laws – not least in discussions of player allowances prior to the 1905 tour. We shall also see shortly that a few in the upper echelons of the New Zealand game developed some sympathy, albeit pragmatic, for the views expressed above. Yet the success of 1905, in terms of both public acclaim and considerable profits, now made preservation of the game more vital than ever. The consequences of a split as had happened in Britain were too terrible to contemplate. Further, as discussed in Chapter Two, there was an increasingly widespread perception by 1907 that elements of gambling and rough play that had blighted the game before 1905 were again coming to prominence. One player had died after a kick to the head in a club match in Wellington, and numerous others were being suspended by the provincial unions for violence and foul language.[18] The spectre of a professional team represented a chance for the NZRFU to reassert firm control over all aspects of its game.

On 27 April, Edgar Wylie, secretary of the NZRFU, stated that any player who went on Baskerville's tour would be disqualified for life. On 7 May, the Hawke's Bay RFU passed a motion urging the national body to do its 'utmost to kill the proposal, as in the opinion of this union it is likely to have a very damaging effect upon amateur Rugby football in the future'.[19] On 16 May, Auckland passed a similar motion expressing 'alarm and indignation' at the proposed tour.[20] On 21 May, the NZRFU announced that all players nominated for the upcoming inter-island match were required to sign a legal declaration confirming their amateur status and promising not to join the touring team.[21]

> I, _____ of _____ do solemnly and sincerely declare as follows – (1) That I have never asked, received or relied on promise, direct or implied, to receive any money consideration whatever, actual or prospective,

for playing football or rendering any service to a football organisation; (2) and particularly that I have not asked, received or relied on any promise, direct or implied, to receive any money consideration whatever, actual or prospective, or to receive any benefit from, nor have I promised or asked to be permitted to take part in any manner whatsoever in a scheme having for its object the sending of a team of rugby footballers from New Zealand to play football against the teams of the Northern Counties' Rugby Union of England. And I make this solemn declaration conscientiously believing the same to be true under and by virtue of the provisions of an Act of the General Assembly of New Zealand entitled The Justice of the Peace Act 1882 – Declared at ____ the ____ day of _____ 1907 before me _____ a Justice of the Peace for the Colony of New Zealand.[22]

Those players eventually selected for the inter-island fixture were required to sign a further declaration stating that they would not become involved with the professional tour in any way and that they would actively assist the NZRFU in stopping it and identifying those involved. On a point of principle, and amid debates as to the legal strength of these documents, 12 Auckland players initially refused to sign. Some claimed that they had enjoyed long careers without their amateur status being questioned, and could not see why it should be now.[23] Six Auckland All Blacks initially claimed that they could not sign – having accepted three shillings per day allowance in 1905. On 29 May a compromise was reached when the Auckland RFU added a clause stating that any such expense payments from the NZRFU did not contravene the amateur laws.[24]

At this point the NZRFU was confident that it had secured victory and that no tour would take place. In London, C. Wray Palliser used his links with *The Times* to paint an unfavourable picture of those behind a 'phantom team' that would never be seen in Britain.[25] Meanwhile, the Wellington RFU banned Baskerville from all grounds under its control and asked the NZRFU for a financial guarantee in case he took civil action. He was also warned off all grounds controlled by the Petone Borough Council.[26]

To take the correspondence columns of the *Evening Post* as one example, there was mixed public reaction to the stance of the NZRFU. On one hand, 'Amateur' claimed the proposed tour was unethical and should not be supported on the grounds that rugby was a pastime and should never become a business. 'Here it is a clean, healthy sport in which all classes can meet in pleasant rivalry. On the other hand, professional rugby, as played by the Northern Union clubs, is run entirely as a money-making concern and is afflicted with the attendant evils of trickery and collusion.[27] The *Post* itself predicted good prospects for a tour, especially for those nearing the end of their playing careers for whom 'it would be a temptation to receive an offer of a final flutter home with a prospect of sharing the profits of the tour instead of making them for a Rugby Union'. Nor would the prospect of losing their amateur status be a serious consideration.[28] 'Southern Englishman' declared himself in favour of the tour on the grounds that the 'wild alarm' of the NZRFU implied that 'the moment a player became a professional he, by the stroke of a magic wand, is straightaway transformed into a dangerous animal'. Yet both cricket and soccer had embraced professionalism without difficulty and had clearly been improved by it. The real issue to consider, according to 'Southern Englishman', was the challenge offered by the Northern Union.

> What it really resolves itself into is this: shall New Zealand teams go home on picnic parties to play in gentle cake-walks, with congratulatory telegrams etc, in what a leading London daily has described as the 'moribund rugby game', or shall they meet 'foemen worthy of their steel' in matches in which both sides will be fully extended, who ever may win?[29]

In short, anyone with a proper understanding of the changes to English rugby after the split of 1895 could hardly get carried away by the performances of the 1905 All Blacks.

The NZRFU was soon to discover that it had entirely failed to suppress the tour. On 10 August, the same day as Jimmy Hunter's All Blacks completed their last fixture in Australia, 15 members of Baskerville's team departed for Sydney, to be joined a few days later by another party from Auckland. The team was to be known as the Professional All Blacks – the name 'All Golds', as they have been more commonly known, only emerging later in Australia as a cynical reference to the playing of rugby for money. Included were eight All Blacks and 14 prominent provincial players. From the 1905 touring team came Massa Johnston, Bill Mackrell, Duncan McGregor and George Smith, along with Tom Cross, Jum Turtill, Eric Watkins and Edgar Wrigley, who had played against Australia at Dunedin in August 1905.[30]

As Baskerville's team arrived in Sydney, the Australian dimension of the player revolt became public. Motivated by the same dissatisfaction with amateur rugby and the miserly approach of its administrators, a group assembled on 8 August 1907 to establish the New South Wales Rugby Football League. Within days they had enlisted more than 130 players and three matches had been arranged with the New Zealanders. Although played under rugby rules – Northern Union rule books had not yet arrived in Australia – these fixtures provided a very positive sign for the future in that the attendance was much larger than expected and the press commented that the methods and sportsmanship of the tourists were superior to what had just been witnessed from the touring amateur All Blacks.[31]

The Professional All Blacks arrived in the north of England to a tumultuous welcome. Tony Collins explains that as much as they were a team from overseas, they also represented a triumph by the Northern Union over an establishment that had for a long time disparaged everything it stood for.[32] Thankfully, despite never having played under Northern Union rules before they arrived in England, the tourists shaped a remarkably good record. After winning eight and drawing one of their first nine games, they eventually finished with 19 wins, two draws and 14 losses, scoring 412 points to 294. Although losing to England and Wales, they won the test series against the full Northern Union representative team.[33]

Meaningful comparisons between the 1905 and 1907 teams are problematic. Although the former had a far superior record on paper, it must be remembered that the Professional All Blacks had to play an unfamiliar game against all of its strongest exponents. The contrast was made clear in a letter from 'Massa' Johnston to Rugby Football League secretary John Wilson in August 1929:

> Smith, Mackrell, MacGregor and [my]self had a good idea in 1905–06 what the Union players were like but not for one minute did we think we would meet such continuous opposition as we did in 1907–08. I tell them here Jack every match we played in England is [sic] a test match and they can't understand it. No place for weaklings or one who has a habit of looking for the easy and flash stuff.[34]

Over 300,000 people watched the tour, and the players eventually divided a profit of £5,641. It was also crucial to stimulating Northern Union interest in Wales and giving a much needed international dimension to the game. The first Kangaroos from Australia visited the following season and a Northern Union team toured Australasia in 1910.[35]

The death of Baskerville from pneumonia in May 1908 while the team was completing its tour in Australia undoubtedly deprived the Northern Union of a superb organiser in New Zealand. Nevertheless, the first game under the new rules, an exhibition match played in Wellington on 13 June 1908 as a benefit for Baskerville's relatives, drew a very positive verdict from the *Evening Post*. The 6,000 spectators witnessed a generally faster game with an absence of the sort of 'bullocking' play that marred rugby, and the NZRFU could learn much from the new rules. 'Some of the time honoured traditions of the orthodox Rugby have outlived their day. Some of the quaint rules are a drag on the game. The Northern common-sense should not be ignored.'[36]

Several of the Professional All Blacks embarked on successful careers with English clubs – including George Smith at Oldham, Massa Johnston at Wigan and Warrington, and Jum Turtill at St Helens. Bronco Seeling signed with Wigan at the end of 1909. George Gillett and 11 other All Blacks also switched codes before 1914.[37] Meanwhile, Northern Union secured a small but significant footing throughout New Zealand – initially through a series of interprovincial matches during 1908-09 and then the establishment of regular club competitions from 1910. Much as the conservative press liked to portray it as a corrupt product of uncouth working-class culture, and the NZRFU imposed a mandatory life ban on anyone associated with it, limited resources and a small population base dictated that this was effectively an amateur game from which players received nothing more than their expenses when playing away from home. What attracted them was not money, but more likely a desire to play an open, attractive game and to escape constraints imposed by middle-class administrators within the NZRFU and the provincial unions. Yet many more working-class players remained within the rugby union fold than ever embraced Northern Union and there was to be nothing to match the dominance of the professional code in New South Wales.[38]

The real impact of the Professional All Blacks was far less in the numbers they attracted to the new game than in the friction that the tour caused within New Zealand rugby union and in its relations with Britain. In 1907–08 it seemed to many rugby followers that where some had gone, more could follow and action must be taken to stop them. Others felt that a rugby culture that could spawn such a team was clearly in need of reform. However, the nature of that reform produced distinct battle lines during 1908 that highlighted long-standing divisions within New Zealand rugby. On one side were 'imperialists', loyal to the amateur traditions and spirit of the game, who favoured a vigorous campaign to suppress Northern Union – not to mention the various 'moral' threats posed by rough play and unethical conduct within rugby union. Opposing them were 'nationalists' who resented control of the local game from Britain and favoured various changes, and perhaps a liberalisation of the rules on amateurism, to increase the popularity of rugby and thereby counter the appeal of Northern Union.[39]

Leading the quest for reform was the Otago RFU, which on 30 March 1908 recommended that the NZRFU carefully evaluate the existing rules of the game with a view to submitting reform proposals to the RFU. The matter was given greater urgency after June 1908 when the first Northern Union matches began to be played and people could compare the two games. Among other things, Otago advocated reducing teams to 14 players, abolishing the wing-forward and modifying the offside rules to encourage a faster game with greater spectator appeal. At the same time, 'broken time' payments should be instituted for touring representative teams in an effort to 'immunise' the amateur game against open professionalism. Finally, it was proposed that the NZRFU should break with the International Board and form a separate alliance with the Australian unions if these proposals were not accepted.[40]

Although a special meeting of delegates to the NZRFU on 9 October 1908 conceded that reform was 'advisable', rather than 'imperatively necessary' as an Otago delegate had proposed, and although some proposals to modify the game were accepted in principle, conservative elements of the NZRFU Management Committee ensured that New Zealand's existing tendency towards a liberal interpretation of the rugby laws would be taken no further. Ever mindful of its lucrative connections with Britain and the consequences of isolation from the rest of the international rugby community, the union decisively rejected all proposals for 'broken time' and insisted that nothing should be done to alter the game in New Zealand without first gaining approval from the Australian unions, the RFU and the International Board. By now the NZRFU was very aware that such approval would never be forthcoming, and this position was confirmed in August 1909 when Ireland and Scotland informed the RFU that they would not discuss any reform proposals with the colonial unions and would only do so with the English and Welsh. As Chapter Six explained, it would be another 40 years before those who viewed themselves as the traditional guardians of the game would allow New Zealand proper representation at international level.[41]

The refusal of Scotland and Ireland to countenance any reform measures generated in New Zealand was an entirely predictable consequence of steadily deteriorating Anglo–Australasian rugby relations since 1905. As this book has consistently argued, many in Britain harboured grave reservations about the methods and attitudes displayed by the All Blacks. The emergence of the Professional All Blacks in 1907 only confirmed their perceptions of a 'moral malaise' afflicting the New Zealand game. Although plans for another British touring team to Australia and New Zealand had been canvassed by George Dixon during 1905,[42] these now became a matter of some urgency as the NZRFU moved to enlist the help of the RFU in 'saving' New Zealand rugby for amateurism. In May 1907, after direct representations from Cecil Wray Palliser, of the New Zealand High Commission, and A. E. G. Rhodes, former president of the NZRFU, the RFU was persuaded to send a team to New Zealand in 1908.[43]

Animosity towards colonial rugby now triggered sharp divisions within the British game. While the more liberal Welsh were happy to lend their support to the RFU, the Irish and Scots flatly refused to become involved with this tour or the proposed visit of an Australian team to Britain at the end of 1908. Both felt that rather than containing professionalism, such ventures merely encouraged it. In January 1908, Ireland announced that, in accordance with its amateur principles, it would not play a fixture against the Wallabies if a profit was to be made out of the tour.[44] Scotland took the same decision on 5 March and passed a further resolution stating that they would take no part in colonial tours except those that were managed by a committee equally representative of the four committees of the British unions. Further, Scotland declined to associate themselves with any proposal for another New Zealand tour until the details of the gates and accounts of the English matches on the 1905 tour, asked for in March 1907, were supplied to them by the RFU or NZRFU. Scotland also opposed any attempt to have colonial representatives on the International Board.[45]

The Irish and Scots, and some like-minded elements within the English game, were further antagonised when the RFU released a report in March 1908 claiming that veiled professionalism did not exist in England to nearly the extent it once had. The union claimed that the remaining problem was simply one of lavish entertainment expenditure by clubs in order to attract players.[46] A motion expressing lack of confidence in the report and condemning it as whitewashing, moved by Moseley RFC at the RFU annual general meeting in May 1908, was defeated amid acrimonious debate. Nevertheless, the RFU president, C. A. Crane, resigned in protest.[47]

Against this background, the RFU made strenuous efforts to select a team that would impart the right sort of 'tone' in New Zealand. The backgrounds and amateur credentials of aspiring tourists were carefully vetted and efforts, although not successful, were made to include Rhodes Scholars such as Colin Gilray and Garnet Portus to reinforce the imperial ideals of the tour. The Anglo-Welsh team eventually selected was decidedly middle class and determinedly amateur in spirit – to the extent that they eschewed shipboard training on the way to New Zealand on the grounds that gentlemen who played a game for its own sake had no reason to prepare for it. This was in stark contrast to the comprehensive training regime of Bedell-Sivright's party in 1904.[48]

What ensued in New Zealand during the Anglo-Welsh tour was an acrimonious clash of cultural and sporting values that served only to accentuate the problems of 1905. From the outset, the tourists developed a strong animosity towards the ferocious competitiveness of New Zealand teams and the fanaticism of their supporters, who seemed to treat the game as something akin to a 'religion'. There were numerous disputes over refereeing and interpretations of the laws, frequent accusations of rough play, and scathing condemnation of the wing-forward. Some of the touring party were also disturbed by the apparent circumvention of the amateur ethos whereby 'working men' were able to devote considerable time to training and playing.[49] To make this concern even more painful, the Anglo-Welsh suffered the indignity of having a player, Fred Jackson, recalled to England and suspended as a professional for allegedly playing Northern Union during the 1901–02 season.[50]

At the end of the tour the team manager George Harnett informed the *Morning Post* that none of the party had any desire to visit New Zealand again. He was also highly critical of the severity and roughness of the New Zealand game and claimed that the wing-forward was even more aggressive on home territory than Gallaher had been in 1905. To the *Daily Express* he added, 'Whatever is done, we should keep in very close touch with the South African players who, besides being amateurs to the core, are genuine sportsmen who play clean and honest rugby.'[51]

The next blow to New Zealand's standing in the rugby world was in part a case of guilt by association, in that they suffered directly from the acrimonious Australian tour of Britain at the end of 1908 and the consequent determination of Scotland in particular to put colonial rugby firmly in its place. When plans for a tour were announced in 1907, the New South Wales Rugby Union (NSWRU) '[noted] with pleasure the expansion of the Imperial character of the Rugby Union game, and trusts that it will continue to expand as a pastime throughout the world'.[52] To counter the growing threat of the professional game and the aspersions cast against them by the refusal of Ireland and Scotland to become involved in the tour, the union established an 'examining committee' to confirm the bona fide amateur status of every touring player.[53] When the Wallabies arrived in England, their captain, Dr H. M. 'Paddy' Moran, insisted that despite the pernicious influence of professionalism in Sydney, 'He was thankful to say that they themselves had remained strong adherents to amateurism, and although they might be beaten in forthcoming encounters they could never be robbed of their amateur status'.[54]

Despite these admirable sentiments, the tour quickly revealed themes very familiar to New Zealand observers. From the earliest matches, the press seized on aspects of apparently rough Australian play, and especially incidents such as the sending-off of a player for punching an opponent in the match against Oxford University. In the first of several newspaper attacks, the football columnist for the *Morning Post* roundly condemned the conduct of the Australians: 'The incident caused something like disgust among those accustomed to see the rugby game played in the proper spirit, and generally their was a feeling of regret that this "ordering off" incident should have occurred on one of the university grounds, of all places.'[55] In slightly more measured tones, the Oxford *Daily Chronicle* lamented the Australians' failure to reveal their true talents:

> Clever as the play of the colonials was, they were so frequently guilty of unfair play that one's admiration of their cleverness was sadly diminished by indignation. They were out to win at all costs, but they were so superior forward that they could have won with ease without recourse to unfair methods.[56]

There were similar reactions when two further players were sent off in later tour matches, and by the midpoint of the tour the *Morning Post* columnist had become trenchant in his criticism of colonial tours in general:

> The rugby game required no 'boom'; it was a great and flourishing sport before the New Zealand invasion. These recurring tours are merely a highway to exhibition and professional football. The football dictum laid down at the Exeter Church congress many years ago was that in football we want players not spectators . . . New Zealand and Australia easily acquired the arts of the game, but they forgot the foundation on which all games of recreation are built; the instincts of sport.[57]

Even the *Daily Mail*, so enamoured of the All Blacks, added that it was 'no secret that lack of *esprit de corps* [was] one of the chief features contributing to the collapse of the Wallabies'.[58] W. L. Sinclair in the *Athletic News* lamented that 'These Australians are such jolly good footballers, when they like, that I marvel at the introduction of these nasty incidents into their game'.[59] But perhaps the most damning criticism came from an unnamed writer during a comparison with the All Blacks and Springboks:

> The South Africans observed morality, canons, traditions and rules, the New Zealanders observed the rules, while the Australians disregard every one of these sacred and holy appurtenances to the game. The result as far as English sides are concerned is just the same. They are always beaten to a frazzle.[60]

Finally, Hamish Stuart observed that 'One is not concerned as to their idea of fair and unfair play. All that is relevant to the issue is that they have been guilty of unfair play according to rules.'[61]

The Wallabies were in no doubt as to the general tone of their reception in Britain. Speaking on his return to Sydney, manager, James McMahon, complained that 'as visitors to the Mother Country, as representatives of part of the British nation, they could not understand and were certainly not prepared for such hostility as was shown them by the section of the press'.[62] One of the players, Tom Richards, mused that 'If we were hostile and treacherous aliens, instead of colonial Britishers playing a national game, some of the criticisms poured upon us would not have been too hot'.[63] Moran, as with Dixon in December 1905, eventually felt obliged to respond directly to the various criticisms. His letter to the *Daily Mail* on 24 November 1908 is an intriguing combination of defence for the Wallabies and scathing contempt for those who questioned their methods:

> This rugby game is a strenuous struggle between physical giants, and we must not refer to gentle ladies for a decision on what constitutes rough play. Our sisters always did think it rough when that horrid man upset us so rudely in the days when they came to watch us at play. Our tackling has been always hard . . . and has no doubt earned the disapproval of men who have never played. The player, however, who objects to a robust tackle should lay aside his jersey and leave it to become moth-eaten in disuse. For him there are other games, and I believe the newest is diabolo.[64]

Moran and several supporters of his team also observed that they were penalised for indiscretions that were not an issue for referees in English club games.[65] Returning to the matter in 1939, Moran had not changed his views on the conduct of rugby or the source of the controversy in 1908:

> The real danger is that in the anxiety to mitigate its brutalities, the game may suffer in those very hard qualities which make for virility in the race. It was surely meant to be vigorous and a little dangerous. From its university centres a nation decays, aspiring to softness. In such struggles as take place in rugby, men's tempers will sometimes boil over. Let us not take these matters too seriously. Above all let us beware of newspaper sleuths who expand misdemeanours into serious crimes in order to satisfy the vicious appetites which they themselves have created.[66]

In another passage, Moran suggested that there was food for thought in the fact that, less than six years after their return from Britain, only seven of his touring party of 31 enlisted to serve the Empire in the Great War.[67]

Inevitably, Moran's stance in 1908 provoked a sharp retort. 'Medico' informed the *Daily Mail* that many ex-players were among the spectators and well understood the game being played by the Wallabies. 'The puerile reference to players objecting to robust tackling and the doctor's advice to them to resort to diabolo are surely indicative of animus unworthy of a medical sportsman.'[68] But the last and longest word went to Hamish Stuart, who insisted that accusations of unfair play were only ever made 'more in sorrow than in anger' when it was apparent that there were players who lacked 'the traditional spirit' and 'hereditary sporting instinct' of the game.

> Every player can not, of course, approach the rugby Corinth through the portals of a public school or university. Hence the principle that conscience is above the referee and its voice shriller than any whistle is never instilled into many players. That is their misfortune, but in some cases at least it is also their fault. It is to be feared that in dealing with the question of unfair play, many writers fall into two errors. One section fails to make allowance for the difference between our idea of how rugby should be played and the colonial idea. Another section confounds the particular act with the spirit that prompts the act. Judged by this standard the New Zealanders were an unfair side because the ruling motives of their game were 'play to win' and 'play to the referee'. The Australians ... seemed to be concerned by the same motive, though it is probable that custom and the national idea have so blunted their moral sense that they are sublimely unconscious of their delinquencies and are sincerely surprised when accused of unfair practice.

Stuart concluded that the Australians were merely 'clumsy imitators' of more scientific illegal methods used by the New Zealanders.[69]

Within six months of their return to Australia, the Wallabies vindicated their critics in a manner that was to retard the development of Australian rugby union for at least two decades. At the end of August 1909 it was announced that 14 of the touring party had agreed to play three exhibition matches against the professional Kangaroos. Acting independently of the New South Wales Rugby League, a private syndicate under the direction of hotelier James Joynton Smith guaranteed the players sums ranging from £50 to £200.[70] In its 1909 annual report, the NSWRU naturally expressed considerable regret that the players had defected after taking the hospitality of the union during the British tour: 'It is to be deplored that the players who deserted should have, for their personal gain and profit, made use of the popular name attached to your team and temporarily cast a slur on the name of Australian amateur sport and Rugby Union football.'[71] The *Sydney Mail*, while acknowledging the difficulties facing working-class players, was at the same time highly critical of the stance taken by the Wallabies, who had 'created quite a revulsion of feeling in the minds of those who are for the strict maintenance of amateur sport'.[72]

Stripped of its best players and their lucrative spectator appeal, the NSWRU was soon in financial crisis as spectator numbers for key fixtures declined from 13–23,000 to 1–2,000 during 1910. In 1911 the union was obliged to sell its prize asset – the Epping racecourse it had purchased in 1907 in order to develop a new ground. The union game lost further ground during the war years and was all but extinct in Queensland during the 1920s.[73]

No sooner had the Wallabies departed Britain in January 1909 than they, and the All Blacks especially, were embroiled in a new controversy. When the Scottish Football Union was finally provided with the various tour expense accounts it had requested, it discovered that both the All Blacks and the Wallabies (no mention is made of the South Africans), as well as the recent Anglo-Welsh tourists to Australasia, were paid allowances of three shillings per day for petty expenses. These were variously described as 'washing and tips' or 'wine money'. Despite an insistence from the RFU that these allowances did not constitute any form of profit to the players, and simply saved team managers having to pay petty expenses as they arose, the Scots saw nothing but a direct breach of the laws regarding professionalism. They promptly cancelled their fixture with England scheduled for March 1909.[74] Eventually the RFU sought to placate Scotland by abolishing direct cash payments to players and agreeing with an International Board resolution that such direct payments were contrary to amateurism. But in a final display of ideological purity, or petulance, Scotland, with support from Ireland, demanded that this decision be made retrospective to include the 1905 tour – thereby meaning the All Blacks would be declared professional. However, the motion was countered by England and Wales, and the matter remained deadlocked. In March 1909, Scotland relented and agreed to play the English fixture.[75]

For their part, observers in Australia and New Zealand detected a good deal of hypocrisy in the Scottish position and the similar stance taken by the Irish against colonial tours. Several pointed out that the practice of paying daily allowances had originated with the 1899 British tour of Australia. 'Wine money' at the rate of three shillings per day was certainly paid to all, including Scottish players, in the 1904 British team and, as we have seen already, it was commonly known and freely stated that the All Blacks received this daily amount in 1905.[76] Inevitably, some felt that the entire dispute stemmed from the desire of the Scots to exact revenge for their lost financial opportunities against the All Blacks in 1905.[77] Australasian observers might also have added, if the self-serving hypocrisy of the RFU had not shrouded it in mystery, that members of the 1888 British touring team to Australasia were also paid substantial sums for their efforts. Clearly the union was rather more interested in rooting out working-class transgressors of the laws than those such as the supposedly amateur paragon Andrew Stoddart, who received £200 for pursuing the game for the sake of the game.[78] Even some British critics were sceptical of Scottish motives. 'J.M.D.' in the *Football Evening News* accused them of nothing more or less than class-based hostility:

> This craze for the amateurism that is almost impossible – the amateurism that must include social position and a University or Public School education – is a serious hindrance to the spread of the imperial sporting spirit ... There is no room for class distinctions in imperial sport and they must be swept away ... The Irish and Scottish Unions did more harm than they were aware of when they refused to meet the Australians, and that fact will be brought home to both bodies before very long.[79]

These were rarely expressed sentiments in the south of England during 1908–09.

After more than three years in which no proposals for tours seem to have circulated, the RFU informed Australia and New Zealand in July 1912 that no team could be invited to Britain without approval of the International Board. As one British report stated:

When the countries approve of the fitness of a New Zealand visit, the men of the Dominion will be invited, and not before. But the conditions will be entirely different from those which obtained in the 1905 itinerary, and it remains to be seen whether the financial proposition, for one thing, would be acceptable to the Maorilanders.[80]

Exactly what the International Board had in mind became clear within days when it was announced that South Africa had accepted an invitation for a second tour of Britain during the 1912–13 season. In a speech praising the sportsmanship of the 1906 Springboks, Rowland Hill, president of the RFU, made it clear that the 1912 tour was not a 'financial speculation'. The British unions would cover all expenses and take all profits, and no allowances would be paid to the players.[81]

The invitation to South Africa was immediately criticised by the London *Referee*, which pointed out that, having started the cycle of tours, New Zealand was entitled to the next invitation and 'it is therefore regrettable that merely because the South Africans are excellent men to meet off and on the field an affront should be placed upon another part of the Empire'. The Sydney *Referee* was sure that Australasians would agree with this view. Although the revival of interest in British rugby owed much to New Zealand, it was evident that England and Wales had been swayed by Scottish and Irish hostility.[82] Of course, the memory of the Anglo-Welsh tour probably ensured that they required little swaying.

In a display of very belated lip service to New Zealand claims, the RFU asked in July 1912, less than three months before the start of the British season, whether a combined Australasian touring team would be acceptable for a triangular tournament involving South Africa. While the NSWRU was willing to consider this as a special case, the NZRFU declined. Aside from being embroiled in a prolonged dispute with New South Wales over the division of profits from the 1910 American Universities tour of Australasia, New Zealanders felt that the superior record of the All Blacks entitled them to a tour in their own right.[83] The pique of the NZRFU was such that when, in October 1912, the NSWRU proposed that they should issue a joint invitation for a British team to tour Australasia in 1915, to be followed by South Africa in 1916, the management committee replied that it had no desire to do so.[84] Yet it is clear that although the NZRFU was publicly aloof, it was privately anxious to secure a thawing of relations with the British unions and arrange another tour as soon as possible. Early in 1913, F. Lysnar, a New Zealander visiting Britain on business, was apparently asked by the NZRFU to promote the idea of an All Black tour. Lysnar in turn enlisted the help of Douglas Sladen, an Anglo-Australian and enthusiastic imperialist with numerous literary and publishing connections. On 31 January, Sladen wrote to Edward Hulton, owner of the *Athletic News*, the *Daily Dispatch* and numerous other high-circulation newspapers, pointing out that 'New Zealand is awfully sick because no arrangement can be made to receive another All Black team here' and asking for Hulton's assistance in using the press to encourage the idea of another tour. As Sladen explained to Lysnar on 9 February: 'In these matters there is nothing like having a millionaire newspaper proprietor behind you and none of the newspaper proprietors are so much interested in sport as Mr. Hulton.' A meeting was then apparently arranged between Lysnar and James Catton, the influential columnist 'Tityrus' of the *Athletic News*.[85] Whether or not Lysnar was able to put the New Zealand case, there were no tangible results in terms of proposals for another tour before the outbreak of war in August 1914.

Such was the impasse with Britain that in 1913 the NZRFU perhaps looked with some optimism towards Benjamin Ide Wheeler's idea for some sort of Pacific Rim rugby organisation with representatives from California, Canada, Australia and New Zealand.[86] However, as we have noted already, the overwhelming superiority of the All Blacks in California at the end of 1913, and the fact that even in victory they felt that Californians went beyond the accepted bounds of robust play by corrupting rugby with too much of the brutality and intensity of American football, dictated that such an outlet for international rugby would amount to nothing.

Ironically, it was the carnage of the Great War that reopened the channels for rugby, as a New Zealand Services team played 36 matches in Britain and two in France from January to May 1919. Even then, it only appeared once each in Ireland, against Queen's University, and Scotland, against a 'Mother Country' XV.[87] The All Blacks did not return to Britain until 1924, and not again until 1935, when they reacquainted with Scotland after 30 years. The New South Wales Waratahs waited until 1927, and only in 1939 did an official Australian team return – only to have its tour cancelled owing to the outbreak of war. South Africa made only one visit to Britain during the inter-war years, in 1931–32, although it received two in return. After 1908 no British team toured Australasia until 1930, and that tour, as Chapter Six explained, became notable for James Baxter's ultimately successful campaign to abolish the wing-forward. For rugby administrators, the novelty of tours and all that they entailed had clearly faded. By contrast, the always financially precarious New Zealand Cricket Council surpassed its wealthy rugby counterpart by dispatching three teams to England during the inter-war period and hosting three full tours in return. There was also a touring cricket team in England every season from 1926 to 1939, and the MCC dispatched numerous teams to various parts of the British Empire and beyond.

What emerges, then, is a picture of Anglo–Australasian rugby relations, and by implication a view of the qualities of colonial manhood, far more complicated than the conventional celebration of the 1905 All Blacks. The early twentieth-century imperial touring network that is commonly assumed to have fostered notions of imperial loyalty and co-operation was instead undercut by bitter antagonisms. Further, any interpretation of the 1905 tour as a vehicle for emergent nationalism struggles to reconcile sharply divergent views. For every admirer willing to sing the praises of New Zealand and its manhood as revealed on the rugby fields of Britain, there were ever-increasing numbers in the decade after 1905 who saw much that was questionable if not entirely undesirable.

CONCLUSION

This book was not written to belittle the 1905 All Blacks. No doubt they would lose to later sides with greater awareness of fitness and a legion of support staff. And of course the fascinating question as to how they would have performed against Northern Union teams can only partly be answered by remembering how remarkably well the Professional All Blacks did two years later in a game that they had never played before leaving New Zealand. But the only criteria by which a team can really be judged in sporting terms is the extent to which it dominated the available opposition of the era in which it played. By this measure, whether it is the number and margin of their victories or the way in which they raised the profile of rugby in Britain and attracted interest from many previously unfamiliar with the game, the contribution of the 'Original' All Blacks was immense. There is equally no question that many in New Zealand, public and politicians alike, were swept along by the success of the tour and fully believed that it would enhance the reputation of their colony within the British Empire.

But all of this is a question of degree. The central contention of this book is that much as there were enthusiastic supporters of all that the All Blacks achieved, there were also counter-arguments, complaints and criticisms that undermine many of the grand claims made for the tour and provide much needed balance to others. For every admirer of the tourists' superior physique, there were many more who retained faith in the quality of Britons and sought other explanations for the New Zealanders' success. Equally, those who praised their tactics must be set against the many who railed against the wing-forward or what was perceived to be an overly developed determination to win at all costs. Finally, for every belated supporter of the Deans 'try' against Wales, there were others who regarded it as only one among many incidents in a dramatic game, or who felt that the All Blacks' overall performance was not worthy of victory. These were not peripheral issues, nor issues that turned up briefly at the beginning of the tour but were rendered irrelevant by the magnificence of the All Blacks' play. They endured, and in some cases gathered a greater momentum after the tour.

The obvious question to ask is why and how the popular portrayal of 1905 has dominated at the expense of many of its contradictions. No one

CONCLUSION

who read the voluminous sports columns of the British or Australasian press in the years immediately after the tour, and especially after the departure of the Professional All Blacks and the acrimonious tour of the Anglo-Welsh, could be in any doubt that the view of New Zealand rugby was less than favourable or that the New Zealand game was in something of a crisis – threatened both by Northern Union and by the conflicting and often class-based ideals of many who chose to remain within the theoretically amateur game. Even in 1924 there was an undercurrent of tension around some aspects of the tactics of the Invincibles, and it was to be renewed with vigour by Bim Baxter and his campaign against the wing-forward in 1930.

But other forces were at work. The service and sacrifice of New Zealanders during the Great War, Gallaher prominent among them, began to shape a conception of New Zealand manhood and of national identity that possessed far greater unity and continuity than anything that could have been offered by the tumultuous rugby environment before 1914. In a conservative wartime environment, rugby union was quick to set aside many of its internal divisions, to emphasise its loyalty to the cause and to create an enduring image in the public mind that it, above all others, was the game that shaped the qualities now being displayed on the battlefield. The quest for unity extended to the reinstatement of defectors to rugby league. At the same time, the incipient rival code lacked the numbers, especially among schoolboys, to sustain public interest and meaningful competitions during the war in the way that rugby union could. The threat of a professional game that many had feared after 1908 quickly evaporated to a few small pockets. Rugby union was therefore able to emerge from the war years with relative unity and increased respectability, and to secure by the early 1920s a much better claim to the title of 'national game' than could have been imagined earlier in the century.[1]

As rugby became a significant cultural force within twentieth century New Zealand society, the 1905 All Blacks grew in status as a major part of its essential 'creation myth'. How else could the importance of rugby to successive generations be understood without recalling those who gave the national team its name and achieved such a startling record on the first tour to the fields of Britain where the game had originated? While George Nicholson and others among the touring team may have believed that the 1903 side to Australia was a better combination, that team was not the 'All Blacks' and did not have the drama of Wales and the ultimate tragedy of Deans and Gallaher or the symbolism of the Mother Country to sustain the same fascination with it. Consequently, so much writing on New Zealand rugby begins with 1905 rather than with the Native team or the early tours to Australia. More importantly, almost all of it displays conventional traits of nostalgia in which selected elements of the past are idealised and in which unpleasant and contradictory aspects are ignored or marginalised because they do not fit the desire to celebrate, or validate, the 'national game'. Every generation of New Zealand rugby followers and critics during the twentieth century, dissatisfied with a particular loss or more generally disillusioned with the dour methods often used by the All Blacks, has looked back to an earlier period when players and tactics were apparently better. In recent years, amid the upheavals of professionalism and the frequent reminders that the All Blacks are not invincible, this nostalgia has seemed stronger than ever. It reveals itself in a hybrid memory of rural rugby imagery and great performances by past All Black teams and individual players – all of which apparently stem from the magnificent men of 1905.[2] The danger of such nostalgia is that it saddles successive generations of players and administrators with unreasonable, if not impossible, public expectations and produces unnecessary scapegoating and vitriol when these are not met.

The determination of some historians to see the tour of the 1905 All Blacks as an embodiment of colonial manhood and emergent New Zealand nationalism, or as the benchmark for everything virtuous in rugby, does not stand scrutiny. What this book suggests is that the tour is, indeed, symbolic of the complexity of New Zealand rugby and its place in the world – symbolic of a game in which the strategies and ideals were, and always have been, contested at every turn. It follows that if we are to understand the undoubted importance of rugby, and sport more generally, within contemporary New Zealand society, and have some sense of what the future may hold, it is crucial to avoid assumptions, clichés and nostalgia when considering where it came from.

THE 1905 TEAM

DIXON, George Henry
Born 24 December 1859, Huddersfield, England
Died 8 March 1940, Auckland
Position team manager

Dixon came to New Zealand in 1879 and played rugby for the Albert club, Auckland, as a halfback. He served as Auckland RFU secretary 1887–1900 and became a life member in 1911. He served on and generally chaired the NZRFU Management Committee 1901–10, 1913–18. He was president of the union 1911–12, and became its first life member in 1921. An accountant, Dixon was a co-founder of the *New Zealand Free Lance* and sometime manager of the *New Zealand Observer* and *New Zealand Times*. In 1906 he wrote *The Triumphant Tour of the New Zealand Footballers*, based on his diary of the All Black tour. Such was his dedication to the game, he named his son Rugby Laurence Dixon.

DUNCAN, James
Born 12 November 1869, Dunedin
Died 19 October 1953, Dunedin
Position coach

A brilliant tactician who is commonly regarded as having devised the five-eighths system, Duncan played 50 matches for Otago 1889–1903. He captained New Zealand against New South Wales in 1901 and on the 1903 tour of Australia, and coached the team that defeated Great Britain in 1904. He served on the Otago RFU Management Committee 1906–11, refereed the first test between the All Blacks and Anglo-Welsh in 1908 and coached various Otago Boys' High School teams during the 1920s and 1930s.

ABBOTT, Harold Louis ('Bunny')
Born 17 June 1882, Camerontown
Died 16 January 1972, Palmerston North
Education Puni School, Taranaki
Occupation farrier

Biographical details are derived from R. H. Chester and N. A. C. McMillan, *Encyclopedia of New Zealand Rugby*, Auckland: Moa, 1981; Biographical Clippings, Alexander Turnbull Library, Wellington.

Height and weight	1.79 m, 82 kg
Province	Taranaki 1904–06, 1914; Wanganui 1907–09
Position	wing three-quarter
New Zealand career	1905–06: 11 matches (1 international)

Abbott initially worked in North Auckland kauri forests before serving in two New Zealand contingents in South Africa and beginning his rugby career in army matches. A poisoned leg limited him to only 10 matches on the 1905 tour, although he played against France and for British Columbia against the All Blacks. He played provincial rugby until 1909 and returned for one game in 1914. A noted professional sprinter, he also became inspector of plating for Central Racing Districts. Still running his own smithy and shoeing horses in his mid-80s, he was the second-to-last survivor of the touring team after Billy Wallace.

BOOTH, Ernest Edward ('General')

Born	24 February 1876, Teschmakers
Died	18 October 1935, Christchurch
Education	Clyde Quay School, Wellington
Occupation	journalist
Height and weight	1.70 m, 74 kg
Province	Otago 1896, 1900–02, 1904–07; New South Wales 1908–09
Position	fullback, wing three-quarter
New Zealand career	1905–06, 1907: 24 matches (3 internationals)

Booth began his provincial career with Otago in 1896 but had only limited opportunities in Britain. He played in the French international. Continuing to represent Otago until 1907, he toured Australia with the All Blacks during that season. Moving to Sydney, Booth played for New South Wales in 1908–09 and accompanied the Wallabies to Britain as a press correspondent. He served with the Australian forces in the First World War as secretary to the YMCA. Returning to New Zealand, he was appointed professional coach by the Southland RFU during the early 1920s, a move that caused controversy with the NZRFU in terms of its amateur regulations. The job description was redefined and Booth continued to coach.

CASEY, Stephen Timothy

Born	20 December 1882, Dunedin
Died	10 August 1960, Dunedin
Education	Christian Brothers' School, Dunedin
Occupation	storeman
Height and weight	1.78 m, 78 kg
Province	Otago 1903–04, 1906–13
Position	hooker
New Zealand career	1905–06, 1907, 1908: 38 matches (8 internationals)

With George Tyler, Casey formed a powerful hooking partnership in the 2-3-2 scrum and played all of the international fixtures in Britain. He toured Australia with the All Blacks in 1907 and played one international against the Anglo-Welsh in 1908, but was not selected again, although he continued to represent Otago until 1913.

CORBETT, John

Born	1 January 1880, Reefton
Died	11 April 1945, Ratapiko
Education	unknown
Occupation	baker
Height and weight	1.80 m, 87 kg
Province	West Coast 1904–07, Buller 1908–10
Position	forward
New Zealand career	1905–06: 16 matches (no internationals)

Corbett had an unusual representative career in that West Coast did not play a game from 1896 to September 1905. Nevertheless, he was selected for Canterbury-West Coast against the 1904 British team, and for the South Island during the same season. His opportunities in Britain were limited in part by injury but also by the superior form of other loose forwards. He played for the South Island in 1906 and 1909 and for West Coast-Buller against the 1908 Anglo-Welsh. Served as a Buller selector in 1915.

CUNNINGHAM, William

Born	8 July 1874, Rangiaohia
Died	3 September 1927, Auckland
Education	unknown
Occupation	blacksmith
Height and weight	1.80 m, 92 kg
Province	Auckland 1899–1902, 1904–13, NZ Maori 1910, 1912
Position	lock
New Zealand career	1901, 1905–06, 1907, 1908: 39 matches (9 internationals)

Cunningham played his early rugby in Waihi, from where he first represented Auckland. Although a very late addition to the touring party, he was indispensable in locking the 2-3-2 scrum and his absence from the Welsh international because of a heavy cold undoubtedly hampered the team. Cunningham toured Australia in 1907 and played throughout the series against the Anglo-Welsh. Under Billy Stead's captaincy, he then toured Australia with the first New Zealand Maori team in 1910. His 103-match first-class career finished at the age of 39. He served as an Auckland selector in 1920.

DEANS, Robert George ('Tussock')

Born	19 February 1884, Christchurch
Died	30 September 1908, Christchurch
Education	Christchurch Boys' High School
Occupation	farmer
Height and weight	1.83 m, 83 kg
Province	Canterbury 1903–04, 1906–08
Position	centre
New Zealand career	1905–06, 1908: 24 matches (5 internationals)

The youngest member of the touring party, Deans will forever be remembered for the controversy of his non-try against Wales, yet he was also one of the best backs on the tour, appearing in all of the British internationals. Work commitments on the family property at Homebush kept him out of the 1907 tour to Australia, and injury kept him out of the first two tests against the Anglo Welsh in 1908, although he returned to score a try in the third. It was a considerable shock to all rugby followers when Deans died two months later, following complications after an appendicitis operation. On his deathbed he reportedly reiterated that he had scored against Wales.

GALLAHER, David

Born	30 October 1873, Ramelton, Ireland
Died	4 October 1917, Passchendaele, Belgium
Education	Katikati School
Occupation	foreman
Height and weight	1.83 m, 84 kg
Province	Auckland 1896–97, 1899, 1900, 1903–05, 1909
Position	wing-forward
New Zealand career	1903, 1904, 1905–06: 36 matches (6 internationals)

Contrary to many accounts, Gallaher (originally Gallagher) was born in 1873, not 1876. His family came to New Zealand from Ireland in 1878 and took up land at Katikati. Gallaher moved to Auckland in the mid-1890s. He then served as a sergeant in the 6th New Zealand Contingent to the South African War in 1901 and finished his service as squadron sergeant major in the 10th Contingent. Selected for the 1903 tour of Australia as a hooker, he ended it as wing-forward – a position he seldom took for Auckland. In Britain, where his wing-forward play was always keenly debated and often savagely criticised, Gallaher missed the Irish international owing to a leg injury. At the end of the tour he and Billy Stead wrote *The Complete Rugby Footballer on the New Zealand System* in less than three weeks to meet a commission by the *Daily Mail*. Gallaher retired from rugby at the end of the tour and served as Auckland sole selector 1906–16 and a New Zealand selector 1907–14. In an emergency, he played one game for Auckland in 1909. After his younger brother was killed in action, Gallaher enlisted in 1916 at the age of 43. He died of wounds received in the attack on Gravenstafel Spur,

Flanders, Belgium, on 4 October 1917, and is buried in the Nine Elms Cemetery at Poperinghe. In 1922 the Auckland RFU honoured his memory with the Gallaher Shield for its senior championship, and internationals between the All Blacks and France are now contested for the Dave Gallaher Trophy.

GILLETT, George Arthur

Born	23 April 1877, Leeston
Died	12 September 1956, Auckland
Education	Hamilton East School
Occupation	tramways employee
Height and weight	1.83 m, 83 kg
Province	Auckland 1899, 1906–09
Position	fullback, wing-forward
New Zealand career	1905–06, 1907, 1908: 38 matches (8 internationals)

Gillett first represented Auckland from the Karangahake club near Waihi. He then spent several years in Kalgoorlie, Western Australia, and is believed to have represented the state at Australian rules. Back in New Zealand by the beginning of 1905, he played for the Merivale club in Christchurch and was selected for the South Island without playing for Canterbury. In Britain, Gillett demonstrated his versatility by playing four internationals at fullback and deputising as wing-forward for Gallaher in other matches. He toured Australia in 1907 and played two internationals against the Anglo-Welsh in 1908. Switching to rugby league in 1911, Gillett was selected for the New Zealand tour to Australia and then toured Britain with an Australasian team during the 1911–12 season. An executive member of the Auckland Rugby League in 1912, he became a full-time organiser for the game in the North Island. Reinstated to rugby union during the First World War, he was a Poverty Bay selector 1917–18. Gillett later became a publican in Hamilton.

GLASGOW, Frederick Turnbull

Born	17 August 1880, Dunedin
Died	20 February 1939, Wellington
Education	Wellington College
Occupation	bank officer
Height and weight	1.78 m, 84 kg
Province	Wellington 1899–1900; Taranaki 1901–04; Hawke's Bay 1906; Southland 1908–09
Position	loose forward
New Zealand career	1905–06, 1908: 35 matches (6 internationals)

Glasgow did not play for the Wellington College XV but frequent transfers as a bank officer led to a varied rugby career with four provinces. He played all of the internationals in Britain as a loose forward and was recalled as a hooker for the last international against the Anglo-Welsh in 1908. His last first-class game was at Trentham Army Camp in 1918, aged 38. After coaching and refereeing in King Country during the 1920s, he served on the NZRFU Management Committee 1931–36, and Executive Council 1937–39. Glasgow was also liaison officer with the 1937 Springbok team.

GLENN, William Spiers

Born	21 February 1877, Greymouth
Died	5 October 1953, Wanganui
Education	Manaia School
Occupation	auctioneer
Height and weight	1.80 m, 82 kg
Province	Taranaki 1901–05, 1912
Position	loose forward
New Zealand career	1904, 1905–06: 19 matches (2 internationals)

Although he played against the 1904 British team, Billy Glenn's injuries and the strong competition for places restricted his opportunities in Britain to 13 matches including the French international. With Eric Harper, he returned home directly rather than accompanying the team to North America. Aside from a surprise appearance for Taranaki against Wanganui in 1912, Glenn effectively retired from all rugby after the tour. Originally an auctioneer, he farmed near Wanganui from 1906 and became prominent in the racing industry as a breeder, owner and trustee of the Wanganui Jockey Club. He served on many other public bodies and on the NZRFU Management Committee 1922–23. Reaching the rank of major with the Royal Field Artillery during the First World War, Glenn was awarded the MC. He was the first All Black to enter Parliament – representing Rangitikei for the Reform Party 1919–28.

HARPER, Eric Tristram

Born	1 December 1877, Christchurch
Died	30 April 1918, Palestine
Education	Christchurch Boys' High School
Occupation	solicitor
Height and weight	1.80 m, 80 kg
Province	Canterbury 1900–02, 1904–05
Position	three-quarter
New Zealand career	1904, 1905–06: 11 matches (2 internationals)

Injuries and disappointing form during the tour restricted Harper's opportunities. He played only four of the first 17 games but won a place in the French international. He played no representative rugby after the tour, although he served on the Canterbury RFU Management Committee for several years. An exceptional track athlete who won national titles in the 440 and 880 yards, he was also a keen mountaineer and played cricket for Canterbury in 1907. Serving with the

Canterbury Mounted Rifles in Palestine, he was killed while quietening horses during an artillery bombardment.

HUNTER, James

Born	6 March 1879, Hawera
Died	14 December 1962, Wanganui
Education	Wanganui Collegiate
Occupation	farmer
Height and weight	1.68 m, 73 kg
Province	Taranaki 1898, 1900–04, 1906–08
Position	second five-eighth
New Zealand career	1905–06, 1907, 1908: 36 games (11 internationals)

Initially a halfback and then a wing or fullback for Taranaki, Hunter developed as a five-eighth whose remarkable try-scoring exploits (44 from 24 matches, including all five internationals) made him a star of the 1905 tour. He captained the New Zealand team on the preliminary tour to Australia in 1905, on the next tour to Australia in 1907 and once against the Anglo-Welsh in 1908. He finished his career with 49 tries in 36 matches for New Zealand. His son Robert Deans Hunter was killed in Greece in 1941.

JOHNSTON, William ('Massa')

Born	13 September 1881, Dunedin
Died	9 January 1951, Sydney
Education	unknown
Occupation	iron worker
Height and weight	1.85 m, 83 kg
Province	Otago 1904
Position	loose forward
New Zealand career	1905–06, 1907: 27 matches (3 internationals)

Johnston's only representative rugby consisted of six games for Otago in 1904. He reportedly liked 'robust' play and was the first man to be sent off in a Ranfurly Shield match. Restricted by illness and injuries in Britain, he appeared in just 13 matches. A throat infection forced him to remain in London at the end of the tour, and he returned home with Seeling. Reappearing in rugby in 1907, he toured Australia and played in all three internationals. Johnston then toured with the Professional All Blacks in 1907–08 and signed for Wigan in 1908, then Warrington in 1910. He spent his later life in Australia and became commissionaire at the Royal Sydney Agricultural Showgrounds.

McDONALD, Alexander

Born	23 April 1883, Dunedin
Died	4 May 1967, Wellington
Education	George St School, Dunedin
Occupation	brewery worker
Height and weight	1.78 m, 83 kg
Province	Otago 1904, 1906-09, 1911-14, 1918-19
Position	loose forward
New Zealand career	1905-06, 1907, 1908, 1913: 41 matches (8 internationals)

One of the most durable contributors to New Zealand rugby both as a player and administrator, McDonald represented Otago for 15 years. In Britain he played 17 matches, including the first four internationals. After touring Australia in 1907 and appearing against the Anglo-Welsh in 1908, he captained the All Blacks to North America in 1913. A member of the Otago RFU Management Committee 1914-15, 1920-28, and vice-president 1928-32, he moved to Wellington in 1933 and served on the NZRFU Management Committee 1935-36 and Council 1937-50. Variously coach of the Kaikorai and Wellington College Old Boys' clubs and the Otago and Wellington provincial teams, McDonald was also a North Island and South Island selector, and a New Zealand selector 1929-32, 1944-48. Co-manager of the 1938 All Blacks to Australia and assistant manager (or, supposedly, coach) of the 1949 team to South Africa, where he was marginalised by the players in the manner of Jimmy Duncan in 1905. McDonald became an NZRFU life member in 1951.

McGREGOR, Duncan

Born	16 July 1881, Kaiapoi
Died	11 March 1947, Timaru
Education	unknown
Occupation	railway worker
Height and weight	1.75 m, 74 kg
Province	Canterbury 1900, 02-03, 06, Wellington 1904-06
Position	three-quarter
New Zealand career	1903, 1904, 1905-06: 31 matches (4 internationals)

McGregor was a prolific try scorer who totalled 66 in 59 first-class games, including 16 from 10 matches for Canterbury and the South Island in 1902, two against the 1904 British team, four against England at Crystal Palace, and 16 from 14 matches in Britain and North America after missing the first 12 matches of the tour owing to injury. McGregor toured with the Professional All Blacks and joined the Merthyr Tydfil club in Wales in 1908. After involvement with a sports shop in Gloucestershire, he suffered an ankle injury that ended his playing career He returned to New Zealand in 1913, refereed rugby league internationals and was made a life member of the New Zealand Rugby League in 1920.

MACKRELL, William Henry Clifton

Born	20 July 1881, Milton, New South Wales
Died	15 July 1917, Auckland
Education	unknown
Occupation	printer
Height and weight	1.78 m, 79 kg
Province	Auckland 1904–05
Position	hooker
Career	1905–06: 7 matches (1 international)

Arriving in Britain with flu, Mackrell did not play until the 23rd match, against Munster on 28 November. By this time Casey and Tyler were established as the hookers, and Mackrell played three of his seven tour games as a loose forward. He went to Britain with the Professional All Blacks in 1907–08 but appeared in only 10 matches on that tour. Mackrell continued to play rugby league until 1912, when a kick to the head ended his career and might also have contributed to his early death from a paralytic seizure in 1917.

MYNOTT, Harold Jonas ('Simon')

Born	4 June 1876, Auckland
Died	2 January 1924, New Plymouth
Education	Central School, New Plymouth
Occupation	tinsmith
Height and weight	1.70 m, 74 kg
Province	Taranaki
Position	first five-eighth
New Zealand career	1905–06, 1907, 1910: 39 matches (8 internationals)

Mynott is perhaps unfairly remembered for his poor performance against Wales in the absence of Stead, but he was a talented player in his own right who enjoyed a long career for Taranaki, especially in combination with Jimmy Hunter, and toured Australia with All Black teams in 1907 and 1910. Among his 20 matches in Britain and France was an appearance on the wing against Ireland when injuries had severely depleted the stocks in that position. At 34 years and 28 days, Mynott was the oldest back to represent New Zealand until Joe Stanley and Frank Bunce during the 1990s. A Taranaki selector 1910–14 and All Black selector in 1913.

NEWTON, Frederick ('Fatty')

Born	7 May 1881, Christchurch
Died	10 December 1955, Christchurch
Education	unknown
Occupation	railway fitter
Height and weight	1.83 m, 95 kg
Province	Canterbury 1901, 1904, Buller 1908

Position	lock, loose forward
New Zealand career	1905–06: 19 matches (3 internationals)

The 1905 tour, in which he played 19 matches including the internationals against England, Wales and France, represented most of Newton's first-class career. He played once for Canterbury in 1901, six times in 1904, and once for the South Island in 1905. His only game after the tour was for Buller against Marlborough in 1908. He was the heaviest player in the touring party.

NICHOLSON, George William ('Long Nick')

Born	3 August 1878, Auckland
Died	13 September 1968, Auckland
Education	Newton East School, Auckland
Occupation	bootmaker
Height and weight	1.91 m, 87 kg
Province	Auckland 1901–04, 1906–09
Position	loose forward
New Zealand career	1903, 1904, 1905–06, 1907: 39 matches (4 internationals)

Nicholson began his rugby career as a three-quarter but switched to loose forward and became something of a lineout specialist. He toured Australia in 1903, played against the British in 1904 and appeared 18 times in Britain. Although he did not appear in any of the internationals, he scored the vital try to defeat Cardiff. Called into the 1907 All Blacks while on holiday in Australia, he became involved in controversy later in the same season when he switched to the Ponsonby club amid rumours that he had been offered inducements to stop him going to rugby league. As a referee, Nicholson controlled the international against Australia in 1913. He was an Auckland selector 1919, 1922–24, 1930–31 and New Zealand selector 1920–21, 1929–30, 1936–37 and became a life member of the Ponsonby club, the Auckland RFU and the Auckland Referees Association.

O'SULLIVAN, James Michael

Born	5 February 1883, Okaiawa
Died	21 December 1960, Hawera
Education	Matapu School, Taranaki
Occupation	farmer
Height and weight	1.78 m, 86 kg
Province	Taranaki 1901–04, 1906, 1908–09
Position	loose forward
New Zealand career	1905–06, 1907: 29 matches (5 internationals)

One of the most consistent players in the touring party, O'Sullivan appeared in 20 matches in Britain, including the four internationals. A broken collarbone against Cardiff ended his tour, although he stayed with the All Blacks during the French and North American legs. O'Sullivan toured Australia in 1907 and later became president and a life member of the Taranaki RFU.

ROBERTS, Frederick

Born	7 April 1881, Wellington
Died	21 July 1956, Wellington
Education	Thorndon School, Wellington
Occupation	clerk
Height and weight	1.70 m, 78 kg
Province	Wellington 1901–04, 1906–12
Position	halfback
New Zealand career	1905–06, 1907, 1908, 1910: 52 matches (12 internationals)

Although he played rugby at school, Roberts turned to soccer for two seasons before coming back to rugby. As the only halfback selected for the 1905 tour, he endured a heavy workload, appearing in 29 matches including four internationals before Billy Stead played as halfback against France. Roberts toured Australia in 1907 and 1910, on the later occasion as captain, and played against the Anglo-Welsh in 1908. A Wellington selector during the 1920s, he also gave long service to the Oriental club.

SEELING, Charles Edward ('Bronco')

Born	14 May 1883, Wanganui
Died	29 May 1956, Stalybridge, England
Education	Wanganui District High School
Occupation	slaughterman
Height and weight	1.83 m, 86 kg
Province	Wanganui 1903; Auckland 1904, 1906–09
Position	loose forward
New Zealand career	1904, 1905–06, 1907, 1908: 39 matches (11 internationals)

Seeling played his early rugby as a back before developing into an outstanding loose forward. On tour he appeared 25 times, including all of the internationals. He remained in England with the ill Massa Johnston, returning to New Zealand in late March. Seeling toured Australia in 1907 and played the three internationals against the Anglo-Welsh in 1908. He switched to rugby league at the end of 1909 and played for Wigan until 1922. His son Charlie jnr was also a leading league player in Britain. The licensee of the Roebuck Hotel, Wigan, Bronco Seeling was killed in a motor accident shortly before his proposed return to New Zealand.

SMITH, George William

Born	20 September 1874, Auckland
Died	8 December 1954, Oldham, England
Education	Wellesley St School, Auckland
Occupation	meatworker
Height and weight	1.70 m, 76 kg
Province	Auckland 1896–97, 1901, 1906
Position	three-quarter
New Zealand career	1897, 1901, 1905–06: 39 matches (2 internationals)

Smith was a renowned sprinter and hurdler who won 14 national titles 1898–1904 as well as two Australasian titles and the 1902 British AAA quarter-mile hurdles, an event in which he also set an unofficial world record. He was also a successful jockey during the 1890s, although he probably did not ride the winner of the 1894 New Zealand Cup as some have claimed. Smith's rugby career was sporadic and brilliant. After a few matches for Auckland, he toured Australia in 1897, scoring 11 tries, including five in one match against New England. Reappearing for Auckland in 1901, he was selected for New Zealand against New South Wales before disappearing from rugby for another four years. In Britain he scored 19 tries in 19 matches – including two vital tries against Scotland, but after severely injuring his shoulder against Munster he made only one further appearance. Omitted from the 1907 tour to Australia, despite good club form, Smith then became one of the leading lights of the Professional All Black team. He returned briefly to New Zealand before signing for Oldham until 1916, when a broken leg ended his playing career at the age of 42. After working for a textile company, he was on the Oldham coaching staff from 1932 until his retirement in 1935.

STEAD, John William

Born	18 September 1877, Invercargill
Died	21 July 1958, Bluff
Education	Southland Boys' High School
Occupation	bootmaker
Height and weight	1.73 m, 64 kg
Province	Southland 1896–1908
Position	five-eighth
New Zealand career	1903, 1904, 1905–06, 1908: 42 matches (7 internationals)

After touring Australia in 1903 and captaining New Zealand against the British in 1904, Stead was appointed Gallaher's vice-captain in 1905. In a remarkably talented backline he still emerged as one of the star players in Britain – appearing in 27 matches, including all of the internationals except that against Wales, from which his absence was decisive. He captained the All Blacks against Ireland in the absence of Gallaher and appeared at halfback against France when Roberts was rested. He did not tour Australia in 1907 but returned to captain the All Blacks against the Anglo-Welsh in 1908 and finished his career as vice-captain of the first New Zealand Maori team to Australia, in 1910. Stead was never in a losing team in his 42 appearances for New Zealand. He coached New Zealand Maori teams and the All Blacks in the first two internationals against the 1921 Springboks. Stead also wrote for the *Southland Times* and was rugby columnist for *New Zealand Truth* during the 1920s.

THOMSON, Hector Douglas ('Mona')

Born	20 February 1881, Napier
Died	9 August 1939, Wellington
Education	Wellington College
Occupation	civil servant
Height	1.73 m, 68 kg
Province	Wellington 1900, 1906, 1908; Auckland 1901–02, Canterbury 1903; Wanganui 1904–05
Position	three-quarter
New Zealand career	1905–06, 1908: 15 matches (1 international)

Frequent transfers as a civil servant saw Thomson play for four provinces and both islands. Leg injuries restricted him to only 11 matches during the 1905 tour, although he scored 14 tries, including six against British Columbia. He was selected for one international against the 1908 Anglo-Welsh, but an arm injury ended his career in that season. He retired as an under-secretary in the Immigration Department.

TYLER, George Alfred ('Bubs')

Born	10 February 1879, Auckland
Died	15 April 1942, Auckland
Education	unknown
Occupation	boatbuilder
Height and weight	1.78 m, 82 kg
Province	Auckland 1899–1907, 1910–11
Position	hooker
New Zealand career:	1903, 1904, 1905–06: 36 matches (7 internationals)

After touring Australia in 1903 and playing against the British in 1904, Tyler partnered Steve Casey as a very effective hooking partnership in the 2–3–2 scrum. He appeared in 23 tour matches including, all five internationals. Selected for the 1907 All Blacks, he was unable to tour owing to his boatbuilding business, but continued to play for Auckland until 1911. Tyler was also a keen swimmer who won Auckland titles and a rower and yachtsman. He later served as dockmaster with the Auckland Harbour Board 1910–42. As rugby columnist for the *New Zealand Herald* during the 1920s, he described the departing 1924–25 All Blacks as 'the weakest team New Zealand has ever had – weak in the scrums, weak on defence and lacking in pace'.

WALLACE, William Joseph ('Carbine')

Born	2 August 1878, Wellington
Died	2 March 1972, Wellington
Education	Mt Cook School, Wellington
Occupation	iron master
Height and weight	1.73 m, 76 kg
Province	Wellington 1897, 1899, 1901–04, 1906–08; Otago 1900
Position	utility back
New Zealand career	1903, 1904, 1905–06, 1907, 1908: 51 matches (11 internationals)

As either a three-quarter or fullback, Wallace quickly established himself as one of the great players of New Zealand rugby. After touring Australia in 1903 and playing against the 1904 British, he appeared 26 times on the 1905 tour, including all of the internationals. A prolific goalkicker and try scorer by the standards of his time, Wallace totaled 246 points on tour, was the first New Zealand player to score 500 points in first-class rugby, and his final record of 379 for the All Blacks was only surpassed by Don Clarke during the early 1960s. He toured Australia in 1907 and played twice against the Anglo-Welsh in 1908 before cartilage problems ended his career. Supporters then gave him 400 sovereigns to establish his own iron foundry. Wallace gave long service to the Poneke club and the Wellington RFU, and became a life member of both. He served on the NZRFU Management Committee 1931–36 and Council 1937–38. He managed the 1932 All Blacks to Australia and co-managed the 1935 New Zealand Maori team to Australia. The last survivor of the touring team, he was the second-to-last survivor of the Welsh international after Willie Llewellyn, who died in 1973.

STATISTICS

Matches in Australia and New Zealand

	Opponent	Venue	Result	Crowd
1 July	Auckland	Auckland	Won 9–3	7,000
8 July	New South Wales	Sydney	Won 19–0	30,000
12 July	Metropolitan Union	Sydney	Won 22–3	10,000
15 July	New South Wales	Sydney	Drew 8–8	35,000
22 July	Otago-Southland	Dunedin	Drew 10–10	10,000
27 July	Canterbury	Christchurch	Won 21–3	5,000
29 July	Wellington Province	Wellington	Lost 0–3	4,000

Matches in the British Isles, France and the United States

	Opponent	Venue	Result	Crowd	Receipts
16 September	Devonshire	Exeter	Won 55–4	8,000	£300
21 September	Cornwall	Camborne	Won 41–0	4,926	£156
23 September	Bristol Club	Bristol	Won 41–0	8,000	£300
28 September	Northampton	Northampton	Won 32–0	5,000	£200
30 September	Leicester Club	Leicester	Won 28–0	15,000	£392
4 October	Middlesex	Stanford Bridge	Won 34–0	16,000	£800
7 October	Durham County	Durham	Won 16–3	5,000	£180
11 October	Hartlepool Clubs	West Hartlepool	Won 63–0	12,000	£388
14 October	Northumberland City Clubs	North Shields	Won 31–0	10,000	£300
19 October	Gloucester City Clubs	Gloucester	Won 44–0	12,000	£569
21 October	Somerset	Taunton	Won 23–0	8,851	£465
25 October	Devonport Albion Club	Devonport	Won 21–3	19,458	£636
28 October	Midland Counties	Leicester	Won 21–5	17,000	£772

Date	Opponent	Venue	Result	Attendance	Receipts
1 November	Surrey	Richmond	Won 11–0	8,000	£536
4 November	Blackheath Club	Blackheath	Won 32–0	15,000	£1000
7 November	Oxford University	Oxford	Won 47–0	6,000	£500
9 November	Cambridge University	Cambridge	Won 14–0	5,000	£450
11 November	Richmond Club	Richmond	Won 17–0	10,000	£700
15 November	Bedford XV	Bedford	Won 41–0	8,000	£450
18 November	SCOTLAND	Inverleith	Won 12–7	21,000	£1,200
22 November	West of Scotland	Glasgow	Won 22–0	10,000	£500
25 November	IRELAND	Dublin	Won 15–0	18,000	£1,000
28 November	Munster	Limerick	Won 33–0	4,000	£100
2 December	ENGLAND	Crystal Palace	Won 15–0	45,000	£2,500
6 December	Cheltenham Club	Cheltenham	Won 18–0	7,768	£529
9 December	Cheshire	Birkenhead	Won 34–0	10,000	£500
13 December	Yorkshire	Headingley	Won 40–0	30,000	£1,600
16 December	WALES	Cardiff	Lost 0–3	50,000	£2,650
21 December	Glamorganshire	Swansea	Won 9–0	16,000	£1,000
23 December	Newport Club	Newport	Won 6–3	15,000	£800
26 December	Cardiff Club	Cardiff	Won 10–8	50,000	£1,861
30 December	Swansea	Swansea	Won 4–3	30,000	£1,200
			830–39		**£25,034**
1906					
1 January	FRANCE	Paris	Won 38–8	7,000	£500
			868–47		
9 February	British Columbia	Berkeley	Won 43–6	1,500	
13 February	British Columbia	San Francisco	Won 65–6	1,500	
			976–59		

An exhibition match was played at Brooklyn, New York on 1 February 1906. Six New Zealanders joined the local side. New Zealand won 43–13.

Statement of accounts: Great Britain, France, North America 1905–06

Dr	£	s	d
Daily allowances to players	1,041	9	0
Board & lodgings	2,209	1	8
Medical expenses	117	6	9
Transit expenses	1,608	19	10
Selectors expenses	28	10	1
Gratitudes to servants, stewards, etc.	232	18	5
Cablegrams	30	6	8
Postage, telegrams & stationary	49	4	0
Laundry	70	18	7
Entertainment	49	18	3
Presentations	19	14	0
Uniforms	150	14	5
Training expenses	11	12	4
Photographs	36	16	3
Presentation of medals to team	152	2	0
Reception expenses at Auckland	162	15	8
Debentures redeemed at guarantee refunded	1,722	13	0
Interests and exchanges on debentures redeemed and guarantees refunded	89	19	5
Sundries	3	0	2
Balance £7,788 15s 4d less £3 4s 2d shown on preliminary expenses 1904–05	**7,785**	**1**	**2**
Cr			
By our share of takings in 35 matches	14,924	4	6
Exchange on remittances	47	12	0
Debentures and guarantees	1,722	3	0
	16,694	9	6
Credit balance	**8,908**	**10**	**4**

Published in *NZ Referee*, 2 May 1906, p. 64.

NOTES

Introduction

1. Keith Sinclair, *A Destiny Apart: New Zealand's search for national identity*, Wellington: Allen & Unwin, 1986, p. 149.
2. Jock Phillips, *A Man's Country? The image of the Pakeha male: A history*, Auckland: Penguin, 1987, p. 109.
3. Ibid, p. 111.
4. John Nauright, 'Sport, Manhood and Empire: British responses to the New Zealand rugby rour of 1905', *International Journal of the History of Sport*, Vol. 8, No. 2 (1991); 'Colonial Manhood and Imperial Race Virility: British responses to post-Boer War colonial rugby tours', in John Nauright & Timothy J. L. Chandler, eds, *Making Men: Rugby and masculine identity*, London: Frank Cass, 1996.
5. In order, J. A. Buttery, comp., *Why the All Blacks Triumphed*, London: Daily Mail, 1906; D. Gallaher & J. W. Stead, *The Complete Rugby Footballer on the New Zealand System*, London: Methuen, 1906; G. Dixon, *1905: The Triumphant Tour of the New Zealand Footballers*, Wellington: Geddis & Bloomfield, 1906.
6. Ron Palenski, *Century in Black: 100 years of All Black test rugby*, Auckland: Hodder Moa Beckett, 2003, pp. 17–18.
7. See Dixon, *The Triumphant Tour*, esp. pp. 81, 143; Gallaher & Stead, *The Complete Rugby Footballer*, esp. pp. 116–18; *Why the All Blacks Triumphed*, esp. pp. 7–8, 10–13; G. T. Alley, *With the British Rugby Team in New Zealand, 1930*, Christchurch: Simpson & Williams, 1930, pp. 21, 29, 46.
8. Among those who have followed Sinclair and Phillips are Geoff Fougere, 'Sport, Culture and Identity: The case of rugby football', in Davit Novitz & Bill Willmott, eds, *Culture and Identity in New Zealand*, Wellington: GP Books, 1989; Piet de Jong, *Saturday's Warriors: The building of a rugby stronghold*, Palmerston North, 1991; Finlay Macdonald, *The Game of Our Lives: The story of rugby and New Zealand – and how they've shaped each other*, Auckland: Viking, 1996; Robin Law, Hugh Campbell and John Dolan, eds, *Masculinities in Aotearoa/New Zealand*, Palmerston North: Dunmore Press, 1999; James Belich, *Paradise Reforged: A history of the New Zealanders from the 1880s to the year 2000*, Auckland: Penguin, 2001, esp. pp. 378–88. The outstanding exception is Caroline Daley, 'The Invention of 1905', in Greg Ryan, ed., *Tackling Rugby Myths: Rugby and New Zealand society 1854-2004*, Dunedin: University of Otago Press, 2005, pp. 69–87.
9. See in particular T. P. McLean, *Silver Fern: 150 years of New Zealand sport*, Auckland: Moa, 1990, pp. 37–42; *New Zealand Rugby Legends: 15 reflections*, Auckland: Moa, 1987, pp. 41–44, 47–48, 52; Palenski, *Century in Black*, p. 36; *The Jersey: The pride & the passion, the guts & the glory: What it means to wear the All Black jersey*, Auckland: Hodder Moa Beckett, 2001, pp. 35–39; *Our National Game*, Auckland: Moa Beckett, 1992, pp. 27–38. The most notable documentaries are *Mud and Glory*, Television New Zealand, 1991; *The Game of our Lives*, George Andrews Productions, 1996; *Legends of the All Blacks*, Television New Zealand, 1999.

NOTES

Chapter 1: Creating the Rugby World

1. Gareth Williams, 'Rugby', in Tony Mason, ed, *Sport in Britain: A social history*, Cambridge: Cambridge University Press, 1989, p. 308; W. J. Baker, 'William Webb Ellis and the Origins of Rugby Football: The life and death of a Victorian myth', *Albion*, Vol. 13, No. 2, 1981.
2. See Eric Dunning & Kenneth Sheard, *Barbarians, Gentlemen and Players: A sociological study of the development of rugby football*, Canberra: Australian National University Press, 1979, pp. 21–64.
3. Richard Holt, *Sport and the British: A modern history*, Oxford: Oxford University Press, 1989, pp. 80–84.
4. Dunning & Sheard, pp. 71–78; Tony Collins, *Rugby's Great Split: Class, culture and the origins of rugby league football*, London: Frank Cass, 1998, pp. 1–7.
5. Holt, pp. 85–86.
6. Williams, pp. 309–12.
7. Holt, pp. 104–06.
8. Ibid., pp. 96–105.
9. Gareth Williams, *1905 and All That: Essays on rugby football, sport and Welsh society*, Llandysul: Gomer, 1991, pp. 17–19; Collins, pp. 7–39, 53–54, 97–106; Holt, pp. 3, 161–73
10. Robert Gate, *Rugby League: An illustrated history*, London: A. Barker, 1989, pp. 14–16.
11. Collins, pp. 40–45, 123–29; Williams, 'Rugby', p. 313.
12. Collins, pp. 53–54, 112–22.
13. Ibid., pp. 57–59, 69, 75–76.
14. Ibid., pp. 132–36.
15. Ibid., pp. 137–48.
16. Ibid., pp. 167–79; P. Greenhalgh, 'The Work and Play Principle: The professional regulations of the Northern Rugby Football Union, 1898–1905', *International Journal of the History of Sport*, Vol. 9, No. 3, 1992.
17. Collins, pp. 155–57, 160–64.
18. See in particular J. O. C. Phillips, 'Rugby, War and the Mythology of the New Zealand Male', *New Zealand Journal of History*, Vol. 18, No. 2, 1984; *A Man's Country?*, pp. 86–130.
19. See J. R. Barclay, 'An Analysis of Trends in New Zealand Sport from 1840 to 1900', BA Hons essay, Massey University, 1977, p. 21; Phillips, *A Man's Country?*, p. 88; rev. edn, Auckland, 1996, p. 88; 'The Hard Man: Rugby and the formation of male identity in New Zealand', in Nauright & Chandler, p. 71. 50,000 affiliated players in 1890 would have constituted 59 per cent of the New Zealand male population aged 15–30. There is no evidence that even 5,000 players is a reliable figure.
20. See Greg Ryan, 'Rural Myth and Urban Actuality: The anatomy of All Black and New Zealand rugby 1884–1938', *New Zealand Journal of History*, Vol. 35, No. 1, (2001), pp. 45–69.
21. Len Richardson, 'The Invention of a National Game: The struggle for control', *History Now*, Vol. 1, No. 1, 1995, pp. 1–2; Geoffrey Vincent, 'To Uphold the Honour of the Province': Football in Canterbury, c.1854–c.1890', in Ryan, ed., *Tackling Rugby Myths*, pp. 15–17.
22. For example, A. C. Swan, *History of New Zealand Rugby Football 1870–1945*, Wellington: A. H. & A. W. Reed, 1948, pp. 1–33.
23. Vincent, pp. 17–21.
24. Phillips, *A Man's Country?*, p. 90.

25. Rollo Arnold, *Settler Kaponga 1881-1914: A frontier fragment of the western world*, Wellington: Victoria University Press, 1997, p. 159.
26. Ryan, 'Rural Myth', pp. 52-54.
27. John E. Martin, *The Forgotten Worker: The rural wage earner in nineteenth century New Zealand*, Wellington: Allen & Unwin/Trade Union History Project, 1990, pp. 14-15.
28. Ryan, 'Rural Myth', p. 55.
29. Greg Ryan, 'The Paradox of Maori Rugby 1870-1914', in Ryan, ed., *Tackling Rugby Myths*, pp. 90-91.
30. Michael King, 'Between Two Worlds', in G. W. Rice, ed., *The Oxford History of New Zealand*, 2nd edn, Auckland: Oxford University Press, 1992, pp. 290-93.
31. Ryan, 'The Paradox of Maori Rugby', p. 92.
32. Richardson, pp. 3-4.
33. R. H. Chester & N. A. C. McMillan, *The Encyclopedia of New Zealand Rugby*, Auckland: Moa, 1981, pp. 272-75, 280-82, 303-05, 321-23.
34. Ryan, 'Rural Myth', pp. 56-57; Swan, pp. 86-139, 176-209, 242-52.
35. Geoffrey T. Vincent, '"A Tendency to Roughness": Anti-heroic representations of New Zealand rugby 1890-1914', *Sporting Traditions*, Vol. 14, No. 1, 1997, pp. 93-97; Richardson, pp. 3-4.
36. A. C. Swan, *The New Zealand Rugby Football Union 1892-1967*, Wellington: A. H. & A. W. Reed, 1967, pp. 16-21; Phillips, *A Man's Country?*, pp. 96-97.
37. Richardson, p. 5.
38. Vincent, 'A Tendency to Roughness', p. 94.
39. Ibid, p. 99; Sean O'Hagan, *The Pride of Southern Rebels: On the occasion of the Otago Rugby Football Union centenary, 1881-1981*, Dunedin: Pilgrims South Press, 1981, pp. 52-53, 56.
40. Phillips, *A Man's Country?*, p. 92.
41. Ryan, 'Rural Myth', pp. 63-65.
42. O'Hagan, pp. 42-45; Irwin Hunter, *New Zealand Rugby Football: Some hints and criticisms*, Auckland: Whitcombe & Tombs, 1929, pp. 6-7.
43. Gallaher & Stead, p. 2.
44. Greg Ryan, *Forerunners of the All Blacks: The 1888-89 New Zealand Native Football Team in Britain, Australia and New Zealand*, Christchurch, Canterbury University Press, 1993, pp. 67-68, 79.
45. T. R. Ellison, *The Art of Rugby Football: With hints and instructions on every point of the game*, Wellington: Geddis & Bloomfield, 1902, pp. 53-54.
46. O'Hagan, pp. 47-50, 59-64; J. J. Stewart, *Rugby: Developments in the field of play*, Palmerston North: Massey University, 1997, pp. 64-66.

Chapter 2: Conflicts on the World Stage

1. R. H. Chester & N. A. C. McMillan, *The Visitors: The history of international rugby teams in New Zealand*, Auckland: Moa, 1990, pp. 16-28; *Centenary: 100 years of All Black rugby*, Auckland: Moa, 1984, pp. 17-20.
2. Chester & McMillan, *The Visitors*, pp. 29-44.
3. Ryan, *Forerunners*, pp. 106, 119-23.
4. Ibid., pp. 13-31.
5. *Press*, 19 July 1888, p. 5; *NZ Referee*, 10 August 1888, p. 140.
6. *NZ Referee*, 22 June 1888, p. 54; 6 July 1888, p. 79; 20 July 1888, p. 78; 23 November 1888, p. 9; *Press*, 18 July 1888, p. 6

NOTES

7. *Otago Witness*, 8 August 1889, p. 27.
8. For example, *The Times*, 11 October 1888, p. 6; 15 October 1888, p. 7; *Field*, 13 October 1888, p. 541; *Lyttelton Times*, 19 December 1888, p. 2.
9. Ellison, p. 68; Ryan, *Forerunners*, pp. 83–86.
10. *Field*, 23 February 1889, p. 272; *Press*, 6 June 1889, p. 5; Rev. F. Marshall, ed., *Football: The rugby union game*, London: Cassell, 1894, p. 506.
11. *Field*, 30 March 1889, p. 451.
12. T. Eyton, *Rugby Football (Past and Present) and the Tour of the Native Team in Britain Australia & New Zealand in 1888-89*, Palmerston North: Hart, 1896, pp. 19, 36, 64; *Lyttelton Times*, 19 December 1888, p. 2.
13. Eyton, p. 77.
14. *Athletic News*, 11 October 1888, p. 1; 25 October 1888, p. 1; *Press*, 16 April 1889, p. 3.
15. Miles Fairburn, *The Ideal Society and its Enemies: The foundations of modern New Zealand society 1850-1900*, Auckland: Auckland University Press, 1989, pp. 171–74; Raewyn Dalziel, 'The Politics of Settlement', in Rice, p. 104.
16. Vincent, 'To Uphold the Honour of the Province', pp. 17–22; Swan, *New Zealand Rugby Football*, passim.
17. Swan, *New Zealand Rugby Football Union*, pp. 15–21.
18. Ibid; pp. 22–28; Richardson, pp. 4–5.
19. Quoted in Chester & McMillan, *Centenary*, p. 44.
20. Chester & McMillan, *The Visitors*, pp. 67–69.
21. *New Zealand Free Lance*, 30 July 1904, p. 16.
22. *Lyttelton Times*, 27 July 1904, p. 5.
23. Chester & McMillan, *The Visitors*, pp. 69–70.
24. *Evening Post*, 15 August 1904, p. 2.
25. *New Zealand Herald*, 15 August 1904, p. 4.
26. *Evening Post*, 15 August 1904, p. 2.
27. *NZ Referee*, 24 August 1904, pp. 54–56; 21 September 1904, p. 52.
28. *Otago Daily Times*, 11 August 1904, p. 5; *Press*, 15 August 1904, p. 6. See also *NZ Referee*, 24 August 1904, pp. 54–56; 21 September 1904, p. 52.
29. *Press*, 15 August 1904, p. 6; *Otago Witness*, 17 August 1904, p. 57.
30. G. T. Vincent, 'Practical Imperialism: The Anglo-Welsh rugby tour of New Zealand, 1908', MA thesis, University of Canterbury, 1996, pp. 1–3, 26.
31. W. F. Mandle, 'Cricket and Australian Nationalism in the Nineteenth Century', *Journal of the Royal Australian Historical Society*, Vol. 59, Pt 4, 1973, pp. 236.
32. See D. Montefiore, *Cricket in the Doldrums: The struggle between private and public control in Australian cricket in the 1880s*, Sydney: Australian Society for Sports History, 1992.
33. *NZ Referee*, 19 October 1888, p. 259; 22 November 1888, p. 8; 15 April 1889, p. 6; 2 June 1889, p. 6; 3 June 1889; pp. 5–6; *Press*, 15 January 1889, p. 5; 27 April 1889, p. 6.
34. Gallaher & Stead, p. 241; *Why the All Blacks Triumphed*, p. 16.
35. Quoted in McLean, *New Zealand Rugby Legends*, pp. 12–13.
36. Collins, pp. 73–74.
37. NZRFU, AGM Minutes, 25 April 1902; *Lyttelton Times*, 26 April 1902, p. 8; 5 May 1902, p. 3.
38. NZRFU, Special Meeting Minutes, 5 June 1902.
39. NZRFU, Management Committee Minutes, 19 June 1902; 24 June 1902; NZRFU to RFU, 25 June 1902. I am grateful to Tony Collins for a copy of this letter.

40. NZRFU, Management Committee Minutes, 30 September 1902.
41. NZRFU, Management Committee Minutes, 2 April 1903; *NZ Referee*, 27 January 1904, p. 56.
42. *NZ Referee*, 2 March 1904, p. 56.
43. *Yorkshire Post*, 30 May 1905, p. 4.
44. NZRFU, Management Committee Minutes, 14 March 1904; *Otago Witness*, 19 April 1905, p. 60.
45. NZRFU, AGM Minutes, 6 May 1904.
46. *Otago Witness*, 11 May 1904, p. 53.
47. Ibid.
48. *Otago Witness*, 20 April 1904, p. 52; *NZ Referee*, 11 May 1904, p. 55.
49. George Henry Dixon, miscellaneous papers, Folder 1, MS 748 (1), Auckland War Memorial Museum.
50. *Yorkshire Post*, 30 June 1906, p. 4.
51. See Chapter Eight.
52. Timothy N. W. Buchanan, 'Missionaries of Empire: 1905 All Black tour', extended MA research essay, University of Canterbury, 1981, p. 4.
53. *NZ Referee*, 14 December 1904, p. 57; NZRFU Management Committee Minutes, 10 May 1905.
54. *Canterbury Times*, 26 July 1905, p. 27.
55. *Otago Witness*, 23 August 1905, p. 57.
56. Swan, *New Zealand Rugby Football*, pp. 145–49; Chester & McMillan, *The Visitors*, pp. 74–79; NZRFU, Annual Report, 1904.
57. *NZ Referee*, 25 May 1904, p. 52.
58. Vincent, 'A Tendency to Roughness', pp. 99–101; Auckland Rugby Football Union, *100 Years of Auckland Rugby: Official history of the Auckland Rugby Football Union Inc.*, Auckland: ARFU, 1983, p. 312.
59. NZRFU, Annual Report, 1905.
60. For example, *NZ Referee*, 18 May 1904, p. 55; 1 June 1904, p. 55; 22 June 1904, p. 53; 3 August 1904, p. 49; 7 June 1905, p. 51.
61. *Otago Witness*, 10 May 1905, p. 57; 18 October 1905, p. 60.
62. *Otago Witness*, 13 April 1904, p. 52.

Chapter 3: Deliberations and Expectations

1. NZRFU, Management Committee Minutes, 11 November 1904.
2. NZRFU, Management Committee Minutes, 9 December 1904; *Auckland Weekly News*, 12 January 1905, p. 44.
3. Chester & McMillan, *Encyclopedia*, pp. 233–34.
4. Ibid, p. 79.
5. *NZ Referee*, 22 February 1905, p. 53; Chester & McMillan, *Enyclopedia*, p. 90.
6. NZRFU, Management Committee Minutes, 27 January 1905; *Otago Witness*, 1 February 1905, p. 57.
7. *Otago Witness*, 15 February 1905, p. 59.
8. *Otago Witness*, 1 March 1905, p. 62.
9. *Auckland Weekly News*, 30 March 1905, p. 44.
10. *Otago Witness*, 7 June 1905, p. 56.
11. *Otago Witness*, 24 May 1905, p. 53.
12. *NZ Referee*, 14 December 1904, p. 57.
13. *Otago Witness*, 18 January 1905, p. 57.

NOTES

14. *Otago Witness*, 1 February 1905, p. 57.
15. Chester & McMillan, *Encyclopedia*, p. 41; Palenski, *Our National Game*, p. 30
16. *Otago Witness*, 10 May 1905, p. 57.
17. *Otago Witness*, 7 June 1905, p. 56; 14 June 1905, p. 56.
18. *Otago Witness*, 2 August 1905, p. 57.
19. NZRFU Management Committee Minutes, 25 July 1905. *NZ Referee*, 2 August 1905, p. 53.
20. *Auckland Weekly News*, 3 August 1905, p. 42; Chester & McMillan, *Encyclopedia*, pp. 100, 187.
21. I am grateful to Ron Palenski for providing a copy of this agreement.
22. *Otago Witness*, 7 June 1905, p. 56.
23. Dixon, *Triumphant Tour*, p. 25.
24. Ryan, 'Rural Myth', pp. 50–57.
25. Phillips, 'Rugby, War', p. 101.
26. N. A. C. McMillan, 'Deans, Robert George', in Claudia Orange, gen. ed., *Dictionary of New Zealand Biography: Vol. Three, 1901–1920*, Wellington, 1996, p. 133.
27. McLean, *New Zealand Rugby Legends*, p. 92.
28. *NZ Referee*, 12 October 1904, p. 56; 14 December 1904, p. 57.
29. Chester & McMillan, *Encyclopedia*, pp. 65–66.
30. *Otago Witness*, 7 June 1905, p. 57; *NZ Referee*, 21 June 1905, p. 57.
31. *Otago Witness*, 5 July 1905, p. 56; 12 July 1905, p. 56.
32. *Otago Witness*, 26 July 1905, p. 57.
33. *Canterbury Times*, 26 July 1905, p. 27.
34. George Henry Dixon, 1905 All Black Tour, Tour Diary 1905–1906, Folder 1, MS 748 (1), Auckland: Auckland War Memorial Museum, 30 July 1905.
35. *Press*, 19 October 1905, p. 57.
36. *Auckland Weekly News*, 21 December 1905, p. 44; McLean, *New Zealand Rugby Legends*, p. 27.
37. *Otago Witness*, 25 November 1905, p. 65.
38. *Otago Witness*, 12 April 1905, p. 56; 24 May 1905, p. 53.
39. *NZ Referee*, 26 July 1905, p. 49.
40. *Auckland Weekly News*, 13 July 1905, p. 43; 20 July 1905, p. 43.
41. *Press*, 28 July 1905, p. 4.
42. *Lyttelton Times*, 31 July 1905, p. 4.
43. *Lyttelton Times*, 6 October 1905, p. 4.
44. *Otago Witness*, 2 August 1905, p. 57.
45. Dixon, *The Triumphant Tour*, p. 26.
46. Dixon, Diary, 5–27 August 1905; Dixon, *The Triumphant Tour*, pp. 26–27; *New Zealand Herald*, 11 October 1905, p. 7; *Otago Witness*, 18 October 1905, p. 61.
47. Dixon, Diary, 5, 15, 16, 20, 27 August, 7 September 1905.
48. Dixon, Diary, 5 August 1905.
49. Dixon, Diary, 7 September 1905.
50. Dixon, *Triumphant Tour*, p. 27.
51. *Cornishman*, 14 September 1905, p. 3.
52. Dixon, *The Triumphant Tour*, p. 27; *Auckland Weekly News*, 19 October 1905, p. 43.
53. W. F. Mandle, 'W. G. Grace as a Victorian Hero', *Historical Studies*, Vol. 19, No. 76, 1981, p. 355.
54. O. L. Owen, *The History of the Rugby Football Union*, London: Playfair Books, 1955, pp. 259–67; Rugby Football Union, AGM Minutes, 1905. I am grateful to

Tony Collins for assistance with these figures.
55. Gate, p. 29; Williams, 'Rugby', pp. 313–14.
56. John Griffiths, *The Book of English International Rugby*, London: Willow, 1982, pp. 436–40. From 1871 to 1891, England won 31, drew 8 and lost 4 international matches. From 1892 to 1910 they won 18, drew 4 and lost 36.
57. Collins, pp. 168–79.
58. Ibid., p. 180-3.
59. Williams, *1905 and All That*, pp. 22–25.
60. Holt, pp. 245–46.
61. Williams, *1905 and All That*, pp. 17–19.
62. Ibid., pp. 19–20; 'How Amateur Was My Valley: Professional sport and national identity in Wales, 1890–1914', *British Journal of Sports History*, Vol. 3, No. 2, 1985. See also, *Yorkshire Post*, 11 September 1905, p. 4.
63. Bill Murray, *Football: A History of the World Game*, Aldershot: Scolar Press, 1994, p. 44; Tony Mason, *Association Football and English Society 1863–1915*, Brighton: The Harvester Press, 1980, p. 31.
64. Collins, pp. 180–82.
65. Ibid., pp. 184, 197–200.
66. Ibid., pp. 208–11.
67. Figures derived from Gate, passim; Griffith, p. 51
68. *Athletic News*, 2 October 1905, p. 1.
69. *Athletic News*, 25 September 1905, p. 4; 30 October 1905, p. 4.

Chapter 4: Making the All Blacks
1. *Athletic News*, 4 September 1905, p. 13.
2. *Western Times*, 16 September 1905, p. 3.
3. Dixon, *The Triumphant Tour*, p. 29.
4. Ibid., pp. 29-31; *Western Times*, 18 September 1905, p. 3.
5. Ibid., p. 3.
6. Dixon, Diary, 16 September 1905.
7. *Western Times*, 18 September 1905, p. 3.
8. *Athletic News*, 18 September 1905, p. 3.
9. Quoted in Dixon, *The Triumphant Tour*, p. 33.
10. *Field*, 23 September 1905, p. 561.
11. *Athletic News*, 18 September 1905, p. 3.
12. *The Field*, 23 September 1905, p. 561.
13. *Otago Witness*, 20 September 1905, p. 60; *New Zealand Herald*, 19 September 1905, p. 8.
14. *Southland Times*, 18 September 1905, p. 2.
15. Phillips, *A Man's Country?*, p. 118.
16. *Cornishman*, 28 September 1905, p. 7.
17. Quoted in *Western Times*, 22 September 1905, p. 3.
18. *Why the All Blacks Triumphed*, p. 20.
19. Dixon, *The Triumphant Tour*, p. 35.
20. Dixon, Diary, 21 September 1905.
21. *Bristol Echo*, 21 September 1905, p. 3.
22. Dixon, Diary, 23 September 1905.
23. *Bristol Echo*, 25 September 1905, p. 3.
24. *Western Daily Press*, 25 September 1905, p. 9.

25. *Northampton Daily Chronicle*, 30 September 1905, p. 3.
26. *Leicester Daily Post*, 29 September 1905, p. 2.
27. *Leicester Daily Post*, 2 October 1905, p. 7.
28. *Why the All Blacks Triumphed*, pp. 23–24.
29. *Sportsman*, 5 October 1905, p. 2.
30. E. H. D. Sewell, 'New Zealand and British Football', *International Review*, Vol. XLVI, February 1906, p. 1074.
31. For example, *Athletic News*, 25 September 1905, p. 4; *Referee* (Sydney), 15 November 1905, p. 7.
32. *Athletic News*, 9 October 1905, p. 3. See also *Yorkshire Post*, 9 October 1905, p. 4.
33. Quoted in Dixon, *The Triumphant Tour*, p. 54. See also *Field*, 21 October 1905, p. 728.
34. *Field*, 14 October 1905, p. 687. See also *Northern Daily Mail*, 12 October 1905, p. 3.
35. Mason, *Association Football*, pp. 141–43.
36. *Field*, 14 October 1905, p. 687; *Taunton Mail*, 25 October 1905, p. 7; *Leicester Daily Post*, 30 October 1905, p. 7; *Cambridge Daily* News, 9 November 1905, p. 3; *Oxford Chronicle*, 10 November 1905, p. 10; *Bedfordshire Mercury*, 17 November 1905, p. 5.
37. *Otago Witness*, 22 November 1905, p. 61.
38. *Otago Witness*, 8 November 1905, p. 62; 15 November 1905, p. 60; *Taunton Mail*, 18 October 1905, p. 7; 25 October 1905, p. 7.
39. Nauright, 'Sport, Manhood and Empire', p. 251; *New Zealand Free Lance*, 3 March 1906, p. 2.
40. For example, *Taunton Mail*, 25 October 1905, p. 7; *Daily Mail*, 2 December 1905, p. 4.
41. Palenski, *Century in Black*, pp. 17–18; *The Jersey*, pp. 40–41. See also the summary of this debate on the New Zealand Rugby Museum website, 'All Blacks – the Name?', 19 January 2001, http://www.rugbymuseum.co.nz
42. *Otago Witness*, 28 March 1906, p. 57.
43. Daley, n. 3.
44. Lappe Laubscher & Gidon Nieman, comps & eds, *The Carolin Papers: A diary of the 1906/07 Springbok tour*, Pretoria: Rugbyana Publishers, 1990, pp. 49-52; H. M. Moran, *Viewless Winds: Being the recollections and digressions of an Australian surgeon*, London: Peter Davies, 1939, p. 63.
45. *NZ Referee*, 27 September 1905, p. 50.
46. *Otago Witness*, 4 October 1905, p. 57.
47. For example, *Otago Witness*, 6 December 1905, p. 56.
48. *Otago Witness*, 13 December 1905, p. 56.
49. *Western Times*, 16 September 1905, p. 3.
50. *Yorkshire Post*, 9 October 1905, p. 4.
51. *Cambria Daily Leader*, 19 December 1905, p. 2.
52. *Lyttelton Times*, 25 October 1905, p. 8.
53. *Times*, 7 May 1927, p. 6.
54. Greg Ryan, *The Making of New Zealand Cricket 1832–1914*, London: Frank Cass, 2004, pp. 219–30.
55. *Cornishman*, 14 September 1905, p. 3.
56. Chester & McMillan, *Encyclopedia*, pp. 57, 186–87.
57. 'The Haka – in the Beginning', 19 January 2001, New Zealand Rugby Museum, http://www.rugbymuseum.co.nz.

58. Moran, pp. 63-4.
59. For example, *Western Times*, 18 September 1905, p. 3; *Otago Witness*, 18 October 1905, p. 57.
60. Dixon, Diary, 20 September 1905; *Otago Witness*, 15 November 1905, p. 61.
61. *Billy's Trip Home*, passim. See also *Otago Witness*, 27 December 1905, p. 57.
62. *Otago Witness*, 21 March 1906, p. 57.
63. For example, *Daily Mail*, 16 October 1905, p. 4.
64. Dixon, Diary, 21, 23 September 1905.
65. Dixon, Diary, 7 October 1905.
66. Quoted *Otago Witness*, 27 December 1905, p. 57. See also *Bedfordshire Mercury*, 17 November 1905, p. 5.
67. *Yorkshire Post*, 13 November 1905, p. 4.
68. *Why the All Blacks Triumphed*, p. 35.
69. *Otago Witness*, 17 January 1906, p. 57.
70. Chester & McMillan, *Encyclopedia*, pp. 19-20, 88, 104, 130, 198.
71. Quoted, ibid., p. 100.
72. Quoted, ibid., p. 205.
73. Quoted, ibid., p. 178.

Chapter 5: Healthy Bodies?

1. Quoted in *Otago Witness*, 25 October 1905, p. 61.
2. Nauright, 'Sport, Manhood and Empire', pp. 239-55. 'Colonial Manhood', pp. 122-39.
3. Frederick Maurice, 'Where to Get Men', *Contemporary Review*, January 1902, pp. 78-86; 'National Health: A soldier's study', *Contemporary Review*, January 1903, pp. 41-56. See also A. Summers, 'Militarism in Britain Before the Great War', *History Workshop Journal*, No. 2, Autumn 1976, p. 111; A. Davin, 'Imperialism and Motherhood', *History Workshop Journal*, No. 5, Spring 1978, pp. 14-22; Robert H. MacDonald, *Sons of the Empire: The frontier and the Boy Scout movement, 1890-1918*, Toronto: University of Toronto Press, 1993, pp. 3-6; Gareth Stedman Jones, *Outcast London: A Study in the Relationship Between Classes in Victorian Society*, London, 1984, pp. 127-51.
4. *Annual Report of the Inspector-General for Recruiting 1900*, (Cd 519: 1901); *Director-General of Army Medical Service – Memorandum*, (Cd 1501: 1903); *Report of the Elgin Commission of Enquiry into the South African War* (Cd 1789, 1903); *Report of the Inter-Departmental Committee on Physical Deterioration*, (Cd 2175, 1904).
5. Quoted in *Evening Post*, 18 November 1905, p. 5. See also Nauright, 'Colonial Manhood', p. 136.
6. Nauright, 'Colonial Manhood', pp. 121-32; 'Sport, Manhood and Empire', pp. 244-47; Phillips, 'Rugby, War', pp. 95-97.
7. Greg Ryan, 'The End of an Aura: All Black rugby and rural nostalgia since 1995', in Ryan, ed., *Tackling Rugby Myths*, pp. 151-59.
8. *Spectator*, 16 September 1905, p. 387; 23 September 1905, p. 423.
9. *Spectator*, 30 September 1905, pp. 466-67.
10. *Yorkshire Post*, 25 September 1905, p. 4; 2 October 1905, p. 4.
11. *Sportsman*, 26 September 1905, p. 4.
12. Daley, p. 76.
13. J. L. Thompson, *Northcliffe: Press baron in politics 1863-1922*, London: John Murray, 2000, pp. 25-26.

NOTES

14. David Smith & Gareth Williams, *Fields of Praise: The official history of the Welsh Rugby Union 1881–1981* Cardiff: University of Wales Press on behalf of the Welsh RFU, 1980, p. 164.
15. Nauright, 'Sport, Manhood and Empire', p. 251.
16. *Daily Mail*, 9 October 1905, pp. 7-8. See also 11 October 1905, p. 7.
17. *Daily Mail*, 9 October 1905, p. 8.
18. *Daily Mail*, 10 October 1905, p. 6.
19. *Times*, 10 October 1905, p. 15.
20. Smith & Williams, p. 147.
21. Quoted in ibid, pp. 146–47.
22. *Annual Report of the Inspector-General for Recruiting 1900*, (Cd 519: 1901), pp. ix, 299; *Director-General of Army Medical Service – Memorandum*, (Cd 1501: 1903), p. 919; *Report of the Inter-Departmental Committee on Physical Deterioration*, (Cd 2175, 1904), pp. 1–6, 92–93.
23. *Committee on Physical Deterioration*, p. 84.
24. See Stephen Koss, ed., *The Pro-Boers: The anatomy of an antiwar movement*, Chicago, 1973, esp. pp. xxxviii, 214–71.
25. Luke Trainor, *British Imperialism and Australian Nationalism*, Cambridge, 1994, pp. 27, 102, 150–52; R. L. Wallace, *The Australians at the Boer War*, Canberra: Australian War Memorial, 1976, pp. 34, 78–79; K. S. Inglis in L. M. Field, *The Forgotten War: Australian involvement in the South African conflict of 1899–1902*, Melbourne: Melbourne University Press, 1979, p. vii.
26. For example, Wallace, pp. 328–34, 352, 354; Field, pp. 180–83. See also J. R. Burns, 'New Zealanders at War?: The mythology of the New Zealand soldier and the beliefs of the New Zealand soldier of the South African War 1899–1902', MA thesis, Victoria University of Wellington, 1996.
27. Wallace, pp. 361–84.
28. *Times*, 17 October 1905, p. 12; *Manchester Guardian*, 18 October 1905, p. 6; 21 October 1905, p. 7. See also the discussion of Vaile's position in Daley, p. 75.
29. Sewell, pp. 1071–77, 1083.
30. *Daily Mail*, 18 October 1905, p. 8.
31. *Daily Mail*, 9 October 1905, pp. 7–8; 11 October 1905, p. 7; 12 October 1905, p. 8.
32. *Referee* (London), 22 October 1905, p. 9; 29 October 1905, p. 12.
33. *Daily Mail*, 12 October 1905, p. 8.
34. Quoted in *Otago Witness*, 17 January 1906, p. 57.
35. *Daily Mail*, 18 October 1905, p. 8.
36. *Daily Mail*, 24 October 1905, p. 9.
37. *Daily Mail*, 19 October 1905, p. 8.
38. Quoted in *Otago Witness*, 27 December 1905, p. 56.
39. *Otago Witness*, 25 October 1905, p. 61. See also *The Press*, 6 October 1905, p. 4.
40. *Daily Mail*, 17 October 1905, p. 8.
41. *Why the All Blacks Triumphed*, pp. 48–49.
42. Ibid, p. 55.
43. *Athletic News*, 16 October 1905, p. 3.
44. *Daily Mail*, 14 October 1905, p. 6.
45. *Daily Mail*, 20 October 1905, p. 9.
46. Ryan, *The Making of New Zealand Cricket*, pp. 220–24.
47. *Spectator*, 28 October 1905, p. 646.
48. *Sportsman*, 16 October 1905, p. 2.
49. *Sportsman*, 23 October 1905, p. 2.

50. *Sporting Life*, 16 October 1905, p. 8.
51. Quoted in *Otago Witness*, 17 January 1906, p. 56.
52. *Field*, 11 November 1905, p. 825.
53. Caroline Daley, *Leisure & Pleasure: Reshaping & revealing the New Zealand body 1900–1960*, Auckland: Auckland University Press, 2003, esp. pp. 13–40.
54. *Sandow's Magazine*, 2 November 1905, p. 483, quoted in Daley, 'The Invention of 1905', p. 76.
55. *New Zealand Herald*, 11 October 1905, p. 7.
56. Quoted in *Referee* (Sydney), 29 November 1905, p. 7.
57. *Punch*, 27 December 1905, p. 452.
58. Daley, 'The Invention of 1905', p. 75.

Chapter 6: Infringing Ideals
1. See Brian Stoddart & Ric Sissons, *Cricket and Empire: The 1932–33 bodyline tour of Australia,* London: Allen & Unwin, 1984.
2. *Daily Mail*, 16 October 1905, p. 4.
3. *Leicester Daily Post*, 30 October 1905, p. 7.
4. Gallaher & Stead, p. 259; *Cambridge Daily News*, 9 November 1905, p. 3.
5. Dixon, *The Triumphant Tour*, pp. 66–92.
6. *Taunton Mail*, 25 October 1905, p. 7.
7. *Oxford Times*, 11 November 1905, p. 11.
8. *Why the All Blacks Triumphed*, p. 55.
9. Palenski, *Our National Game*, p. 38; *Century in Black*, p. 36; See also Phillips, *A Man's Country?*, p. 124; Nauright, 'Sport, Manhood and Empire', pp. 240, 248; Macdonald, *The Game of our Lives*, pp. 20–29; T. P. McLean, *Great Days in New Zealand Rugby*, Wellington: A. H. & A. W. Reed, 1959, p. 18; Joseph Romanos, ed., with Keith Quinn, *Legends of the All Blacks*, Auckland: Hodder Moa Beckett, 1999, pp. 92–94.
10. Dixon, *The Triumphant Tour*, p. 81.
11. Ibid, p. 143.
12. Collins, pp. 93–97.
13. *Yorkshire Post*, 9 October 1905, p. 4. See also *NZ Referee*, 17 January 1906, p. 50.
14. Collins, p. 209.
15. Quoted in Hamish Doig, 'New Zealand Alone: Rugby union and the 2-3-2 scrum', Hist 490 research essay, University of Otago, 1997, p. 24. See also *Otago Witness*, 8 November 1905, p. 60.
16. Ellison, pp. 53–56.
17. Gallaher & Stead, pp. 116–17.
18. Swan, *New Zealand Rugby Football*, p. 123.
19. O'Hagan, pp. 47–48, 59–64.
20. Swan, *New Zealand Rugby Football*, p. 139.
21. Ellison, p. 53.
22. O'Hagan, p. 74.
23. For discussion of the range of interpretations, see B. E. Haley, *The Healthy Body and Victorian Culture*, Harvard: Harvard University Press, 1978; J. A. Mangan & James Walvin, eds, *Manliness and Morality: Middle-class masculinity in Britain and America 1800–1940*, Manchester: Manchester University Press, 1987; David Newsome, *Godliness and Good Learning: Four studies on a Victorian ideal*, London: John Murray, 1961; Norman Vance, *The Sinews of the Spirit: The ideal*

NOTES

of Christian manliness in Victorian literature and religious thought, Cambridge: Cambridge University Press, 1985, pp. 189–206.
24. *Morning Post*, 18 September 1905, p. 3.
25. *Manchester Guardian*, 18 September 1905, p. 4.
26. Dixon, Diary, 22 September 1905.
27. *Illustrated Sporting and Dramatic News*, 30 September 1905, p. 151.
28. Dixon, *The Triumphant Tour*, p. 66.
29. Quoted in *Otago Witness*, 25 October 1905, p. 60.
30. *Daily Mail*, 2 November 1905, p. 8. See also Dixon, *The Triumphant Tour*, pp. 73–75; *Why the All Blacks Triumphed*, p. 52.
31. *Field*, 4 November 1905, p. 788.
32. Sewell, p. 1076; Daley, 'The Invention of 1905', pp. 80–84.
33. Quoted in *Otago Witness*, 3 January 1906, p. 7.
34. *Athletic News*, 4 December 1905, p. 2.
35. *Athletic News*, 25 December 1905, p. 4.
36. *Northern Daily Mail*, 9 October 1905, p. 4.
37. *Durham County Advertiser*, 13 October 1905, p. 6.
38. *Sportsman*, 2 October 1905, p. 2.
39. *Sporting Life*, 5 October 1905, p. 4. See also 4 December 1905, p. 8.
40. *Sporting Life*, 1 October 1906, p. 8.
41. *Why the All Blacks Triumphed*, p. 13.
42. Sewell, pp. 1076–77.
43. Ibid., p. 1077.
44. *Northern Daily Mail*, 12 October 1905, p. 3.
45. *Why the All Blacks Triumphed*, pp. 7–9.
46. Gallaher & Stead, p. 118.
47. *Otago Witness*, 2 January 1907, p. 58.
48. Terry Godwin, *The International Rugby Championship 1883–1983*, London: Willow, 1984, pp. 80–81.
49. *Canterbury Times*, 4 May 1910, p. 60.
50. Quoted in *NZ Referee*, 10 July 1907, p. 59.
51. R. A. Barr, *British Rugby Team in Maoriland*, Dunedin: Otago Daily Times and Witness Newspapers Co., 1908, p. 137.
52. *Morning Post*, 17 November 1924, p. 9.
53. *Field*, 20 November 1924, p. 794.
54. *New Zealand Herald*, 1 December 1924, p. 8.
55. *New Zealand Herald*, 22 May 1930, p. 14.
56. *New Zealand Herald*, 26 May 1930, p. 14. See also *Times*, 23 October 1930, p. 7.
57. For example, *New Zealand Herald*, 26 May 1930, p. 8; *Manawatu Evening Standard*, 27 May 1930, p. 2.
58. Alley, pp. 21, 29, 46.
59. *Referee* (Sydney), 14 February 1906, p. 9.
60. Read Masters, *With the All Blacks in Great Britain*, Christchurch: Christchurch Press Company, 1928, pp. 162–63.
61. *Times*, 6 December 1925, p. 6.
62. *Times*, 20 March 1926, p. 7.
63. *Times*, 30 April 1931, p. 6; Chester & McMillan, *Centenary*, p. 196.
64. *Press*, 30 April 1931, p. 6.
65. Swan, *New Zealand Rugby Football Union*, pp. 33–51.

Chapter 7: Big Matches and Bigger Legends

1. Sinclair, *A Destiny Apart*, p. 147.
2. *Otago Witness*, 1 November 1905, p. 56; 8 November 1905, p. 62; 6 December 1905, p. 57.
3. Dixon, *The Triumphant Tour*, p. 102.
4. Daley, 'The Invention of 1905', p. 84.
5. Tony Collins to author 28 November 2004.
6. Allan Massie, *Portrait of Scottish Rugby*, Edinburgh: Polygon, 1984, p. 15.
7. *Athletic News*, 6 November 1905, p. 4.
8. *Yorkshire Post*, 20 November 1905, p. 4.
9. *Otago Witness*, 28 November 1906, p. 62.
10. For example, Winston McCarthy, *Haka: The All Black story*, London: Pelham, 1968, p. 46.
11. *Otago Witness*, 28 November 1906, p. 62; Laubscher, & Nieman, p. 97.
12. Palenski, *Century in Black*, pp. 74–75, 78.
13. Quoted in *Otago Witness*, 7 March 1906, p. 60.
14. Palenski, *Century in Black*, p. 74–75.
15. *Daily Mail*, 18 November 1905, p. 8.
16. *Field*, 25 November 1905, p. 940; Chester & McMillan, *Encyclopedia*, p. 233.
17. Dixon, Diary, 18 November 1905.
18. *Otago Witness*, 10 January 1906, p. 57; R. H. Chester & N. A. C. McMillan, *Men in Black*, Auckland: Moa, 1988, pp. 24–25.
19. *Glasgow Herald*, 23 November 1905, p. 6.
20. *Athletic News*, 20 November 1905, p. 4.
21. *Scotsman*, 20 November 1905, p. 10.
22. *Yorkshire Post*, 20 November 1905, p. 4.
23. *Field*, 25 November 1905, p. 940.
24. *Otago Witness*, 3 January 1906, p. 58.
25. Dixon, *The Triumphant Tour*, p. 95.
26. *Otago Witness*, 10 January 1906, p. 57.
27. Quoted in *Otago Witness*, 24 January 1906, p. 65.
28. *Sportsman*, 27 November 1905, p. 8.
29. Dixon, *The Triumphant Tour*, p. 105.
30. *Field*, 2 December 1905, p. 53.
31. *Otago Witness*, 17 January 1906, p. 57; Chester & McMillan, *Men in Black*, pp. 26–27.
32. *Irish Times*, 27 November 1905, p. 5.
33. *Yorkshire Post*, 27 November 1905, p. 4.
34. *Sporting Life*, 4 December 1905, p. 8.
35. Dixon, *The Triumphant Tour*, pp. 105–06.
36. *Sport*, 2 December 1905, p. 3; *Limerick Leader*, 1 December 1905, p. 3.
37. *Otago Witness*, 24 January 1906, p. 64.
38. *Otago Witness*, 31 January 1906, p. 61; Chester & McMillan, *Men in Black*, pp. 28–29.
39. *Athletic News*, 4 December 1905, p. 2.
40. *Yorkshire Post*, 4 December 1905, p. 4.
41. *Field*, 9 December 1905, p. 1026.
42. Dixon, *The Triumphant Tour*, pp. 110–12.
43. *Yorkshire Post*, 11 December 1905, p. 4; *Why the All Blacks Triumphed*, p. 80.
44. Ibid., p. 83.

45. Williams, *1905 and All That*, p. 71.
46. Ibid., pp. 72–81.
47. *Otago Witness*, 3 January 1906, p. 57.
48. *Taunton Mail*, 25 October 1905, p. 7.
49. *Western Mail*, 4 December 1905, p. 8.
50. *Western Mail*, 16 December 1905, p. 4.
51. *Cambria Daily Leader*, 15 December 1905, p. 2.
52. *Cambrian*, 15 November 1905, p. 5.
53. Dixon, *The Triumphant Tour*, p. 119. See also *Western Mail*, 15 December 1905, pp. 5–6.
54. *South Wales Echo*, 16 December 1905, p. 3; Dixon, *The Triumphant Tour*, p. 119.
55. *Evening Post*, 16 December 1905, p. 5.
56. For the occupations and education of those who opposed the All Blacks in 1905, see Vincent, 'Practical Imperialism', pp. 33–35, 58–59.
57. Smith & Williams, pp. 148–52.
58. Chester & McMillan, *Men in Black*, p. 30.
59. Dixon, *The Triumphant Tour*, p. 122.
60. McLean, *Great Days in New Zealand Rugby*, p. 17.
61. Chester & McMillan, *Centenary*, p. 66.
62. Chester & McMillan, *Men in Black*, p. 30.
63. For example, *Cambria Daily* Leader, 18 December 1905, p. 4; *Otago Witness*, 31 January 1906, p. 62; Dixon, *The Triumphant Tour*, pp. 122–29.
64. *Otago Witness*, 31 January 1906, p. 62; Dixon, *The Triumphant Tour*, p. 122.
65. Chester & McMillan, *Centenary*, pp. 66–68.
66. *Otago Witness*, 31 January 1906, p. 62; Chester & McMillan, *Men in Black*, p. 31.
67. *Sportsman*, 18 December 1905, p. 2.
68. *Western Mail*, 18 December 1905, p. 4.
69. *Cambria Daily Leader*, 18 December 1905, p. 4.
70. *Cambrian*, 22 December 1905, p. 3.
71. Quoted in *Cambrian*, 22 December 1905, p. 3.
72. Ibid.
73. Quoted in *Otago Witness*, 31 January 1906, p. 62.
74. *The Field*, 23 December 1905, pp. 1071–72.
75. Quoted in *Cambrian*, 22 December 1905, p. 3.
76. Ibid.
77. Ibid. See also *Western Mail*, 18 December 1905, p. 4; *Field*, 23 December 1905, p. 1099.
78. Quoted in *Cambrian*, 22 December 1905, p. 3.
79. *South Wales Echo*, 18 December 1905, p. 2.
80. Sewell, p. 1077.
81. Quoted in *Otago Witness*, 31 January 1906, p. 60.
82. Quoted in *Cambrian*, 22 December 1905, p. 3.
83. Quoted in *Otago Witness*, 31 January 1906, p. 61.
84. *Why the All Blacks Triumphed*, p. 7.
85. *Otago Witness*, 20 December 1905, p. 36. See also *Otago Daily Times*, 18 December 1905, p. 4.
86. *Waikato Times*, 18 December 1905, p. 2.
87. *Press*, 18 December 1905, p. 6.
88. *NZ Referee*, 20 December 1905, p. 52.
89. For example, *Otago Witness*, 31 January 1906, pp. 60–62; *Press*, 27 January 1906,

p. 8; 17 February 1906, p. 5.
90. Smith & Williams, p. 163.
91. Chester & McMillan, *Men in Black*, pp. 30–31; *Centenary*, pp. 66–68.
92. Smith & Williams, pp. 164–67; McCarthy, pp. 48–50.
93. McCarthy, p. 50.
94. Smith & Williams, p. 164.
95. McCarthy, p. 38; McLean, *Great Days in New Zealand Rugby*, p. 23; Gordon Slatter, *On the Ball: The centennial book of New Zealand Rugby*, Christchurch: Whitcombe & Tombs, 1970, pp. 277–78.
96. Dixon, Diary, 16 December 1905; *The Triumphant Tour*, p. 123.
97. *Otago Witness*, 20 December 1905, p. 36.
98. *Press*, 18 December 1905, p. 6. See also *Otago Witness*, 3 January 1906, p. 56.
99. *Otago Witness*, 3 January 1906, p. 56.
100. *Otago Witness*, 31 January 1906, pp. 60–61.
101. *Auckland Weekly News*, 8 February 1906, p. 44.
102. *Otago Witness*, 28 February 1906, p. 62.
103. *Otago Witness*, 14 March 1906, p. 61.
104. Daley, 'The Invention of 1905', pp. 84–85.
105. Quoted, Dixon, *The Triumphant Tour*, p. 128.
106. Masters, p. 86.
107. Slatter, pp. 282–83; Paul Verdon, *The Power Behind the All Blacks: The untold story of the men who coached the All Blacks*, Auckland: Penguin, 1999, p. 44.
108. Gallaher & Stead, p. 267.
109. Dixon, Diary, 16 December 1905.
110. Ibid.

Chapter 8: Serving the Minister for Football

1. Cables, Dixon to NZRFU, 19 December 1905; Dixon to Rowland Hill, 20 December 1905, Dixon papers.
2. *Cambria Daily Leader*, 20 December 1905, p. 3.
3. Dixon, Diary, 20 December 1905; *The Triumphant Tour*, pp. 130–31.
4. *Athletic News*, 25 December 1905, p. 4.
5. Quoted in Dixon, *The Triumphant Tour*, p. 132.
6. Ibid, p. 130.
7. *Yorkshire Post*, 26 December 1905, p. 7.
8. *South Wales Daily Post*, 30 December 1905, p. 6.
9. Dixon, Diary, 26 December 1905.
10. Quoted in Dixon, *The Triumphant Tour*, p. 135.
11. Quoted in *Otago Witness*, 14 February 1906, p. 56.
12. *South Wales Echo*, 26 December 1905, p. 3.
13. *South Wales Echo*, 30 December 1905, p. 3.
14. Dixon, Diary, 30 September 1905.
15. *Why the All Blacks Triumphed*, p. 96.
16. Philip Dine, *French Rugby Football: A cultural history*, Oxford: Berg, 2001, pp. 19–52.
17. Chester & McMillan, *Men in Black*, pp. 32–33.
18. *Otago Witness*, 21 February 1906, p. 57.
19. Ibid.; Chester & McMillan, *Men in Black*, pp. 32–33.
20. *Otago Witness*, 21 February 1906, p. 57; 28 February 1906, p. 59.

NOTES

21. Dixon, *The Triumphant Tour*, p. 140.
22. Quoted in *Otago Witness*, 21 February 1906, p. 57.
23. Quoted in *Otago Witness*, 7 March 1906, p. 62.
24. *Otago Witness*, 21 February 1906, p. 57.
25. Dine, pp. 61–94.
26. Masters, p. 118.
27. *Press*, 8 November 2000, p. 67; 19 November 2004, p. D7; *Dominion Post*, 29 November 2004, p. 1.
28. Dixon, *The Triumphant Tour*, pp. 140-2.
29. *Otago Witness*, 20 December 1905, p. 35; Chester & McMillan, *Centenary*, p. 70.
30. *NZ Referee*, 7 March 1906, p. 54
31. *Otago Witness*, 24 January 1906, p. 64; Dixon, *The Triumphant Tour*, p. 152.
32. Dixon, *The Triumphant Tour*, p. 152.
33. Chester & McMillan, *Centenary*, pp. 70–71.
34. Dixon, *The Triumphant Tour*, p. 143.
35. A. W. Pullin to George Dixon, 18 January 1906, Dixon papers.
36. *Sportsman*, 8 January 1906, p. 2.
37. *Referee* (London), 31 December 1905, p. 2.
38. Quoted in *Otago Witness*, 22 February 1906, p. 56.
39. Collins, pp. 209–13.
40. Phillips, *A Man's Country?*, p. 110.
41. *Evening Post*, 16 December 1905, p. 5.
42. *Otago Witness*, 13 December 1905, p. 57.
43. *Otago Witness*, 20 December 1905, p. 35.
44. *Otago Daily Times*, 18 December 1905, p. 4.
45. *Evening Post*, 2 January 1906, p. 7.
46. David Hamer, 'Seddon, Richard John 1845–1906', in Claudia Orange, gen. ed., *Dictionary of New Zealand Biography Vol. Two 1870–1900*, Wellington: Bridget Williams Books/Department of Internal Affairs, 1993, pp. 447–51.
47. *Evening Post*, 2 January 1906, p. 6.
48. Quoted in *Evening Post*, 4 January 1906, p. 8.
49. Ibid.
50. *Press*, 3 January 1906, p. 6; *Otago Witness*, 10 January 1906, p. 56.
51. *New Zealand Times*, 3 January 1906, p. 4.
52. *NZ Referee*, 2 May 1906, p. 64; *Yorkshire Post*, 30 June 1906, p. 4.
53. Ronald A. Smith, *Sports and Freedom: The rise of big-time college athletics*, New York: Oxford University Press, 1988, p. 4.
54. Benjamin G. Rader, *American Sports: From the age of folk games to the age of televised sports*, Upper Saddle River, NJ: Prentice Hall, 1999, pp. 174–76.
55. Smith, *Sports and Freedom*, pp. 14–25, 26–48, 147–64, 172–74.
56. Ibid., pp. 67–82.
57. Ibid., pp. 84–95.
58. M. Oriard, *Reading Football: How the popular press created an American spectacle*, Chapel Hill: University of North Carolina Press, 1993, pp. 35–43.
59. Ibid, p. 84.
60. Ronald A. Smith, 'Harvard and Columbia and a Reconsideration of the 1905–06 Football Crisis', *Journal of Sport History*, Vol. 8, No. 3, 1981, pp. 5–19.
61. Roberta J. Park, 'From Football to Rugby – and Back, 1906–1919: The University of California-Stanford University response to the "football crisis of 1905"', *Journal of Sport History*, Vol. 11, No. 3, 1984, pp. 9–17.

62. Ibid., pp. 14–15.
63. Ibid., p. 20. See also *NZ Referee*, 10 July 1907, p. 54; *Athletic News*, 20 December 1909, p. 3.
64. *NZ Referee*, 31 January 1906, p. 50
65. Park, p. 20.
66. Dixon, *The Triumphant Tour*, p. 153.
67. *Daily Californian*, 5 February 1906, p. 4.
68. *Daily Californian*, 9 February 1906, p. 1.
69. *San Francisco Chronicle*, 11 February 1906, p. 41. See also *Daily Californian*, 12 February 1906, p. 1.
70. Dixon, *The Triumphant Tour*, p. 157.
71. Park, pp. 21–22.
72. *NZ Referee*, 26 December 1906, p. 58; 20 February 1907, p. 58.
73. *NZ Referee*, 10 July 1907, p. 59.
74. *NZ Referee*, 5 June, 1907, p. 51.
75. *Referee* (Sydney), 17 April 1912, p. 13; 12 June 1912, p. 12. For a full discussion of these tours, see Greg Ryan, '"Brawn against Brains": Australia, New Zealand and the American "football crisis" 1906–13', *Sporting Traditions*, Vol. 20, No. 2, May 2004.
76. Quoted in *Daily Californian*, 19 November 1913, p. 4.
77. Ryan, '"Brawn against Brains"', pp. 34–35.
78. *Otago Witness*, 14 March 1906, p. 61.
79. Ibid.; Chester & McMillan, *Centenary*, p. 71.
80. *Evening Post*, 7 March 1906, p. 6.
81. *Otago Witness*, 14 March 1906, p. 62.
82. *Otago Witness*, 21 March 1906, pp. 57–58; 28 March 1906, p. 57; 4 April 1906, p. 56.
83. See player biographies, pp. 186–98.

Chapter 9: The Fabric Unravels

1. *Referee* (Sydney), 24 June 1908, p. 8.
2. *Yorkshire Post*, 10 December 1906, p. 3.
3. Vincent, 'Practical Imperialism', pp. 21–22.
4. *Field*, 6 October 1906, p. 582. See also 5 January 1907, p. 2
5. *Times*, 13 October 1906, p. 11.
6. *Athletic News*, 8 October 1906, p. 2. See also Laubscher& Nieman, *The Carolin Papers*, pp. 87, 103.
7. Quoted in *Otago Witness*, 24 October 1906, p. 57. See also 28 November 1906, p. 62.
8. *Sporting Life*, 2 January 1907, p. 8.
9. C. Berkeley Cowell & E. Watts Moses, *Durham Country Rugby Union: Sixty years records of the county fifteen 1876–1936*, Newcastle Upon Tyne: Andrew Reid & Co., 1936, p. 215.
10. *Cambrian*, 22 December 1905, p. 3; *Otago Witness*, 21 March 1906, p. 57.
11. Gallaher & Stead, pp. 220–21.
12. John Haynes, *From All Blacks to All Golds: New Zealand's rugby league pioneers*, Christchurch: Ryan & Haynes, 1996, pp. 31–36.
13. Ibid; Collins, p. 217.
14. *New Zealand Herald*, 27 April 1907, p. 8; 27 May 1907, p. 8; *Athletic News*, 7 October 1907, p. 4; Haynes, pp. 36–38; Collins, p. 218.

NOTES

15. *Yorkshire Post*, 13 November 1908, p. 5.
16. Quoted in Bernard Wood, *Lion Red Rugby League Annual '96*, Wellington: B. J. Wood, 1996, p. 104.
17. Jo Smith, 'All That Glitters: The All Golds and the advent of rugby league in Australasia', MA thesis, University of Canterbury, 1998, pp. 32-33.
18. Vincent, 'A Tendency to Roughness', pp. 61-64.
19. *New Zealand Herald*, 8 May 1907, p. 8.
20. *New Zealand Herald*, 18 May 1907, p. 8.
21. *New Zealand Herald*, 27 May 1907, p. 8; Haynes, pp. 21-23.
22. *New Zealand Herald*, 28 May 1907, p. 6.
23. Ibid.
24. *New Zealand Herald*, 30 May 1907, p. 6.
25. Haynes, p. 43; *New Zealand Herald*, 21 October 1907, p. 5.
26. *New Zealand Herald*, 28 May 1907, p. 6; Haynes, pp. 24-25.
27. *Evening Post*, 16 May 1907, p. 4. See also 18 May, p. 14.
28. *Evening Post*, 11 May 1907, p. 14.
29. *Evening Post*, 6 June 1907, p. 2.
30. Haynes, pp. 45-53. The registered name of the team was 'The New Zealand All Black Rugby Football Team'.
31. Haynes, pp. 67-70.
32. Collins, p. 219.
33. Haynes, Appendix 5
34. Massa Johnston to Jack Wilson, August 1929. I am grateful to Tony Collins for a copy of this letter.
35. Collins, pp. 219-21.
36. *Evening Post*, 15 June 1908, p. 8.
37. Chester & McMillan, *Encyclopedia*, p. 239.
38. Haynes, pp. 160-3.
39. G. T. Vincent & T. Harfield, 'Repression and Reform: Responses within New Zealand rugby to the arrival of the 'Northern Game, 1907-8', *New Zealand Journal of History*, Vol. 31, No. 2, 1997, pp. 234-40.
40. Ibid, pp. 241-45.
41. Ibid, pp. 246-49.
42. Edgar Wylie, Secretary NZRFU, to George Dixon, 29 November 1905; George Dixon to Percy Coles, Secretary RFU, 19 December 1905. Dixon papers.
43. Vincent, 'Practical Imperialism', pp. 37-40.
44. *Times*, 13 January 1908, p. 13.
45. *Referee* (Sydney), 21 April 1908, p. 9; 13 May 1908, p. 8.
46. *Times*, 3 March 1908, p. 12.
47. *Times*, 29 May 1908, p. 14.
48. Vincent, 'Practical Imperialism', pp. 167-70.
49. Ibid, pp. 171-73.
50. Ibid, pp. 186-89.
51. *New Zealand Herald*, 26 November 1908, p. 8.
52. *New South Wales Rugby Union Annual Report: 1907*.
53. *NZ Referee*, 12 August 1908, p. 53.
54. *Referee* (Sydney), 11 November 1908, p. 9. See also 18 November 1908, p. 9; 16 December 1908, p. 9; *Sporting Life*, 10 November 1908; Pollard, p. 861.
55. *Morning Post*, 19 November 1908, p. 11.
56. *Daily Chronicle*, 19 November 1908, p. 8.

THE CONTEST FOR RUGBY SUPREMACY

57. Quoted in *Otago Witness*, 13 January 1909, p. 62.
58. Quoted in *Sydney Mail*, 6 January 1909, p. 54.
59. *Athletic News*, 23 November 1908, p. 4.
60. Quoted in *Referee* (Sydney), 6 January 1909, p. 9.
61. Quoted in *Referee* (Sydney), 30 December 1908, p. 9.
62. *Referee* (Sydney), 31 March 1909, p. 9.
63. Ibid.
64. *Daily Mail*, 24 November 1908, p. 9. Diabolo involved throwing and catching a spinning top on a cord fastened to two sticks held in the hands.
65. For example, *Daily Mail*, 27 November 1908, p. 7; *Sportsman*, 23 November 1908, p. 2.
66. Moran, pp. 78–79.
67. Ibid., p. 70.
68. *Daily Mail*, 27 November 1908, p. 7.
69. *Otago Witness*, 3 January 1909, p. 63.
70. *Sydney Mail*, 28 September 1909, p. 59; Max Howell, '1909: The great defection', in David Headon & Lex Marinos, eds, *League of a Nation*, Sydney: ABC Books, 1996, pp. 29–34.
71. *New South Wales Rugby Union Annual Report: 1909*.
72. *Sydney Mail*, 8 September 1909, p. 59.
73. Howell, p. 36; Wray Vamplew, et al., eds, *The Oxford Companion to Australian Sport*, Melbourne, 1992, p. 304.
74. *Times*, 14 January 1909, p. 15; *NZ Referee*, 27 January 1909, p. 54.
75. C. Wray Palliser to J. D. Avery, secretary NZRFU, 5 November 1908; 5 February 1909; 12 February 1909; 26 February 1909.; *NZ Referee*, 10 February 1909, p. 56; *Field*, 27 February 1909, p. 365; 6 March 1909, p. 410.
76. For example, *Referee* (Sydney), 20 January 1909, p. 9.
77. *NZ Referee*, 14 April 1909, p. 55.
78. For example, Arthur Shrewsbury to Alfred Shaw, 14 March 1888, Arthur Shrewsbury Letter Book. I am grateful to Tony Collins for a copy of this correspondence. See also Collins, pp. 73–74.
79. Quoted in *Referee* (Sydney), 23 December 1908, p. 9.
80. Quoted in *Otago Witness*, 3 July 1912, p. 60.
81. *Otago Witness*, 26 June 1912, p. 60; *Referee*, (Sydney), 23 October 1912, p. 13.
82. *Referee* (Sydney), 18 September 1912, p. 12.
83. *Referee* (Sydney), 17 July 1912, p. 12; *Otago Witness*, 24 July 1912, p. 32; 31 July 1912, p. 60.
84. *Referee*, (Sydney), 30 October 1912, p. 13.
85. Douglas Sladen to Edward Hulton, 31 January 1913; Douglas Sladen to F. Lysnar, 9 February 1913, Douglas Sladen Papers 1886–1920, Canberra: Australian Joint Copying Project, Microfilm M1977-1978. I am grateful to Luke Trainor for this correspondence.
86. Park, pp. 21–22.
87. Swan, *New Zealand Rugby Football*, pp. 526–29.

Conclusion

1. Richardson, pp. 7–8.
2. See Ryan, 'The End of an Aura', pp. 170–72.

BIBLIOGRAPHY

OFFICIAL SOURCES

British Parliamentary Papers:
Annual Report of the Inspector-General for Recruiting 1900 (Cd 519: 1901)
Director-General of Army Medical Service – Memorandum (Cd 1501: 1903)
Report of the Elgin Commission of Enquiry into the South African War (Cd 1789, 1903).
Report of the Inter-Departmental Committee on Physical Deterioration (Cd 2175, 1904),

MANUSCRIPT SOURCES

Alexander Turnbull Library, New Zealand Biographical Clippings, Alexander Turnbull Library, Wellington.
Dixon, George Henry, 1905 All Black Tour, Tour Diary 1905–1906/Personal Papers, Folder 1, MS 748 (1), Auckland War Memorial Museum.
New South Wales Rugby Union, Annual Reports 1905–09, Mitchell Library, Sydney.
New Zealand Rugby Football Union, Minutes/Annual Reports/Correspondence 1902–14, New Zealand Rugby Union, Wellington.
Shrewsbury, Arthur, Correspondence 1887–88, in possession of the author.
Sladen, Douglas, Papers 1886–1920, Canberra: Australian Joint Copying Project, Microfilm M1977-1978.

WEB SITES

New Zealand Rugby Museum, http://www.rugbymuseum.co.nz

NEWSPAPERS

Athletic News (Manchester)
Auckland Star
Auckland Weekly News
Bedfordshire Mercury
Bristol Echo
Cambria Daily Leader (Swansea)
Cambrian (Swansea)
Cambridge Daily News
Cheltenham Examiner
Contemporary Review (London)
Cornishman (Penzance)
Daily Californian (Berkeley)
Daily Chronicle (Oxford)
Daily Mail (London)
Daily Telegraph (London)
Durham County Advertiser
Edinburgh Evening News
Evening Post (Wellington)
Field (London)
Glasgow Herald
Glasgow News
Gloucester Journal
Illustrated London News
Irish Evening Times
Leicester Daily Mercury
Leicester Daily Post
Limerick Leader
Los Angeles Times
Manawatu Evening Standard (Palmerston North)

Manchester Guardian
Morning Post (London)
New Zealand Free Lance (Wellington)
New Zealand Herald (Auckland)
New Zealand Times (Wellington)
Northampton Daily Chronicle and Evening Herald
Northampton Mercury
Northern Daily Mail and South Durham Herald
NZ Referee (Christchurch)
Otago Daily Times
Otago Witness
Oxford Chronicle & Berks & Bucks Gazette
Oxford Times and Midland Counties Advertiser
Press (Christchurch)
Referee (London)
Referee (Sydney)
San Francisco Chronicle
San Francisco Examiner
Scotsman (Edinburgh)
South Wales Echo (Cardiff)
South Wales Weekly Post (Cardiff)
Sport (Dublin)
Sporting Life (London)
Sportsman (London)
Star (Christchurch)
Taunton Mail
Times (London)
Western Daily Mercury (Plymouth)
Western Daily Press (Bristol)
Western News (Taunton)
Western Times (Exeter)
Western Mail (Cardiff)
Yorkshire Post (Leeds)

SECONDARY SOURCES

Alley, G. T., *With the British Rugby Team in New Zealand,1930*, Christchurch: Simpson & Williams, 1930.
Arnold, Rollo, *Settler Kaponga 1881-1914: A frontier fragment of the western world*, Wellington: Victoria University Press, 1997.
Auckland Rugby Football Union, *100 Years of Auckland Rugby: Official history of the Auckland Rugby Football Union Inc.*, Auckland: ARFU, 1983.
Baker, W. J., 'William Webb Ellis and the Origins of Rugby Football: The life and death of a Victorian myth', *Albion*, Vol. 13, No. 2, 1981.
Barclay, J. R., 'An Analysis of Trends in New Zealand Sport from 1840 to 1900', BA Hons essay, Massey University, 1977.
Barr, R. A., *British Rugby Team in Maoriland*, Dunedin: Otago Daily Times and Witness Newspapers Co., 1908.
Barrow, Graeme, *Up Front: The story of the All Black scrum*, Auckland: Heinemann, 1985.
Belich, James, *Paradise Reforged: A history of the New Zealanders from the 1880s to the year 2000*, Auckland: Penguin, 2001.
Berkeley Cowell, C. & E. Watts Moses, *Durham Country Rugby Union: Sixty years records of the county fifteen 1876-1936*, Newcastle Upon Tyne: Andrew Reid & Co, 1936.
Billy's Trip Home: The remarkable diary of an All Black on tour, Dunedin, New Zealand Sports Hall of Fame, 2005.
Buchanan, Timothy N. W., 'Missionaries of Empire: 1905 All Black Tour', extended MA research essay, University of Canterbury, 1981.
Burns, J. R., 'New Zealanders at War?: The mythology of the New Zealand soldier and the beliefs of the New Zealand soldier of the South African War 1899-1902', MA thesis, Victoria University of Wellington, 1996.
Buttery, J. A., comp., *Why the All Blacks Triumphed*, London: Daily Mail, 1906.
Chester, R. H. & N. A. C. McMillan, *The Encyclopedia of New Zealand Rugby*,

BIBLIOGRAPHY

Auckland: Moa, 1981.

———, *Men in Black*, Auckland: Moa, 1988.

———, *Centenary: 100 years of All Black rugby*, Auckland: Moa, 1984.

———, *The Visitors: the history of international rugby teams in New Zealand*, Auckland: Moa, 1990.

Coffey, John, *Canterbury XIII: A rugby league history*, Christchurch: Canterbury Rugby League, 1987.

Collins, Tony, *Rugby's Great Split: Class, culture and the origins of rugby league football*, London: Frank Cass, 1998.

Crawford, Scott A. G. M., 'A History of Recreation and Sport in Nineteenth Century Colonial Otago', PhD thesis, University of Queensland, 1984.

Daley, Caroline, *Leisure & Pleasure: Reshaping & revealing the New Zealand body 1900–1960*, Auckland: Auckland University Press, 2003.

———, 'The Invention of 1905', in Greg Ryan, ed., *Tackling Rugby Myths: Rugby and New Zealand society 1854–2004*, Dunedin: University of Otago Press, 2005.

Dansey, R., comp., *Special Souvenir: All Blacks in England, Ireland and Wales*, Leeds: J. Waddington for the New Zealand Advertising Agency, 1925.

Davin, Anna, 'Imperialism and Motherhood', *History Workshop Journal*, No. 5, Spring 1978.

de Jong, Piet, *Saturday's Warriors: The building of a rugby stronghold*, Palmerston North: Dunmore Press, 1991.

Dine, Philip, *French Rugby Football: A cultural history*, Oxford: Berg, 2001.

Dixon, G., *1905: The Triumphant Tour of the New Zealand Footballers*, Wellington: Geddis & Bloomfield, 1906.

Dobbs, B. *Edwardians At Play: Sport 1890–1914*, London: Pelham, 1973.

Doig, Hamish, 'New Zealand Alone: Rugby union and the 2-3-2 scrum', Hist 490 research essay, University of Otago, 1997.

Dunning, E. & K. Sheard, *Barbarians, Gentlemen and Players: A sociological study of the development of rugby football*, Canberra: Australian National University Press, 1979.

Ellison, T. R., *The Art of Rugby Football: With hints and instructions on every point of the game*, Wellington: Geddis & Bloomfield, 1902.

Eyton, T., *Rugby Football (Past and Present) and the Tour of the Native Team in Britain Australia & New Zealand in 1888–89*, Palmerston North: Hart, 1896.

Fairburn, Miles, *The Ideal Society and its Enemies: The foundations of modern New Zealand society 1850–1900*, Auckland: Auckland University Press, 1989.

Field, L. M., *The Forgotten War: Australian involvement in the South African conflict of 1899–1902*, Melbourne: Melbourne University Press, 1979.

Fougere, Geoff, 'Sport, Culture and Identity: The case of rugby football', in David Novitz & Bill Willmott, eds, *Culture and Identity in New Zealand*, Wellington: GP Books, 1989.

Gallaher, D. & J. W. Stead, *The Complete Rugby Footballer on the New Zealand System*, London: Methuen, 1906.

Garnham, N., 'Rugby and Empire in Ireland: Irish reactions to colonial rugby tours before 1914', *Sport in History*, Vol. 23, No. 1, 2003.

Gate, Robert, *Rugby League: An illustrated history*, London: A. Barker, 1989.

Godwin, Terry, *The International Rugby Championship 1883–1983*, London: Willow, 1984.

———, *The Complete Who's Who of International Rugby*, Poole, Dorset: Blandford Press, 1987.

Greenhalgh, Paul, 'The Work and Play Principle: The professional regulations of the Northern Rugby Football Union, 1898–1905', *International Journal of the History of sport*, Vol. 9, No. 3, 1992.

Griffiths, John, *The Book of English International Rugby 1871 to 1982*, London: Willow, 1982.

Growden, Greg, *Gold, Mud and Guts: The incredible Tom Richards, footballer, war hero, Olympian*, Sydney: ABC Books, 2001.

Haley, B. E., *The Healthy Body and Victorian Culture*, Harvard: Harvard University Press, 1978.

Haynes, John, *From All Blacks to All Golds: New Zealand's rugby league pioneers*, Christchurch: Ryan & Haynes, 1996.

Headon, David & Lex Marinos, eds, *League of a Nation*, Sydney: ABC Books, 1996.

Heads, Ian, *True Blue: The story of the NSW Rugby League*, Sydney: Ironbark Press, 1992.

Holt, Richard, *Sport and the British: A modern history*, Oxford: Oxford University Press, 1989.

Hunter, Irwin, *New Zealand Rugby Football: Some hints and criticisms*, Auckland: Whitcombe & Tombs, 1929.

Jenkins, John M., *A Rugby Compendium: An authoritative guide to the literature of Rugby Union*, Weatherby: The British Library, 1998.

Johnston, P., *Blue and Black: Bruised but unbowed – 100 Years of Wanganui rugby*, Wanganui; Wanganui RFU, 1989.

Jones, Lloyd, *The Book of Fame*, Auckland: Penguin, 2000.

Jones, S. G., *Sport, Politics and the Working Class*, Manchester: Manchester University Press, 1988.

Koss, Stephen, ed., *The Pro-Boers: The anatomy of an antiwar movement*, Chicago: University of Chicago Press, 1973.

Laubscher, Lappe & Gidon Nieman, comp. & eds, *The Carolin Papers: A diary of the 1906/07 Springbok tour*, Pretoria: Rugbyana Publishers, 1990.

Law, Robin, et al., eds, *Masculinities in Aotearoa/New Zealand*, Palmerston North: Dunmore Press, 1999.

McCarthy, Winston, *Haka: The All Black Story*, London: Pelham, 1968.

McDevitt, Patrick F., *May the Best Man Win: Sport, masculinity, and nationalism in Great Britain and the empire, 1880–1935*, New York: Palgrave Macmillan, 2004.

Macdonald, Finlay, *The Game of Our Lives: The story of rugby and New Zealand – and how they've shaped each other*, Auckland: Viking, 1996.

Mackenzie, J. M., *All Blacks in Chains*, Wellington: Truth Ltd, 1960.

Black, Black, Black, Auckland: Minerva, 1969.

McLean, T. P., *Great Days in New Zealand Rugby*, Wellington: A. H. & A. W. Reed, 1959.

———, *Red Dragons of Rugby: Wales v. All Blacks 1905–69*, Wellington: Reed, 1969.

——— *New Zealand Rugby Legends: 15 reflections*, Auckland: Moa, 1987.

——— *Silver Fern: 150 years of New Zealand sport*, Auckland: Moa, 1990.

Mangan, J. A. & James Walvin, eds, *Manliness and Morality: Middle-class masculinity in Britain and America 1800–1940*, Manchester: Manchester University Press, 1987.

Marshall, Rev. F., ed., *Football – The Rugby Union Game*, London: Cassell, 1894.

Martin, John E. *The Forgotten Worker: The rural wage earner in nineteenth century New Zealand*, Wellington: Allen & Unwin, 1990.

Mason, Tony *Association Football and English Society 1863–1915*, Brighton: The Harvester Press, 1980.

BIBLIOGRAPHY

———— ed., *Sport in Britain: A social history*, Cambridge: Cambridge University Press, 1989.
Massie, Allan, *Portrait of Scottish Rugby*, Edinburgh: Polygon, 1984.
Masters, Read, *With the All Blacks in Great Britain*, Christchurch: Christchurch Press Company, 1928.
Montefiore, D., *Cricket in the Doldrums: The struggle between private and public control in Australian cricket in the 1880s*, Sydney: Australian Society for Sports History, 1992.
Moran, H. M., *Viewless Winds: Being the recollections and digressions of an Australian surgeon*, London: Peter Davies, 1939.
Murray, Bill, *Football: A history of the world game*, Aldershot: Scolar Press, 1994.
Nauright, John, 'Sport, Manhood and Empire: British responses to the New Zealand rugby tour of 1905', *International Journal of the History of Sport*, Vol. 8, No. 2, 1991.
————, & Timothy J. L. Chandler, eds, *Making Men: Rugby and masculine identity*, London: Frank Cass, 1996.
Newsome, David, *Godliness and Good Learning: Four studies on a Victorian ideal*, London: John Murray, 1961.
Nicholls, Sydney, *All Black Tour 1953–54 and the Story of Our Famous All Blacks in Their five main tours*, Auckland: Graham Beamish, 1953.
O'Hagan, Sean, *The Pride of Southern Rebels: On the occasion of the Otago Rugby Football Union centenary, 1881–1981,* Dunedin: Pilgrims South Press, 1981.
Orange, Claudia, gen. ed., *Dictionary of New Zealand Biography: Vol. Two 1870–1900*, Wellington: Bridget Williams Books/Department of Internal Affairs, 1993.
Oriard, Michael, *Reading Football: How the popular press created an American spectacle*, Chapel Hill: University of North Carolina Press, 1993.
Owen, O. L., *The History of the Rugby Football Union*, London: Playfair Books, 1955.
Palenski, Ron, *Century in Black: 100 years of All Black test rugby*, Auckland: Hodder, Moa, Beckett, 2003.
————, *New Zealand Rugby: Stories of heroism and valour*, Auckland: Cumulus, 2002.
————, *The Jersey: The pride & the passion, the guts & the glory: What it means to wear the All Black jersey*, Auckland: Hodder Moa Beckett, 2001.
————, *Our National Game*, Auckland: Moa Beckett, 1992.
————, ed., *Between the Posts: A New Zealand rugby anthology*, Auckland: Hodder & Stoughton, 1989.
Park, Roberta J., 'From Football to Rugby – and Back, 1906–1919: The University of California-Stanford University response to the "football crisis of 1905"', *Journal of Sport History*, Vol. 11, No. 3, 1984.
Phillips, J. O. C., 'Rugby, War and the Mythology of the New Zealand Male', *New Zealand Journal of History*, Vol. 18, No. 2, 1984.
————, *A Man's Country? The image of the Pakeha male – a history*, Auckland: Penguin, 1987.
Pollard, Jack, *Australian Rugby Union: The game and the players*, North Ryde, NSW: Angus & Robertson, 1984.
Rader, Benjamin G., *American Sports: From the age of folk games to the age of televised sports*, Upper Saddle River NJ: Prentice Hall, 1999.
Richardson, Len 'Rugby, Race, and Empire: The 1905 All Black tour', *Historical News*, No. 47, December 1983.
————, 'The Invention of a National Game: The struggle for control', *History Now*, Vol. 1, No. 1, 1995.

Rice, G. W., ed., *The Oxford History of New Zealand*, 2nd edn, Auckland: Oxford University Press, 1992.
Romanos, Joseph, ed., with Keith Quinn, *Legends of the All Blacks*, Auckland: Hodder Moa Beckett, 1999.
Ryan, Greg, *Forerunners of the All Blacks: The 1888-89 New Zealand Native Football Team in Britain, Australia and New Zealand*, Christchurch: Canterbury University Press, 1993.
———, '"A Lack of Esprit de Corps": The 1908-09 Wallabies and the legacy of the 1905 All Blacks', *Sporting Traditions*, Vol. 17, No. 1, Nov. 2000.
———, 'Rural Myth and Urban Actuality: The anatomy of All Black and New Zealand rugby 1884-1938', *New Zealand Journal of History*, Vol. 35, No. 1, April 2001.
———, *The Making of New Zealand Cricket 1832-1914*, London: Frank Cass, 2003.
———, '"Brawn against Brains": Australia, New Zealand and the American "football crisis" 1906-13', *Sporting Traditions*, Vol. 20, No. 2, May 2004.
——— ed, *Tackling Rugby Myths: Rugby and New Zealand society 1854-2004*, Dunedin: University of Otago Press, 2005.
Sinclair, Keith, *A Destiny Apart: New Zealand's search for national identity*, Auckland: Penguin, 1986.
Slatter, Gordon, *On the Ball: The centennial book of New Zealand rugby*, Christchurch: Whitcombe & Tombs, 1970.
Smith, David, 'People's Theatre: A century of Welsh rugby', *History Today*, No. 31, March 1981.
———, & Gareth Williams. *Fields of Praise: The official history of the Welsh Rugby Union 1881-1981*, Cardiff: University of Wales Press on behalf of Welsh RFU, 1980.
Smith, Jo, 'All That Glitters: The All Golds and the advent of rugby league in Australasia', MA thesis, University of Canterbury, 1998.
Smith, Ronald A., 'Harvard and Columbia and a Reconsideration of the 1905-06 Football Crisis', *Journal of Sport History*, Vol. 8, No.3, 1981.
———, *Sports and Freedom: The rise of big-time college athletics*, New York: Oxford University Press, 1988.
Stedman Jones, Gareth, *Outcast London: A study in the relationship between classes in Victorian society*, London: Penguin, 1984.
Stewart, J. J., *Rugby: Developments in the field of play*, Palmerston North: Massey University, 1997.
Stoddart, Brian & Ric Sissons, *Cricket and Empire: The 1932-33 bodyline tour of Australia*, London: Allen & Unwin, 1984.
Stone, R. A., *Rugby Players Who Have Made New Zealand Famous*, Auckland: Scott & Scott, 1938.
Summers, Anne, 'Militarism in Britain Before the Great War', *History Workshop Journal*, No. 2, Autumn 1976.
Swan, A. C., *History of New Zealand Rugby Football 1870-1945*, Wellington: A. H. & A. W. Reed, 1948.
———, *The New Zealand Rugby Football Union 1892-1967*, Wellington: A. H. & A. W. Reed, 1967.
Thompson, J. Lee, *Northcliffe: Press baron in politics 1865-1922*, London: John Murray, 2000.
Triumphant Tour! The All Blacks in England, Ireland and Wales 1924-25 . . . memories of 1905, Wellington: L. T. Watkins, 1925.

BIBLIOGRAPHY

Trainor, Luke, *British Imperialism and Australian Nationalism*, Cambridge: Cambridge University Press, 1994.

Vamplew, Wray, et al., eds, *The Oxford Companion to Australian Sport*, Melbourne: Oxford University Press, 1992.

Vance, Norman, *The Sinews of the Spirit: The ideal of Christian manliness in Victorian literature and religious thought*, Cambridge: Cambridge University Press, 1985.

Verdon, Paul *The Power Behind the All Blacks: The untold story of the men who coached the All Blacks*, Auckland: Penguin, 1999.

———, *Born to Lead: The untold story of the All Black test captains*, Auckland: Celebrity Books, 2000.

———, *Tribute: Ranking the greatest All Blacks of all time*, Auckland: Cumulus, 2001.

———, *Heritage: Golden years of All Black rugby*, Auckland: Hill-Verdon Publishers, 2002.

Vincent, G. T., 'Practical Imperialism: The Anglo-Welsh rugby tour of New Zealand, 1908', MA thesis, University of Canterbury, 1996.

———, '"A Tendency to Roughness": Anti-Heroic Representations of New Zealand Rugby 1890–1914', *Sporting Traditions*, Vol. 14, No. 1, 1997.

———, '"To Uphold the Honour of the Province": Football in Canterbury, c. 1854–c. 1890', in Greg Ryan, ed., *Tackling Rugby Myths: Rugby and New Zealand society 1854–2004*, Dunedin: University of Otago Press, 2005.

———, & T. Harfield, 'Repression and Reform: Responses within New Zealand rugby to the arrival of the 'Northern Game, 1907–8', *New Zealand Journal of History*, Vol. 31, No. 2, 1997.

The Wales Test 1905: Match reports & commentary on the first Wales v. New Zealand rugby test played at Cardiff Arms Park, 16 December 1905, Christchurch, Nag's Head Press, 1983.

Wallace, J. M., *All Blacks and Lions: An examination of rugby tactics and players*, Wellington: Reed, 1959.

Wallace, R. L., *The Australians at the Boer War*, Canberra: Australian War Memorial, 1976.

Williams, Gareth, 'How Amateur Was My Valley: Professional sport and national identity in Wales, 1890–1914', *British Journal of Sports History*, Vol. 3, No. 2, 1985.

———, 'Rugby' in Tony Mason, ed., *Sport in Britain: A social history*, Cambridge: Cambridge University Press, 1989.

———, *1905 and All That: Essays on rugby football, sport and Welsh society*, Llandysul: Gomer, 1991.

Wood, Bernard, *Lion Red New Zealand Rugby League Annual 1996*, Wellington: B. J. Wood, 1996.

Wooller, W. & D. Owen, *Fifty Years of the All Blacks: A complete history of New Zealand rugby touring teams in the British Isles, 1905–54*, London: Phoenix House, 1954.

Zavos, S., *Ka Mate Ka Mate!: New Zealand's conquest of British rugby*, Auckland: Viking, 1998.

INDEX

Abbott, Bunny 55, 83
Adams, Alan 113
Adams, Dr G. J. 117
advertising 77
Aikman Smith, James 120
Alderson, F. H. R. 110
Alexander, Harry 94, 111
All Blacks (1905)
   internal discipline 63
   name 77–78
   off-field activities 64, 82–83
   player expectations for tour 69, 70
   reactions to success 74, 102
   relations between players 60–61, 63
   staleness 119–20, 139, 142–43, 148
   (1913) 157, 180
   (1924) 14, 114, 121, 138, 146
   (2004) 146
Alley, G. T. 115
amateurism 23–26, 107, 148, 163, 166–67
American football 150, 152–57
Anglo-Welsh (1908) 172–73
Arnold, Thomas 21–22
Auckland RFU 50–51, 59–60
Australian tour 50, 61–62

Barr, R. A. 113–14
Baskerville, Albert 163–64, 167–69
Baxter, James 114–15, 116, 180
Bedell-Sivright, D. R. 41, 43, 49
Bennet, Bob 54
'bodyline' 101
Booth, E. E. 164–65
British and Irish Lions (2005) 14
British teams
   (1888) 34, 37–38, 178
   (1904) 14, 41–44, 50, 148, 173, 178
   (1930) 114–15
broken time 24, 26, 33, 165, 171
Buttery, J. A. 77, 83

Calnan, Joseph 54
Camp, Walter 153, 154, 156

Campbell, G. F. C. 48
Canterbury RFU 41, 50, 51
captaincy 55, 63–64
class relations 23–25, 32–33
Clowes, Jack 46
coaching 59–61
Corbett, John 63, 84
Coffey, W. 46–47
Coles, Percy 94
Cooper, F. W. 163
Coventry, R. G. T. 75, 88
cricket tours 64
criticism of All Blacks 147–48, 161–63;
   see also rough play, tactics,
   wing-forward
crowds 76–77, 88
Cunningham, Bill 54, 63, 81, 129

daily allowance 49, 165, 167, 177–78; *see
   also* financial arrangements
Daily Mail 85, 88, 91–92, 136
Dallas, John 129–30, 136, 139–40
Dave Gallaher Trophy 146
Dean, S.S. 116
Deans, Bob 59, 118, 130, 135–39
debentures 48–49; *see also* financial
   arrangements
departure from Britain 147–48
Dixon, George 47, 49, 53, 55–56, 60, 62–
   63, 70, 73–74, 77, 82, 102, 104–05, 108,
   112, 119, 122, 128, 136–37, 139, 144,
   152, 158
Duncan, Jimmy 41, 59–61, 106–07

Ellison, Tom 30, 35, 38, 46, 106
Eyton, Thomas 38–39
environmental determinism 88–90, 100
expectations for tour 61–62

Fache, George 52
Fell, Nolan 122
financial arrangements 47–49, 77, 121,
   151–52, 172; *see also* guarantees

228

INDEX

fitness 93, 103
Fookes, Ernest 52–53

French tour 144–46
Gabe, Rhys 41, 43, 130, 135–37
Gaelic Athletic Association 66
Galbraith, Neil 60, 61
Gallaher, David 15, 52, 53, 55, 61, 63–64, 70–71, 84, 107–10, 112, 124, 132–34, 138, 143, 146, 149
gambling 33, 50–51
Garrard, Walter 52
gate revenue 48, 77
Gillett, George 165, 170
Gilray, Colin 53, 173
Glasgow, Frank 64, 84
Glenn, Billy 84, 100, 147
Gould, Arthur 66, 113
government funding of tour 47, 49, 149–52
guarantees 47–48, 49

haka 81–82, 158
Harnett, George 173
Harper, Eric 59, 83, 147, 148
Harris, Henry 52
Harvey, Peter 53
Hawke's Bay RFU 38, 60, 166
Hay-McKenzie, Scobie 53, 54
Hill, George Rowland 39, 47, 179
historiography 15–16
Hoben, E. D. 40–41
Hulton, Edward 180
Hunter, Jimmy 55, 59, 60, 70, 84, 103
Hunter, Dr Thomas 51

imperial touring network 44–45, 118–19, 180–81
imperialism 42–43, 80–81
injuries 83–84, 119
international matches 118–19
 England 125–26
 France 144–46
 Ireland 124
 Scotland 122–23
 Wales 126–40
International Board 66–67, 115–16, 121, 171, 179
Irish rugby 65–66
Irish Rugby Union 124, 171, 172, 178

itinerary 68, 119
Jackson, Fred 173
Johnston, Massa 83–84, 147, 168, 169, 170
Jones, A. O. 74–75, 93
Jordan, David Starr 154–56

King, James 55

Llewellyn, Willie 41, 136
Lowry, T. C. 81
Lysnar, F. 179

MacCormick, C. E. 60
McGregor, Duncan 42, 83, 125, 130, 145, 168
Mackrell, Bill 83, 168
McMahon, James 175
male stereotype 14–15, 86
Masters, Read 138
matches:
 Bedford 102
 Blackheath 102
 Bristol 73–74
 British Columbia 145, 155
 Cambridge University 102–03
 Cardiff 143, 145
 Cheshire 126
 Cheltenham 126
 Cornwall 73
 Devon 71–72
 Devonport Albion 101, 102
 Durham 75–76, 110
 Glamorgan 141–42
 Gloucester City Clubs 102
 Hartleepool Clubs 76
 Leicester 74
 Middlesex 74–75
 Midland Counties 101, 102
 Munster 124
 New York 155
 Newport 142–43
 Northampton 74
 Northumberland City Clubs 76
 Oxford University 102
 Richmond 102
 Somerset 120
 Surrey 102, 108–09
 Swansea 143–44
 West of Scotland 123
 Yorkshire 126

Maurice, Sir Frederick 86, 91
Meads, Colin 87
Moran, Paddy 81–82, 174–76
Morant, 'Breaker' 92
Morgan, Teddy 41, 44, 129–30, 145–47
Muscular Christianity 107–08
Mynott, Simon 49, 129, 130, 132, 147
mythology of 1905 14–17

nationalism 14–15, 43, 80–81, 85–86, 126–27
Nauright, John 15, 86, 91–92
New South Wales RFL 169, 177
New South Wales RFU 173–74, 179–80
New Zealand Native team (1888–89) 30, 35, 37–40, 45, 65, 68, 71, 106, 149
New Zealand Rugby Football Union (NZRFU) 33, 40, 41, 45–47, 50–54, 59, 77, 106, 116–17, 121, 150, 164–72, 179–80
New Zealand rugby teams
   (1884) 37
   (1893) 41, 78
   (1903) 41, 57
   (1904) 42–43
Newton, Fred 82
Nicholls, Gwyn 136
North American tour 149–57
Northcliff, Alfred Lord 88
Northern Union 17, 25–26, 65, 67–68, 93–94, 105, 126, 149, 163–70, 177
nostalgia 14, 148

O'Brien, Arthur 43
occupations of players 32, 57–58
origins of 1905 tour 45–50
O'Sullivan, Jimmy 59
Otago RFU 33–34, 39, 41, 45, 48, 51, 106

Palliser, C. Wray 45–46, 64, 121, 145, 147, 167, 172
Parata, Ned 81
Phillips, Jock 14–15, 26–27, 34, 86
physical attributes of players 87–88, 119
physical deterioration debates 15, 86–93, 96–100, 119–20; *see also* environmental determinism
playing numbers 50
Porter, Cliff 114
Portus, Garnet V. 160, 173

press coverage 16, 63, 78–79, 83, 100, 103–04, 141–42, 147–48
Pritchard, Charlie 129, 130
Pritchard, Cliff 136
Professional All Blacks 168–70, 172
professionalism 23–26, 39, 46–50, 66–67, 152, 164–70, 172–73, 177
provincial rivalries 40, 60
Pullin, A. W. 148

reactions to tour 72, 79, 85, 134–35
Reeves, William Pember 47, 90, 99, 147, 158
refereeing 139–42
reform debates 170–72
return to New Zealand 157–59
Rhodes, A. E. G. 172
Richards, Tom 175
Roberts, Fred 70, 84, 156, 164
Roosevelt, Theodore 154
rough play 50, 110–11, 123, 132–33, 144, 166
rugby
   California 154–57
   decline in England 65, 93
   growth in New Zealand 26–32, 50–51
   Maori 29–30
   north of England 24–6, 39–40
   origins 21–23
   provincial 31, 40, 50
   urban growth 29–32, 57
Rugby Football Union (RFU) 21, 23–26, 38, 44, 46–47, 50, 51, 65, 93, 116–17, 121, 145, 171–75, 178
rugby league *see* Northern Union
Rugby School 21–22
rural myth 26–32, 57–9, 86–90

Scottish Football Union (SFU) 66–67, 120–22, 171, 172–73, 177–78
Scottish rugby 65–66
Seddon, Richard 42, 49, 62, 85–86, 99–100, 135, 137–38, 149–52, 157–59
Seeling, 'Bronco' 84, 147, 170
selection of touring team 52–59, 83, 120
Sewell, E. H. D. 75, 92, 109, 111–12, 133
Sinclair, Keith 14, 86, 118
Sladen, Douglas 180
Smith, George 53, 63, 84, 129, 163–64, 168, 170

230

INDEX

soccer 21–23, 25, 67, 93
South African War (1899–1902) 86, 91–92, 161
Southland RFU 41, 51, 60
Springboks
  (1906) 161–63, 175
  (1912) 179
Stead, Billy 49, 55, 61, 63–64, 70, 81, 82, 84, 129, 132, 147, 159
Stoddart, Andrew 39, 45, 178
Stuart, Donald 53, 54
Stuart, Hamish 71–72, 95, 109–10, 121, 123, 125, 133, 142, 162, 176

tactics 32–39, 59, 71–72, 75–76, 97, 105–06, 128, 148, 161–62
Taranaki RFU 48, 49
Thompson, Mona 83
Tom Brown's Schooldays 22
tour agreement 55–56
training 98–99, 101
Trevor, Major Philip 109, 111, 123, 148

Vaile, P. A. 87–90, 92, 96, 137

Victorian Rules 27–28
voyage to Britain 63–64

Ward, Ernest 93
Welsh rugby 14, 15, 16, 66–67, 71, 74, 118, 126–40, 148
Welsh Rugby Union (WRU) 66, 141–42, 172–73
Wallabies (1909) 172–77
Wallace, Billy 42, 70, 78, 84, 130, 135–37, 156
Warbrick, Joseph 38–39
Webb Ellis, William 21
Wellington RFU 54, 167
Wheeler, Benjamin Ide 154–56, 180
Wiley, Edgar 51, 166
Williams, Gareth 126–27
Williams, Tom 129
Winfield, H. B. 130, 135–37
wing-forward 35, 43, 72, 73, 76, 101–17, 143, 158, 162, 173, 180
Woods, S. M. J. 103